The
HIDDEN INNS
of
LANCASHIRE & CHESHIRE

Edited by
Peter Long

Published by:
Travel Publishing Ltd
7a Apollo House, Calleva Park
Aldermaston, Berks, RG7 8TN
ISBN 1-902-00771-9
© Travel Publishing Ltd

First Published: *2001*

Regional Titles in the Hidden Inns Series:

Central & Southern Scotland	Heart of England
Lancashire & Cheshire	Southeast England
South of England	Wales
Welsh Borders	West Country
Yorkshire	

Regional Titles in the Hidden Places Series:

Cambridgeshire & Lincolnshire	Chilterns
Cornwall	Derbyshire
Devon	Dorset, Hants & Isle of Wight
East Anglia	Gloucestershire & Wiltshire
Heart of England	Hereford, Worcs & Shropshire
Highlands & Islands	Kent
Lake District & Cumbria	Lancashire and Cheshire
Lincolnshire	Northumberland & Durham
Somerset	Sussex
Thames Valley	Yorkshire

National Titles in the Hidden Places Series:

England	Ireland
Scotland	Wales

Printing by: Ashford Colour Press, Gosport
Maps by: © MAPS IN MINUTES ™ 2001 © Crown Copyright, Ordnance Survey 2001
Line Drawings: Sarah Bird
Editor: Peter Long
Cover Design: Lines & Words, Aldermaston
Cover Photographs: White Lion Inn, Barthomley, Cheshire; The Red Lion, Moore, Cheshire; The Basset Hound, Wirral, Cheshire

FOREWORD

The *Hidden Inns* series originates from the enthusiastic suggestions of readers of the popular *Hidden Places* guides. They want to be directed to traditional inns "off the beaten track" with atmosphere and character which are so much a part of our British heritage. But they also want information on the many places of interest and activities to be found in the vicinity of the inn.

The inns or pubs reviewed in the *Hidden Inns* may have been coaching inns but have invariably been a part of the history of the village or town in which they are located. All the inns included in this guide serve food and drink and many offer the visitor overnight accommodation. A full page is devoted to each inn which contains a line drawing of the inn, full name, address and telephone number, directions on how to get there, a full description of the inn and its facilities and a wide range of useful information such as opening hours, food served, accommodation provided, credit cards taken and details of entertainment. *Hidden Inns* guides however are not simply pub guides. They provide the reader with helpful information on the many places of interest to visit and activities to pursue in the area in which the inn is based. This ensures that your visit to the area will not only allow you to enjoy the atmosphere of the inn but also to take in the beautiful countryside which surrounds it.

The *Hidden Inns* guides have been expertly designed for ease of use. *The Hidden Inns of Lancashire and Cheshire* is divided into 6 regionally based chapters, each of which is laid out in the same way. To identify your preferred geographical region refer to the contents page overleaf. To find a pub or inn simply use the index and locator map at the beginning of each chapter which refers you, via a page number reference, to a full page dedicated to the specific establishment. To find a place of interest again use the index and locator map found at the beginning of each chapter which will guide you to a descriptive summary of the area followed by details of each place of interest.

We do hope that you will get plenty of enjoyment from visiting the inns and places of interest contained in this guide. We are always interested in what our readers think of the inns or places covered (or not covered) in our guides so please do not hesitate to write to us using the form at the back of the book. This is a vital way of helping us ensure that we maintain a high standard of entry and that we are providing the right sort of information for our readers. Finally if you are planning to visit any other corner of the British Isles we would like to refer you to the list of Hidden Inns and Hidden Places guides to be found at the rear of the book.

Travel Publishing

LOCATOR MAP

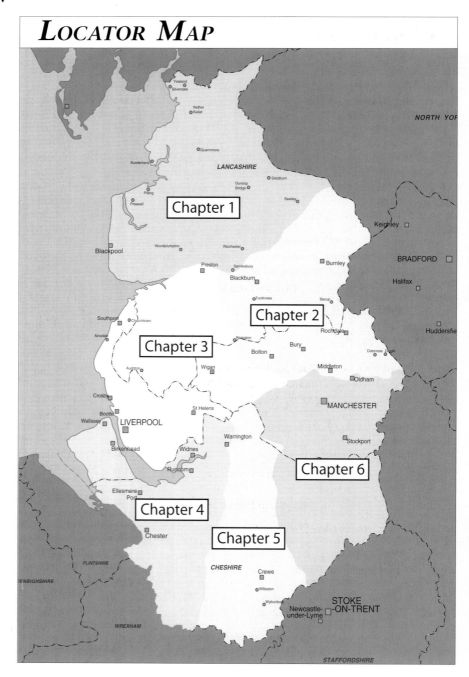

CONTENTS

1 North Lancashire

PLACES OF INTEREST:

PUBS AND INNS:

The Hidden Inns of Lancashire and Cheshire

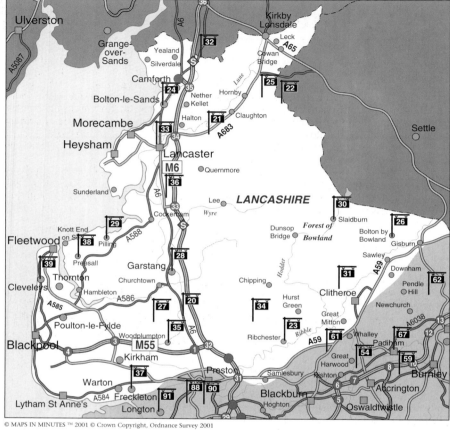

© MAPS IN MINUTES ™ 2001 © Crown Copyright, Ordnance Survey 2001

20	The Barton Fox, Barton
21	The Black Bull, Caton
22	Black Bull Hotel, High Bentham
23	Black Bull Inn, Ribchester
24	The Blue Anchor Hotel, Bolton-le-Sands
25	The Bridge Inn, Lower Tatham
26	The Coach & Horses, Bolton by Bowland
27	The Derby Arms, Inskip, nr Preston
28	The Eagle & Child, Garstang
29	The Golden Ball Hotel, Pilling

30	Hark to Bounty, Slaidburn, nr Clitheroe
31	Higher Buck Inn, Waddington
32	The Kings Arms Hotel, Burton-in-Kendal
33	The Lord Ashton, Bury
34	The Old Oak, Longridge
35	The Plough at Eaves, Woodplumpton
36	The Plough at Galgate, Galgate
37	The Plough Hotel, Freckleton
38	The Ranch House, Poulton-le-Fylde
39	The Travellers Rest, Cleveleys

Please note all references refer to page numbers

North Lancashire 3

The county of Lancashire is know to many people but, perhaps, more than any other area in the country it has suffered from cliched images of its landscape and people: the harsh life of the mill towns and the brashness of Blackpool. Before the reorganisation of the county boundaries in 1974, this large area also included Liverpool and Manchester in the south and the Furness Peninsula to the north. Those parts have been lost, but the county still has a great deal to offer in terms of both history and scenic attraction. Key moments in history include the Wars of the Roses; the old Catholic families and their support of Charles I during the Civil War; the trials of the Pendle Witches; and the innovators that started the Industrial Revolution in the textile industry.

The ancient county town of Lancaster, in the north, is an excellent place to start any journey of discovery. With a variety of museums and a wealth of interesting buildings, the life of Lancastrians through the ages is mapped out for any visitor to explore. Small and compact, it has the added advantage of having, as yet, been off the general tourist routes which has made its larger, White Rose equivalent somewhat hard going in the height of the season. To the northeast lies Leck Fell, just south of Kirkby Lonsdale and Cumbria. It is easy for the visitor to mistake this for the Yorkshire Dales as there is a typical craggy limestone gorge along the little valley of Leck Beck, as well as one of the most extensive cave systems in the British Isles for the experienced potholer to explore. A natural route from Kirkby Lonsdale back to the county town is marked by the River Lune. For those who enjoy walking, the best way to enjoy this won-

River Ribble

derful green and hilly area of Lancashire is to follow the Lune Valley Ramble which travels the valley's intimate pastoral setting, with through woodland, meadows, and along the riverside itself.

To the west of Lancashire lies Morecambe Bay, a treacherous place, where over the centuries, many walkers have lost their lives in an attempt to make the journey to the Furness Peninsula considerably shorter. The bay offers superb views, including glorious sunsets, as well as being an important habitat for a wide variety of birds. Extending across much of the north of the county is the Forest of Bowland, an ancient royal hunting ground that is dotted with small, isolated villages. With no major roads passing through the area, it has remained little changed and, with so many splendid walks and fine countryside, it is also relatively quiet even during the busiest summer weeks. Flowing between the Forest of Bowland in the north and the hill country of Pendle in the south, the River Ribble cuts a pleasant and green course along a narrow valley. The Ribble Way middle-distance footpath follows the full 70 miles of the river, from its source in Yorkshire to the flat, tidal marshes of its estuary.

A beautiful, unspoilt yet small area, the Ribble Valley has long been a favourite with the people of Lancashire. Not only is it easily accessible but there are numerous gentle walks in the sheltered valley and a wealth of wildlife is supported by the lush countryside. It is also

4

a place of pretty, untouched villages which the modern era has left relatively unspoilt. The central point of the valley is Clitheroe, a typical ancient Lancashire market town that is also home to one of the smallest Norman castles in the country. At the mouth of the river lies Preston, the county's administrative centre and a town with more to offer than first appearances would suggest. Known to many as the home of the World Snooker and World Indoor Bowls Championships, this ancient town also saw one of the key battles of the Civil War and it still continues the tradition of the Guild Celebrations. Dating back to medieval times and occurring once every 20 years, the week long festival is well worth seeing.

The historic area of coastal Lancashire called The Fyldes is known to many as the home of Blackpool: the brash, seaside resort that has been entertaining holidaymakers for generations. To the south lies another resort, Lytham St Anne's, which is not only somewhat more genteel but also the home of one of the country's most well known golf courses and host to the British Open Championships. Both places grew up as the result of the expansion of the railway system in the Victorian age, when they were popular destinations for the mill workers of Lancashire and Yorkshire. However, the Fylde is also an ancient region that was known to both the Saxons and the Romans. To the north of this region, around the Wyre estuary, the salt marshes have been exploited for over 2,000 years and the process continues at the large ICI plant. Fishing and shipping too have been important sources of revenue here. Fleetwood is still a port though small than it was whilst, surprisingly though it might seem today, Lytham was also an important port along the Ribble Estuary. Inland, the fertile, flat plain has been farmed for many centuries and, with few major roads, the quiet rural communities lie undisturbed and little changed. A haven for wildlife, and particularly birds and plants, the two estuaries, of the Ribble and the Wyre, provide habitats that abound with rare and endangered species of plants and birds. A relatively undiscovered region, the Fylde has much more to offer than a white knuckle ride and candy floss and is well worth taking the time to explore.

PLACES OF INTEREST

BLACKPOOL

Probably Britain's liveliest and most popular resort, certainly it is a place that everyone in the country has heard of even if they do not know where it is, Blackpool, like it or loath it, is definitely an experience. A typical British resort, with piers, funfairs, gardens, amusement arcades, and a promenade, although they all appear much bigger here, not even the rather wet northwest coast weather is able to dampen the spirits of the many who flock here for their two weeks holiday or just for a day out by the sea. It is hard to believe that, just over 150 years ago, Blackpool was little more than a fishing village among the sand dunes of the Fylde coast. At that time, travel to and from the village involved considerable discomfort, taking a day from Manchester and two days from York. However, it was the arrival of the great Victorian railway companies that put Blackpool well and

truly on the map by laying the railway lines right to the coast and building the grand stations, the town had three. The quiet fishing village was quickly transformed into a vibrant resort as day-trippers from the mill towns of Lancashire and Yorkshire took advantage of the cheap excursion rail fares. It was the late 19th century which saw the building of many of the resort's now famous attractions. At that time it was estimated that Blackpool's 7,000 dwellings could accommodate 250,000 holidaymakers in addition to a permanent population of 35,000. As these visitors would also need entertainments and amusements the town's development began in earnest.

In 1889, the original Opera House was built in the Winter Gardens complex and two years later a start was made on the world famous Tower. Completed in 1894, the world famous **Blackpool Tower**, modelled on the Eiffel Tower in Paris, stands some 518 feet high and for over

100 years it has been a well-known landmark, visible from many miles away. The North Pier, designed by Eugenius Birch, was opened at the beginning of the 1863 season. It soon became *the* place to promenade and it is now a listed building. The Pleasure Beach, which boasts its own railway station, is an attraction that continues to be extended and improved. Home to the tallest, fastest, and possibly the most expensive roller coaster ride in the world, some of its delights are not for the fainthearted. Close to the Pleasure Beach is a relatively new attraction that the British weather cannot spoil. The Sandcastle provides all-weather fun in a water environment, with waves, waterslides, and flumes in a tropical indoor setting. Further down the Golden Mile, The Sea Life Centre, again reflecting the water theme, proves popular with all ages and gives visitors a close-up view of the creatures of the underworld.

Despite its reputation as a brash and lively resort, Blackpool also has its quiet, secluded corners where visitors can escape the hustle of the crowds. There are seven miles of sea front, from the North Shore down as far as Squire's Gate and Lytham, where the pace of life gentle and the beaches are quieter. Blackpool Tramways have provided a most enjoyable way of exploring these less busy sides the town and it environs for many years. And, it should also be remembered that the world's first electric street tram system opened here in 1885. They are still a popular means of transport here today, with many of the tramcars date from the 1930s or 1950s, and the managing company has a special selection of vintage cars which they run on special occasions. One of these occasions is the now annual Illuminations which, following a ceremonial lighting much like that of the Christmas lights in London, is a splendid end to the season. An eagerly awaited free show, running the full length of the promenade, the lights have, over the years, provided many spectacular shows and incorporated many themes.

Bolton By Bowland

Close to the River Ribble, this tranquil village with its ancient green, stone cross, and old stocks, lies on the southern edge of the forest area. The village church is home to the famous Pudsey tomb, with its engraved figure of Sir Ralph Pudsey in full armour alongside figures of his three wives and 25 children! Also here are many ornamental carvings.

Carnforth

5

The town lies around what was once a major crossroads on the A6 but it is, perhaps, its fame as a busy railway junction town - whose station was used as the setting for the 1940s film classic *Brief Encounter* - by which most people know Carnforth. Though the station has declined in importance, now an unstaffed halt, the old engine sheds and sidings are now occupied by **Steamtown**, one of the largest steam railway centres in the north of England. Visitors are likely to see such giants of the Age of Steam as the Flying Scotsman or an A4 Pacific being stabled here, together with a permanent collection of over 30 British and Continental steam locomotives. There are steam rides in the summer months on both standard gauge and miniature lines.

Chipping

This picturesque village overlooking the River Loud is now a conservation area and it is also home to a post office, built in 1668, which claims to be Britain's oldest shop. Very much at the heart of the local agricultural communities, the annual village show is one of the best in Lancashire and its very name comes from the old English for market place. In medieval times there were no less than five watermills along the banks of Chipping Beck and, later, one of the mills, Tweedies Mill, made ships' portholes which were used on the clipper ships bringing tea back from the east. There are also a number of attractive inns here and one in particular, the Sun Inn, also associated with a sad tale. Lizzy Dean, a serving wench at the inn, became engaged to a local man. On the morning of their wedding, on hearing the church bells ringing, Lizzie looked out of the window of her room at the inn and saw her bridegroom leaving the church with another bride on his arm. In deep despair, she hanged herself in the pub's attic and her last request was that her grave be dug in the path to the church so that her would-be groom had to walk over her grave each Sunday. This sad event took place in 1835 and Lizzie is said to haunt the inn to this day.

Churchtown

This delightful village has many buildings of both architectural and historic interest and none more so than the **Church of St Helen** which dates back to the days of the Norman

6

Conquest. Featuring architectural styles from almost every period since the 11th century, this church is well worth exploring. The oldest parts of the building are the circular pillars near the nave which date from around 1200 and the roof is the original Tudor structure. Built on the site of a Saxon church, St Helen's is dedicated to the mother of Emperor Constantine and the circular churchyard is typical of the Saxon period. Known as the Cathedral of the Fylde, the church has been subjected to flooding by the River Wyre and, in 1746, such was the damage caused by the rising waters that the rebuilding of the church looked necessary. However, the builder brought in to survey the scene, suggested that moving the river would be a cheaper option and this method of preserving the church was undertaken. The original course of the river can be seen by taking the footpath from the churchyard in the direction of the new river course.

Clitheroe Castle & Museum

CLAUGHTON

The Old Toll House Garage, on the road into this village (which is pronounced Clafton), found fame when a garage owner, earlier this century, painted the first white lines on the road the nearby corner because of the many accidents that had occurred there. After much debate their value was recognised by George V and from then onwards the use of white lines became accepted as a means of road marking, eventually spreading worldwide.

CLITHEROE

This old stone town, just south of the Forest of Bowland and in the valley of the River Ribble, has always been considered the forest's capital. It is also Lancashire's oldest borough after Wigan, receiving its first charter in 1147, and since then Clitheroe has served the surrounding villages of the Ribble Valley as their market town. Like Lancaster, it too is dominated by an 800-year-old **Clitheroe Castle** standing on a limestone crag high above the town. It is now little more than a ruin, set in a small park, and as visitors stand inside the keep, hidden voices relate the history of the castle, with suitable sound effects. During the Civil War, Clitheroe was a staunchly Royalist town but, fortunately, it and the castle survived the ravishes of the victorious Parliamentarians. The Castle Museum, as well as holding collections of local

geology and local history, also has reconstructions of a clogger's workshop, a printer's shop, and a lead mine. On a neighbouring hill stands the parish Church of St Mary Magdalen which, though it was rebuilt by the Victorians, was founded in the 13th century. At this time too the town also had a school, however, the present Royal Grammar School was not established until 1554. The school's official charter, granted by Mary Tudor, was eventually found, in the vaults of a local solicitor's office, in 1990. The town's narrow, winding streets are full of character and charm and, amidst the ancient buildings, is the rather incongruous Civic Hall Cinema. Built in the 1920s, this unspoilt monument to the golden days of the silver screen is still lined with plush velvet, has retained its grand piano that was used to accompany the silent films, and remains the town's cinema. Just outside the town can be found Edisford Picnic Area, a popular place for family outings that stands on the site of a battle ground where the Scots fought the Normans. Also close to Clitheroe, at Brungerley, is a set of stepping stones across the river that are said to be haunted. Apparently the evil spirit living in the water drags a traveller to his watery death every seven years.

COCKERHAM

Home to Cockerham Hall, a fine and rare example of a medieval timber-framed building

7

that dates from the late 15th century, the village is also famous for its local custom of fluke fishing.

COWAN BRIDGE

The school attended by the Brontë sisters, and immortalised in Jane Eyre as Lowood, can still be seen though it is now part of a row of terraced cottages. The school, which moved to Casterton in 1833, was founded some 10 years earlier by Carus Wilson, the vicar of neighbouring Tunstall. His rather plain house too can still be seen here.

DOWNHAM

One of the most attractive villages in the area, Downham was purchased by the Assheton family in 1558 at the same time as they acquired

Downham Village

Whalley Abbey. Beautifully maintained by the family, the present squire, Lord Clitheroe of Downham, still refuses to permit the skyline to be spoilt by television aerials, satellite dishes, and even dormer windows. The village phone box has also come under the influence of the family and it is not painted a distinctive pillar box red but grey, to tone in with the surroundings. The extent of the village's conservation has led to its use as a location for many films, the most famous being *Whistle Down the Wind*.

DUNSOP BRIDGE

Often known as the 'Gateway to the Trough of Bowland', Dunsop Bridge is, despite its remote location, the centre of the British Isles. The actual centre point, worked out by the Ordnance Survey, lies near Whitendale Hanging Stones and, to confirm the claim, the explorer Sir Ranolph Fiennes unveiled the commemorative plaque. British Telecommunications have also offered the village a unique honour by putting their 100,000th phone box here.

FLEETWOOD

This fishing town, on the northern tip of the Fylde coast, is a planned town founded in the early 19th century around the Wyre deepwater port. Based on a form street pattern radiating from the Mount, the development was undertaken by the then landowner, Sir Peter Hesketh-Fleetwood, who wished to create a new holiday resort for working class people from the industrial mill towns of east Lancashire. Prior to the commencement of the building work in 1836, this had been a small settlement of a few fishermen's cottage. The opening of the railway extension from Preston to Fleetwood was a key player in the town's development and the North Euston Hotel, which opened in 1842, reflects those railway links. Queen Victorian used Fleetwood as she travelled to Scotland for her annual holiday. However, this was all before the railway companies managed to lay a railway over Shap fell in Cumbria in 1847 and thus provide a direct rail link to Scotland. The town's Museum, overlooking the River Wyre, illustrates the town's links with the fishing industry which suffered greatly from the Icelandic cod wars. However, Fleetwood's real claim to fame is the

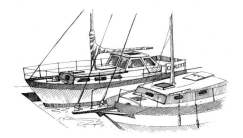

Fleetwood Harbour

The Hidden Inns of Lancashire and Cheshire

8

Fisherman's Friend - a staggeringly successful lozenge that was used by fishermen to relieve sore throats and bronchial trouble caused by the freezing conditions found in the northern Atlantic waters. In 1865, James Lofthouse, a chemist in the town, combined the ingredients of liquorice, capsicum, eucalyptus, and methanol, into a liquid for the town's fishermen but, as the seas were invariably rough, the bottles were broken before the men could benefit from the mixture. So Lofthouse, undefeated, combined the same ingredients into a lozenge that proved much more practical on board ship and, in a very short space of time his shop was inundated with customers. Today, Fishermen's Friends, which remain unchanged from the original recipe, are still produced by the same family business and their sales are worldwide.

FOREST OF BOWLAND

Designated an Area of Outstanding Natural Beauty in February 1964, this large scenic area is a veritable paradise for walkers and country lovers that is dotted with picturesque villages. The 11th largest of such designated areas, the Forest of Bowland is something of a misnomer: the term 'forest' is derived from the Latin 'foris' which was formerly used to denote a royal hunting ground, an unenclosed tract of land, rather than a distinct wooded area. In fact, even this description is not entirely correct as, in the 11th century the area was a chase - a private rather than a royal hunting ground. Before 1066, Bowland was in the ownership of Earl Tostig of Northumbria, a brother of King Harold. Banished from his earldom, Tostig, with the help of the King of Norway, attempted to regain his lands and both he and the Norwegian king were killed at Stamford Bridge, just weeks before the fateful Battle of Hastings. Following the Norman Conquest, Bowland became part so the Honour of Clitheroe and the vast estates that belonged to the de Lacy family. In time, by marriage, they came into the hands of the Earls of Lancaster and, in 1399, when the then Duke of Lancaster ascended the throne as Henry IV, Bowland finally became one of nearly a hundred royal hunting forests. The remains of a Roman road can be clearly seen traversing the land and many of the village's names in this area date back to the Saxon period. Perhaps the most celebrated of the many routes across

Bowland is the minor road from Lancaster to Clitheroe which crosses the Abbeydale Moor and the Trough of Bowland before descending into the lovely Hodder Valley around Dunsop Bridge. This is a popular route in the summer months, with most lay-bys and parking places filled as people pause to take in the breathtaking moorland views.

GARSTANG

This is an ancient, picturesque town whose market dates back to the time of Edward II, who granted the monks the right to hold the market. Thursday is still market day and both the High Street and the Market Hall become a hive of activity. As the town is situated close to a ford over the River Wyre, visitors will not be surprised to learn that the town dates back to the 6th century when a Saxon, named Garri, made his base here. The town's name comes from the Old Scandinavian words of 'geirr' meaning spear and 'stong' meaning pole. The town is also home to an excellent Discovery Centre which deals with a variety of aspects of the region, including the history of the nearby Forest of Bowland and the natural history of the surrounding countryside. Just to the east of the town, on the top of a grassy knoll, are the remains of **Greenhalgh Castle**, built in 1490 by Thomas Stanley, the first Earl of Derby. Severely damaged in a siege against Cromwell in 1645-46, the castle is reputed to be one of the last strongholds in Lancashire to have held out against the man. A little to the north, on the A6, are the remains of a stone-built Toll House which probably dates from the 1820 when parts of the turnpike from Garstang to Lancaster were realigned. Although a ruin, the toll house is more than usually interesting as the posts for the toll gates can still be seen on either side of the road. This stretch of road is also home to some of the finest Turnpike Milestones in the county. To the south of Garstang, they are round-faced stones with cursive lettering dating from the 1750s and, to the north, the stones are triangular, with Roman lettering, and date from the time of the turnpike's realignment in the early 19th century.

GISBURN

Now within the boundaries of Lancashire, this village was once in Yorkshire and, as many locals would like to believe, it still is! One of the Ribble Valley's most pleasant and picturesque villages, its recent history is dominated by the Lister family who, from humble beginnings rose to become the Lords of Ribblesdale. Their house, built in the early 17th century in Gisburne Park, is still standing though it is now a private hospital. Over the years, many people were given shelter by the family and, in 1648, Cromwell is said to have rested at the house whilst on his way to fight at Preston. During the late 18th century, the family were rewarded for their loyalty to king and country, when they raised an army against Napoleon, by the creation of the title Lord of Ribblesdale in 1797. Coincidentally, the 4th and last Lord of Ribblesdale, who died in 1925 having lost both his sons in World War I, shared the same name, Thomas, as the 1st Lord.

GREAT MITTON

Standing opposite the Three Fishes Hotel, which takes its name from the three fishes on the Whalley Abbey coat of arms, is the attractive All Hallows' Church. Housing some of the finest relics to be seen in any British church, this is most certainly worth a visit. Built in around 1270, though undoubtedly there was a wooden Saxon structure hereabouts, little has been done to the building since although a tower was added in 1438 and the pews are Jacobean. However, it is the Shireburn Chapel that draws most visitors to the church. Added in the mid-15th century by the Shireburn family of Stonyhurst they claimed to be the direct descendants of the first rector, Ralph the Red of Mytton. Among the many memorials in the chapel, perhaps the most impressive is the fine alabaster tomb of Sir Richard Shireburn and his wife Maude. Confirmation that a settlement existed here before the days of the land ownership by the abbey comes with the name of the village itself. Mitton is derived from the Saxon word 'mythe' which means a farm at the junction of two rivers - perfectly describing the location as, close by, the River Hodder feeds into the River Ribble.

HALTON

The high mound, Castle Hill, which rises above this ancient village, was, firstly, the site of a Roman camp, and later a Saxon castle. The village's parish **Church of St Wilfrid** was founded in the 7th century and, although nothing can be seen from that time, there are some stone crosses, both inside the building and out, that date from the 9th century. One in particular

bears both pagan and Christian symbols and it is the only known cross to do so. Roman remains, in the form of a votive altar (where offerings were made before a military operation began), were found on the site in the late 18th century.

HAMBLETON

A centre for ship building in medieval times, Hambleton is now a quiet village on the banks of the River Wyre from which radiate a network of narrow lanes that wind through the charming north Fylde countryside. The village also stands on one of the narrowest parts of the river and there was certainly a ford here in Roman times, as relics have been found here. However, it is probable that the ford goes back even further, to the Iron Age, around 500 BC. On the site of the ford now stands the 325-yard-long Shard Bridge, built in 1864 and which still operates as a toll bridge.

HEYSHAM

It is worth strolling along the promenade in a southerly direction as far as Heysham, Morecambe's twin, with its quaint old main street that winds down to the shore. It is also a town with considerable historic associations, because it was here in the 8th century that Christian missionaries arrived from Ireland to convert the heathen Viking settlers in the north of England. They built the chapel of St Patrick on a rock on the sea edge and it is likely that this is the county's oldest religious house. Its ruins, with coffin-shaped rocks - one of the most curious graveyards in England - can still be seen. The little **Church of St Peter** on the headland below the chapel is equally interesting. It dates back to Saxon and Norman times, with an Anglo-Saxon cross on which the Madonna and other figures have been crudely carved by 9th century masons, and there is a rare Viking hog-back gravestone. It is one of the oldest churches in western Europe to have been in continuous use. Alongside these antiquities is the modern port of Heysham, with regular car-ferry sailings to the Isle of Man and to Northern Ireland and, of course, the two modern nuclear power stations, Heysham A and Heysham B.

HORNBY

The situation of this village, by a bluff overlooking the valley of the River Lune, not only

10

gives Hornby panoramic views of the surrounding countryside but also makes this a strategic position that has been utilised over the centuries. Just to the north of the village is the attractive stone-built Loyn Bridge, which takes the road over the River Lune and on to Gressington. Constructed in 1684, it replaced a ford and beside the bridge is Castle Stede, the best example of a Norman motte and bailey castle in Lancashire. The romantically situated **Hornby Castle**, which can be viewed from the village, was immortalised in a painting by Turner. Although is was only built in the 19th century, the castle incorporates the ruins of an older castle and it is now a grand and picturesque country house. The Church of St Margaret of Antioch dates from around 1300 when it was built as a chapel of easy to the parish church at Melling. The octagonal tower is said to have been ordered by Sir Edward Stanley after the victory of Flodden Field in 1513.

Hurst Green

A pretty village of stone-built cottages nestling in the Ribble Valley that is best known for its nearby public school. **Stonyhurst College**, the world famous Roman Catholic school, began life as the residence of the local lords of the manor. The present building, begun in around 1523, was the work of Hugh Shireburn although additions were made in 1592 by Sir Richard Shireburn. An ambitious man, Sir Richard served the Tudor monarchy and, as well as being the Chief Forester of Bowland, he was also one of Henry VIII's commissioners studying the state of the monasteries and he was an eager participant in the suppression of Whalley Abbey. Though the family took on the new Protestant religion under Elizabeth I, it was with little spirit and in a short time the Shireburn family, like many other Lancashire families, returned to their Catholic faith. It seems strange then that Cromwell, on his way to and from the Battle of Preston, should take shelter at Stonyhurst and rumour has it that the ardent Puritan slept with a pistol at his side and his guards around him. In 1794, after the house had been left for some considerable time and had fallen into a state of disrepair, the owner, Thomas Weld, offered the property to the Jesuits who had set up an English Catholic School in Flanders. Unwelcome in France following the

revolution, the Jesuits gladly accepted and, after restoring the original building, they extended it during the 19th century. Their finest addition must be the replica of King's College in Cambridge: St Peter's Church was built in 1835 and it includes many treasures including a 7th century copy of St John's Gospel and a cope of Henry II that was used by Henry VIII at the battle of the Field of the Cloth of Gold. One of the college's most famous sons is Sir Arthur Conan Doyle, the creator of Sherlock Holmes.

Kirkham

Mentioned in the Domesday Book, there was a settlement here in Saxon times, known as Ciricham, and, before that, the Romans had a fort here though it is now lost under a modern housing estate. Kirkham was first granted a charter to hold a weekly market in 1296 and, since then, it has been serving the needs of the surrounding farming communities. The Fishstones are still to be seen; the flat stone slabs are set on stone uprights to form a semi-circle and were the counters from which fish was sold. However, Kirkham was also touched by the Industrial Revolution and by the middle of the 18th century there were flax-spinning mills and sailcloth was manufactured and, by the 19th century, there were also come cotton mills.

Kirkham

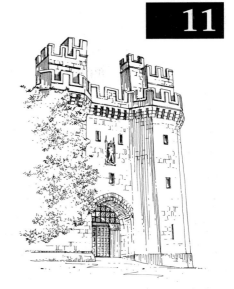

Knott End-On-Sea

This small coastal resort, on the River Wyre estuary, grew into a substantial fishing settlement in the 17th and 18th centuries. It was also a pilot base for the upstream ports of Wardleys and Skippool and later developed into a ferry port. However, today, its broad flat sands and bracing sea air, along with the decline in the fishing industry, have turned the town into a small, quiet holiday resort that is also favoured by those who have retired. Looking out to sea, at low tide, a rocky outcrop can be seen which, some historians have suggested, is the remains of the masonry of a Roman port. Whether this is the port that in the 2nd century Ptolemy marked on a map as Portus Setantiorum is certainly in doubt, but it is undeniable that such a building existed as the Romans were planning an invasion of Ireland from this stretch of coast.

Lancaster

The capital of this beautiful county, Lancaster proudly boasts of its legacy, which extends back many centuries. Unlike York its White Rose cousin, which has long been internationally known as a tourist attraction, this Red Rose city has taken longer to be discovered. In fact, Lancaster has an equally important place in English history and it has retained close links with the monarchy. As early as the 10th century, Athelstan, the grandson of Alfred the Great, had lands in the area and it was during the reign of William the Conqueror that large areas of what is now Lancashire were given, by the grateful king, to his cousin Roger of Pitou, who made his base at Lancaster. The first Earl of Lancaster was Edmund, the youngest son of Henry III and, in time, the title passed to John of Gaunt who persuaded Richard II to give him the right to pass the title on to his highest male descendent. Now a dukedom, to this day the present Queen still retains the title of Duke of Lancaster.

There is much in this historic place for the serious visitor to explore and, as it is also a surprisingly compact city, easily reached by either road, just off the M6, or by rail, it is also a pleasure. Within yards of the railway station lies **Lancaster Castle**, a great medieval fortress, founded by the Normans to keep out Scottish invaders, and strengthened by John of Gaunt, Duke of Lancaster, in the 15th century. Standing proudly on its hilltop position, this great

Lancaster Castle

castle has an imposing presence and dominates the skyline over Lancaster. Its huge square keep dates back to 1200 and was raised in height and impregnability at the time of the Armada. Astonishingly perhaps, most of the building still functions as a prison, but certain sections are open to the public, including the 18th century Shire Hall, the cells where the witches of Pendle were imprisoned, and the Crown Court which not only saw the trials of the Pendle witches but also those of John Paslew (last abbot of Whalley) in 1536, numerous Catholic priest during the 16th and early 17th centuries and, more recently, the Birmingham pub bombers in 1975. Hadrian's Tower and - a touch of the macabre - the Drop Room where prisoners were prepared for the gallows can also be viewed by the public.

Close by, sharing the hill with the castle, is a building with less grim associations - the lovely Priory Church of St Mary, which once served a Benedictine Priory established here in 1094. Most of the present church dates from the 14th and 15th centuries and of particular interest here are the fragments of Anglo-Saxon crosses, the magnificent medieval choir stalls, and some very fine needlework. The Priory Tower, also on the hilltop, was rebuilt in 1759 as a landmark

12

for ships navigating their way into the River Lune. Nearby is one of Lancaster's links with its Roman past - the remains of a bath house which also served soldiers as an inn.

A short walk from the castle leads into the largely pedestrianised city centre, full of shops, the market, and much besides. The City Museum in the Market Place occupies the Old Town Hall, built between 1781-3 by Major Jarrett and Thomas Harrison. As well as the city's art collection and an area of changing exhibitions, there are displays and collections of material illustrating aspects of the city's industrial and social history. Also here is the Museum of the King's Own Royal Regiment, a regiment which was based in Lancaster from 1880 onwards. In Church Street is the Judge's Lodging, a beautifully proportioned building dating from the 1620s when it was built as a private house for Thomas Covell then, later, used by judges during the Lancaster Assizes. It now houses two separate museums: the Museum of Childhood containing the Barry Elder doll collection; and the Gillow and Town House Museum containing many examples of the fine workmanship of Gillows, the famous Lancaster cabinet-makers. In fact, it was Richard Gillow who designed the city's Maritime Museum. Close by is the Cottage Museum in a house built in 1739 that was divided into two dwellings in the 19th century. Just around a corner or two, in Sun Street, is the Music Room, an exquisite early Georgian building originally designed as a pavilion in the long vanished garden of Oliver Marton. It is notable for some superb decorative plasterwork.

Lancaster grew up along the banks of the River Lune, which is navigable as far as Skerton Bridge, so there has always been a strong association between the town and its watery highway. Documents from 1297 make reference to the town's small-scale maritime trade, but it was not until the late 17th and early 18th centuries that Lancaster's character as a port fully emerged. The splendid buildings of the 18th century Golden Age were born out of the port wealth, and the layout and appearance of the town was much altered by this building bonanza. Lancaster as a port gradually declined throughout the 19th century so that many buildings put up for specific maritime purposes were taken over for other uses.

Naturally, the city has been affected by the arrival of the Lancaster Canal, the railways, and

19th century industry; yet the hallmark of Lancaster, its Georgian centre, remains as the product of this maritime prosperity. Lancaster's rich maritime history is celebrated at St George's Quay which, with its great stone warehouses and superb Custom House, is now an award-winning Maritime Museum. In Georgian times this was a thriving port with the warehouses receiving ship loads of mahogany, tobacco, rum, and sugar from the West Indies. Visitors today are given a vivid insight into the life of the mariners and quayside workers, with opportunities for knot-tying and the practising of other maritime skills. Every year, over the four days of the Easter weekend, St George's Quay is home to the Lancaster Maritime Festival with smugglers, sea songs, and shanties. Built between 1797 and 1819, the Lancaster Canal stretches 57 miles from Preston through the centre of Lancaster to Kendal. Today, it is navigable between Preston and Tewitfield, north of Lancaster, the longest lock-free stretch of canal in the country.

The canal offers a diversity of scenery and wildlife with opportunities for long-distance trips and short, circular walks with fine views through peaceful countryside. With 41 lock-free miles it offers relaxed boating with canalside pubs, restaurants, and boat-hire facilities. It provides a good touring route for canoeists and is excellent for coarse fishing. One of the first sights visitors see of the city is the great green

Ashton Memorial

copper dome of the impressive **Ashton Memorial**, a landmark for miles around. A kind of miniature St Paul's - standing on a hilltop in the centre of the wonderful Edwardian Williamson Park - this is a magnificent viewpoint from which Morecambe Bay, the Lakeland Hills, and the Forest of Bowland are all visible. The building now houses exhibitions and multi-screen presentations about the life and times of Lancaster's Lord Ashton and the Edwardians.

The park and the memorial all commemorate the life and works of Lancaster's most famous son, James Williamson. He was born in the town in 1842 and took over the running of the family business, linoleum and textile manufacture, which went on to become Lancaster's largest employer. Williamson was the Liberal MP for the town for many years and, in 1895, he became Lord Ashton. Williamson Park was Lord Ashton's own personal idea as a means of providing work for local people during the cotton famine crisis in the textile industry during the American Civil War in the 1860s. Constructed on the site of old quarries, which gives the park its undulating contours, the park was opened in 1896. As well as the magnificent Ashton Memorial there is also a delightful Butterfly House in the now restored Edwardian Palm House and the Conservation Garden and Wildlife Pool which opened in 1991.

LECK

To the northeast of this village lies Green Hill, surrounded by moorland and the highest point, at 2,060 feet, in the county. At just over three feet higher than the top of the neighbouring fell, Gragarth, it was only a recent, more accurate survey, that distinguished Green Hill as the higher. In the northernmost part of Lancashire, from the summit there are superb views of both Cumbria and North Yorkshire, as well, of course, as Lancashire.

LEE

To the northwest of this typical Bowland village lies the highest summit in the forest, Ward's Stone. Dotted with outcrops of gritstone boulders, the top of the fell is marked by two triangulation pillars: one of which is just over three feet higher than the other though, on first inspection, they look the same height. The panoramic views from this point are magnificent and, to the north and east, the Three Peaks of Yorkshire can be seen.

LYTHAM ST ANNE'S

13

Situated on the coast, Lytham St Anne's is, in fact, two towns which now share their name but have quite distinctive characteristics. Linked together in 1923, St Anne's evolved in just over a century, while Lytham was mentioned in the Domesday Book. Before the development of the resort, in the Victorian age, Lytham was an important port on the Ribble estuary and it was home to the first fishing company on this stretch of the northwest coast. Shipbuilding also continued here until the 1950s, when the last vessel constructed in the shipyards was the Windermere Car Ferry. During the 1940s, parts of the famous Mulberry harbour were constructed here in secret in preparation for the invasion of Normandy in 1944.

The arrival of the railway, linking Lytham with Preston, prompted a group of Lancashire businessmen to plan the construction of a health resort between the old established port and the rapidly expanding town of Blackpool to the north. There was scarcely a cottage on their chosen site when, in 1875, the work began but the growth of the carefully planned town was spectacular. In just 30 years the population increased from just 1,000 to 17,000 inhabitants. The Promenade, running the full length of the seafront from St Anne's to Lytham was constructed in 1875 and, on the landward side, there are several fine examples of Victorian and Edwardian seaside villas. Beyond the attractive Promenade Gardens, laid out by a local character, Henry Gregson, is St Anne's Pier. Opened in 1885, the elegant pier was built in a mock Tudor style and, up until 1897, fishing smacks and pleasure boats were able to tie up at the end of the jetty. Lytham also had a pier, built in 1865, but during a gale in 1903, two sand barges dragged their anchors and sliced the structure in two. Undeterred, and with the Pavilion still standing at the far end the pier was rebuilt only to be almost entirely destroyed by fire in 1928.

In fact, the town has had its fair share of disasters associated with the sea but, by far the worst, occurred in 1886 and it is still Britain's greatest lifeboat disaster. The crew of the St Anne's lifeboat, with the help of the Southport lifeboat, set out to answer a distress signal put up by a German ship, the Mexico. During the rescue some 15 lifeboat crew were lost and the tragedy led to the improvement of lifeboat de-

14

sign. Situated in the Alpine Garden, on the Promenade, is a monument which pays tribute to the men who lost their lives. The statue features the stone figure of a coxswain looking out to sea with a rope in one hand and a lifebelt in the other.

As well as being an elegant place full of fine Victorian and Edwardian architecture, Lytham St Anne's also contains some reminders to the more distant past. Lytham Hall, now privately owned by a large insurance company, started life has a farming cell of the Durham cathedral in 1190. After the Reformation, the estate changed hands several times, until, in 1606, it became the property of Sir Cuthbert Clifton, the first squire of Lytham. The fine Georgian hall standing today was the building that John Carr of York built for Thomas Clifton between 1757 and 1764. The extensive grounds, once part of the estate, is now Lytham Hall Country Park, where visitors can follow several nature trails to discover the birds and wildlife living here which includes three species of woodpecker, the lesser whitethroat, and the hawfinch.

There has been a **Windmill** at Lytham for over 800 years though the present structure dates from 1805. A well known landmark along the coast, the building has a solid white tower with a cap that looks rather like an upturned boat. In 1929, the wind set the four sails turning the wrong way, ruining the machinery and firing the mill, which has never worked since. Now renovated the windmill is home to a per-

manent exhibition on the building's history and on the process of breadmaking. Adjacent to the windmill, and the original home of the Lytham lifeboat, Old Lifeboat House is home to the Lifeboat Museum. Two other museums worthy of a visit are the Lytham Motive Power Museum, with its large model railway layout and an outdoor display of rolling stock, and the Toy and Teddy Museum, housed in the Porrit Victorian building and a varied collection of childhood memorabilia.

For those interesting in discovering more about the abundant wildlife of the dune system here a visit to **Lytham St Anne's Nature Reserve** is a must. Established in 1968, the reserve is an important scientific site as well as being just a small part of what was once a very extensive sand dune system. As well as the rich plant life, the dunes are home to several rare species of migrating birds including osprey, black redstart, and Lapland buntings. No description of Lytham St Anne's is complete without a mention of the **Royal Lytham and St Anne's** golf course. The club originated after a meeting, held in 1886, where a group of 19 keen golfers sought to furnish themselves with suitable facilities. The course opened in 1898 and it is still considered by many to be one of the finest golf links in the country; it is a regular host of the British Open.

MORECAMBE

Featuring prominently on the Lancashire coastline, Morecambe has long been one of the most successful and popular seaside resorts in the North, and it can truly be said to enjoy one of the finest views from its promenade of any resort in England - a magnificent sweep of coastline and bay, looking across to the Lakeland mountains. Like other resorts, Morecambe has changed with the times, and major new attractions include the multi-million pound Bubbles Leisure Park and Superdome, as well as a Wild West Theme Park. WOMAD, Morecambe's annual world music festival, attracts visitors from across the globe. There are also popular seafront illuminations in late summer, together with all the usual lively shops and variety of entertainment associated with a busy seaside resort. However, Morecambe is a relatively recent town, that grew up as a direct result of the expansion of the railways to the north Lancashire coast. Originally three villages, Bare, Poulton, and Torrisholme that were quiet fishing communities, in 1848 all this changed as the railways

Windmill, Lytham St Anne's

brought visitors from the textile towns of Lancashire, and especially Yorkshire, to what was jokingly called 'Bradford-by-the-Sea'. Hotels and boarding houses were built as well as the usual seaside amenities, such as parks and promenades, and soon the villages were lost into one thriving resort. Of the many buildings dating from Morecambe's heyday as a holiday destination, one in particular, the Midland Hotel stands out. Situated on the seafront, at the southern end of the promenade, the hotel, which was built in the early 1930s to designs by Oliver Hill, is concave towards the sea and convex facing inland. The elegant, sweeping balconies to the luxurious rooms remain a superb feature of the hotel and, whilst filming Brief Encounter, at nearby Carnforth, both Celia Johnson and Trevor Howard made their home here along with others working on the film. The railway also turned Morecambe into a thriving port and, in the mid-19th century it was handling twice as much cargo as Glasson Dock. However, as it had first outgrown its neighbour, Heysham, the docks in the town further south again took over and the port of Morecambe died as quickly as they had grown. Fortunately, though, the local delicacy, shrimps, that were so loved by the Victorians with their afternoon tea, are still available and they make a delicious savoury dish. **Morecambe Bay**, a vast wide, flat tidal plain situated between Lancashire and Cumbria, is the home of many forms of marine life as well as being a very popular and important habitat for birds. The Rivers Lune, Kent, Keer, Leven, and Crayke create the gulleys, mud, and sandbanks that make this not only one of the most important ornithological sites in Europe but also a great source of mussels and shrimps. It is also a treacherous place for the unwary as, though it looks a simple walk across the bay, the sands are extremely hazardous and a crossing should not be made, in any circumstances, without the direct supervision of a sand pilot. Over the centuries, many have perished whilst attempting the crossing and, at one time, the monks of the Furness peninsula acted as guides to those wishing to make their way to Cumbria without taking the long overland route.

NETHER KELLET

This farming village has a traditional village green which, as well as being the central focus of the community, also features several old wells and pumps. Quarrying has too taken place here

for many centuries and lime burning has been an important local industry and its remains, in the form of lime kilns, can still be seen around the village.

15

PILLING

A quiet, scattered village, on the edge of rich, fertile marshland, was, for many years, linked to the market town of Garstang by a little, winding, single-track railway known affectionately as the 'Pilling Pig'. Said to be the second largest village in Britain, Pilling is steeped in history. The Olde Ship Inn, for example, was built in 1782 by George Dickson, a slave trader. Now a listed building, the inn is reputed to be haunted by a lady dressed in Georgian attire, wandering around with a pale and worried look on her face.

POULTON-LE-FYLDE

This is one of the oldest towns in the ancient area known as Amounderness. The Romans were known to have been in the area and it was probably their handiwork that constructed the Danes Pad, an ancient trackway. The town developed as a commercial centre for the surrounding agricultural communities and its Market Place remains its focal point. In 1732, a great fire, started by sparks from the torches of a funeral procession, destroyed most of the thatched cottages that surrounded the market square in those days and a nationwide appeal was launched to help meet the rebuilding costs. Consequently, little of old Poulton can be seen in the centre of the town. The present **Church of St Chad** dates from the early 17th century, though the majority of the building is Georgian, and it stands on the site of the original Norman church. Inside, which is true Georgian, there is a splendid staircase, unusual for a church, leading up to the gallery which runs around three sides of the building. As Poulton was a key town in the area for centuries, it is not surprising that there are several magnificent memorials to the local Fleetwood-Hesketh family also to be found here. Fire seems to have played an important role in the life of the town and one ancient custom still kept is Teanlay Night, which involves the lighting of bonfires on Hallowe'en. Each bonfire is encircled with white-coloured stones which are then thrown into the flames by the onlookers and left until the next day. The successful retrieval of one's own stone is considered a good omen for fu-

16

ture prosperity. Strolling around Poulton-le-Fylde now, it is hard to imagine that the town was once a seaport. But until relatively recently ships sailed up the River Wyre to Skippool Creek. Today, the creek is home to the Blackpool and Fleetwood Yacht Club and from here the ocean-going yachts compete in major races around Britain. The town had a rail link long before Blackpool and it was here that the early holidaymakers alighted from their trains to take a horse and trap the remaining few miles. Fortunately for Poulton, in 1846, the railway reached Blackpool and the town could, once again, return to a more peaceful existence. It is this quiet and charm, as well as sensitive approaches to planning, that have led it to become, in recent years, a much sought after residential area for businessmen now able to travel the M55 to Manchester and Liverpool.

Clougha Pike

forest - it is just over 1300 feet - the walk up Clougha Pike is very pleasant and one which offers splendid views at the summit, not only of the Lakeland Fells but also of Morecambe Bay and, on a clear day, Blackpool Tower.

PREESALL

The village's original name, Pressoude, as it was mentioned in the Domesday Book, is thought to mean a salt farm near the sea and certainly in 1872 rock salt deposits were discovered beneath the village. From then on, for around 30 years, Preesall became a centre for salt mining and, in 1883, the Fleetwood Salt Company was established to develop the field. The bulk of the salt was extracted in the form of brine and, by the end of 1891, there was a reliable pipeline pumping the salt under the River Wyre to Fleetwood. However, as much of the salt was extracted from underneath the expanding village, subsidence soon became a problem and, in 1923, this lead to the opening up of a huge pit, known locally as 'Bottomless' to the west of the village.

QUERNMORE

Lying at the head of the Conder Valley, this farming village had a pottery industry as well as slate quarrying in the 17th century. The word 'quern' refers to a particularly ancient form of hand-mill that was hewn from the rocks found on the nearby moorside and, indeed, corn milling continued here until World War II. To the east of the village lies **Clougha Pike**, itself on the western edges of the Forest of Bowland Area of Outstanding Natural Beauty and one of the few places in the area that is accessible to walkers. Although it is not the highest peak in the

RIBCHESTER

Situated on the banks of the River Ribble, the village is famous for its Roman Fort, **Bremetannacum**, on the northern river bank. It was the Roman governor, Gnaeus Julius Agricola, in AD 79, who first established a fort here at the junction of the two important roads between Manchester and Carlisle, and York and the west coast. Although little of the fort's walls remain, the granary or storehouse, with its hypocaust (underfloor heating), has been excavated and has revealed some interesting coins, pottery, sculptures, and inscriptions. The fort's Roman Museum is designed to transport visitors back to the days of the Roman occupation and it offers an excellent insight into those times. Unfortunately, the finest artefact found on the site, an ornate helmet, is not on display here (though they do have a replica) but it can be seen in the British Museum in London. Back in the village proper, the discovery of some pre-Norman Conquest crosses in and around St Wilfrid's Church would suggest that this 13th-century building occupies the site of a Saxon church. The church is named after the first Bishop of Ripon, who in the 7th century took a prominent role in the Synod of Whitby, and this would seem to confirm the earlier buildings existence in the absence of any direct evidence. A great place for tourist during the summer months, Ribchester not only has these two sights to offer but also several excellent pubs, restaurant, and cafés which provide much needed refreshment. Finally, Ribchester has one further attraction, the **Museum of Childhood** housed in the village's old Co-op building. The collection is diverse and goes back to the days of the Victorian music hall, with many of the models still in working order.

SAMLESBURY

To the east of the village, close to the busy main road, lies **Samlesbury Hall**, built by the Southworth family. The hall seen today it actually the second house they built as their original hall was burned to the ground by Robert the Bruce in the early 14th century. Thinking that the original position, close to a crossing of the River Ribble was too vulnerable to attack, the family built their subsequent home in what was then an isolated location. More peaceful times followed and the hall, surrounded by a moat and with a drawbridge, was a reflection of the family's wealth. A staunchly Catholic family, their 15th century chapel contains a mullioned Gothic window that was rescued from Whalley Abbey after the Dissolution in the 1530s. However, it was the loyalty to their faith that finally saw the demise of the Southworth family. Their continued practice of Catholicism saw Sir John Southworth imprisoned in Manchester in the late 16th century and, by the time of his death a few years later, the family, having kept their faith, had seen their fortune dwindle away. The hall was sold to the Braddyll family who, having a house near Ulverston, simple stripped Samlesbury Hall of its assets. Some how the hall survived though, by the 1870s it was in a shocking state of repair. First, Joseph Harrison stepped in and began a successful restoration programme, to the point where he was able to entertain the likes of Charles Dickens. However, the building work took all his money and, facing ruin, Harrison committed suicide. Once more in need of rescue, the hall was saved by the Samlesbury Hall Trust, a group who are still managing the property today. The hall's unusual history is only equalled by the unconventional manner in which it, quite literally, earns its keep. With no assets left, after being stripped by the Braddylls, the hall is once again full of antiques but these are all for sale. As salerooms go, this has to be one of the most atmospheric.

SAWLEY

17

At the centre of this historic village, easily missed as the main road by passes it, is **Sawley Abbey**, founded in the 13th century by the Cistercian monks of Fountains Abbey. As well as building their religious house, the monks had great influence over the whole of the surrounding area. Clearing their immediate surroundings, the monks cultivated the land and their ridge and furrow patterns can still be made out in the fields. Although during the reigns Edward I and II, the abbots of Sawley were called to the House of Lords, none of the abbots were men of note except, perhaps, William Trafford, the last head of the community. With his colleague and neighbour, the last Abbot of Whalley, Trafford took part in the Pilgrimage of Grace in 1536 and, for his part in the failed uprising, he was taken prisoner. Tried for treason at Lancaster in 1537, Trafford, with others like him, was found guilty and executed. During the 18th and 19th centuries, the land around the village, as elsewhere, was enclosed by drystone walls and, less so here, hedgerows. Today, seen much as it was then, the landscape has changed little from those days and it continues to support a wealth of wildlife.

SILVERDALE

The village lies at the northwesternmost corner of the county and has the Lakeland hills as a backdrop as well as superb views over Morecambe Bay. The latter half of the 19th century saw Silverdale develop as a quiet seaside resort where those so inclined could take medicinal baths of fresh sea water in the one of the many small villas situated along the coast. One frequent visitor was Elizabeth Gaskell, who is said to have written at least part of all her books whilst holidaying here. However, Silverdale's history goes back well beyond the days of a genteel Victorian resort. Its name comes from a Viking family which settled here and which signifies that this was Sigward's or Soevers' valley. Fishing, naturally, was the key provider of local income, but in the 18th century, a copper smelting works was built here. All, however, that remains of the foundry is the chimney near Jenny Brown's Point, said to be named after an old woman who lived here in the 18th century. Essentially now a small residential village, Silverdale is well worth visiting for the network of footpaths from here that pass through the

18

limestone woodlands that are such a joy for the botanist, being rich in wild flowers in spring - primroses, violets, orchids, bird's eye primroses, rockroses, and eglantines abound. **Leighton Moss** near Silverdale is a nationally known RSPB bird sanctuary. The reed beds are the most important part of the reserve because they have become a northern stronghold of the rare bearded tit and are also the major British breeding centre for the bittern.

SLAIDBURN

Slaidburn is a pretty village of stone cottages and cobbled pavements lying in the heart of the Forest of Bowland. The village's focal point is the 13-century public house, **Hark to Bounty**, the name of which recalls the days when deer hunting was common in the area. The inn also contains an old court room, with its original oak furnishings, where, from around 1250, the Chief Court of Bowland, or Halmote, was held. The only courtroom between York and Lancaster, it was used by visiting justices from the 14th century onwards and is said to have been used by Oliver Cromwell when he was in the area. From the village a network of beautiful, little used lanes radiates westwards up into the fell country and some of the best walking that Lancashire has to offer. One walk in particular, that offers solitude as well as an excellent taste of the Bowland landscape, is that to the lonely valley of the River Whitendale, to the northwest of the village. To the northeast of Slaidburn lies Stocks Reservoir, another walker's destination.

SUNDERLAND

Sunderland is, unbelievably, an old port and seaside resort, which flourished until larger-berthed ships, silting channels, and the growth last century of rail-served Morecambe caused it to decline. A little wharf, quiet cottages, some with faded and evocative elegance, a sandy shore where sea thrift flourishes among the pebbles, are all that remains. The River Lune estuary is now a Site of Special Scientific Interest because of its wildlife value - visitors are likely to see such birds as redshank feeding on the rich food supplies of worms, shellfish, and shrimps on the saltmarshes, while a variety of wildfowl such as shelduck, wigeon, and mallard, are to be seen in autumn. A particularly

sad story acts as a reminder of Sunderland's time as a port. Sambo was a sea captain's servant at the time of the slave trade into Lancaster, who probably died of a fever in 1736 after a long and difficult voyage from the West Indies. Because he was not a baptised Christian, Sambo was not allowed to be buried in consecrated ground. In later years, his death and grave, marked by a simple cross and stone, became a potent local symbol of the anti-slavery cause. His grave can be still seen, in a field at the west side of Sunderland Point. It can be reached by walking along The Lane from the village foreshore, past Upsteps Cottage where Sambo died, and turning left at the shore then over a stile on the left which gives access to the simple gravestone. Fresh flowers are usually to be seen here, mysteriously placed on the grave.

THORNTON

Situated in the west bank of the Wyre estuary, this small town is dominated by **Marsh Mill**, which stands over 100 feet high and was constructed in 1794. The grinding of corn ceased here soon after World War I but the building has been restored and it is now a tourist attraction. At this point the Wyre estuary is wide and provides shelter for shipping, an advantage that was utilised by both the Romans and the Sandinavians. They both, also, took advantage of the salt deposits here and, today, the large ICI plant is still extracting salt. The **Wyre Estuary Country Park**, taking the whole estuary from Fleetwood up river as far as Shard Bridge, is an excellent place from to discover the area. An initial stop at the Wyreside Ecology Centre, which provides all manner of information about the estuary, is a sensible starting point. From here a number of footpaths take in many of the places along the river as well as leading visitors through important areas of salt marsh which contain a wide range of plants, insects, and birds.

WOODPLUMPTON

This charming little village, centred around its church, still has its well preserved village stocks, behind which is a mounting block that is now categorised as a historic monument. St Anne's Church is also a building of historic note and the keen-eyed will be quick to spot the octagonal cupola shape of tower that is reminiscent of the architecture of Christopher Wren. Completed in 1748, the tower was built to house a new timepiece, a clock, which replaced the sundial that for many years adorned the old tower. Bearing the date 1637, this can now be found in the churchyard. Also in the churchyard is a huge boulder that is said to mark the grave of Margaret Hilton. Locally known as Meg Shelton she is best remembered as Meg the Witch! She lived in a cottage at nearby Catforth and, so it is said, she entered into a bet with her landlords, the Haydock family, that she could turn into a hare and outrun their dogs. This she did but one of the dogs managed to nearly catch up with the hare, biting its ankle as it fled back to Meg's cottage. From then on Meg not only limped but she was also, always, in a foul temper and was accused of turning milk sour and laming cattle. Apparently crushed between a water barrel and a well, her body was buried in the churchyard and to prevent it rising, the huge boulder was placed on top.

YEALAND

To the south of the village lies **Leighton Hall** - a fine early 19th-century house which is open to the public. In the Middle Ages, this land, and much of the surrounding area, was owned by the d'Avranches family. Over the centuries, the house and the land passed through many hands before becoming the property of the Gillow family of Lancaster. Now in the hands of the Reynolds family, a branch of the Gillows, the fine furniture see in the hall reflects the trade that made the family fortune. As with many estates in Lancashire, Leighton Hall was a Catholic house and, one owner, Sir George Middleton, was fined heavily by Cromwell after the Civil War for his loyalty to Charles I and to his religion. Later, another owner of the hall, Albert Hodgson, suffered for his loyalty to Catholicism and the Stuart claim on the throne of England. Taking part in the Jacobite rebellion of 1715, Hodgson was captured at Preston and the Government troops inflicted such damage on the hall that little remained of the Tudor structure. The hall, today, dates from 1800 when it was built out of pale, local sandstone to the Gothic designs of Harrison, a Chester architect. One of the finest houses in the county, the views from the extensive grounds are magnificent and take in the nearby Leighton Moss bird reserve.

20 · The Barton Fox

Garstang Road, Barton, Nr. Preston,
Lancashire PR3 5AB
Tel: 01772 867901 Fax: 01772 867902

Directions:
From J32 of the M6, follow signs to Garstang (A6). Pub is 2 miles from motorway junction on left hand side.

Having served a number of functions since its origins in 1930's, the premises were totally refurbished in 1996 and given their present name. The current landlord, Chris Jones, has been here for 2 years, following a long and varied career within the licensing trade, and offers a warm welcome to visitors. The history of the site is displayed in the bar, where eye-catching features include exposed brickwork, wooden beams and handsome wood panelling. Also a variety of quirky quotations are scattered throughout, on beams and chalkboards and one of the many inscriptions is above the hearth and states, rather gloomily, 'The English winter - ending in July to recommence in August'.

You can sit in front of one of the three real log fires with a glass of real ale before settling down to a meal, which can be enjoyed between noon and 10pm throughout the pub, including a 50-seat non-smoking section. the choice is very varied, and the good food can be accompanied by something from a wine list that offers both variety and quality. Quiz night is Tuesday, from 9 o'clock, and other events include special theme days, which always attract a good following. The pub is set back from the road in extensive grounds with front and rear beer gardens and a large off-road car park.

Among the nearby attractions are the Lancaster Canal, Chingle Hall at Goosnargh and Myerscough College (which specialises in unusual plants), whilst just an hours drive away is the beautiful Lake District.

Opening Hours: All day, every day.

Food: Bar meals all day.

Credit Cards: Amex, Mastercard, Visa.

Accommodation: None.

Facilities: Car Park, beer gardens.

Entertainment: Quiz Tuesday.

Local Places of Interest/Activities: Lancaster Canal, Preston 4 miles, Woodplumpton 3 miles, Beacon Fell 4 miles, Myerscough College, National Football Museum

The Black Bull · 21

Brookhouse,
Caton,
Nr. Lancaster,
Lancashire
LA2 9PJ
Tel: 01524 770329

Directions:

From Lancaster, or
junction 34 of the
M6, take the A6 to
Caton (3 miles from
Lancaster). In Caton
take the minor road
signposted
Brookhouse.

Built in the 16th century and later extended by incorporating adjoining cottages, the **Black Bull** stands on Brookhouse Bridge, where Bull Beck flows on its way to join the River Lune. In the early 19th century the inn was used as a courthouse where the Lord of the Manor would summon his tenants to appear for trial.

Now, in the care of Trevor and Janet Latus, regulars and visitors do not need to be summoned to partake of the excellent hospitality offered in the cosiest and most atmospheric of surroundings. Thwaites Brewery provides the real ale and a Dark Smooth, and there's also a good selection of draught lagers. Tables and chairs are set throughout the brick-walled, low-beamed bars, and food is served daily from noon to 2.30 and from 6 till 8 (till 9 on summer nights). Most of the dishes are home-cooked, and the pub does a really good line in curries. Booking is advisable on Sunday. Quiz night is every Tuesday, and the occasional weekend sees a disco and/or live singers. There's a pleasant beer garden and off-road parking at the Black Bull, which is open every session and all day Saturday and Sunday.

It stands on the corner of Littledale Lane, which leads to one of the lesser known scenic gems of Lancashire. Littledale, tucked away among the hills on the northern edge of the Forest of Bowland, is mainly wooded, and it's a real delight to take a walk along Artle Beck to Littledale Hall and enjoy the handsome buildings and the splendid views.

Opening Hours: Lunchtime and evening; all day Sat & Sun.

Food: Bar meals.

Credit Cards: Diners, Mastercard, Visa.

Accommodation: None.

Facilities: Car Park.

Entertainment: Quiz Tuesday.

Local Places of Interest/Activities: Lancaster 3 miles, Morecambe 5 miles, Littledale 2 miles.

22   Black Bull Hotel

13 Main Street,
High Bentham,
Nr. Lancaster,
Lancashire
LA2 7HF
Tel: 01524 261213

Directions:

From Lancaster take the A683 about 5 miles then take the right fork on to the B6480. The pub is on the main street of the village, about 4 miles along.

Two handsome signs of a **Black Bull** identify this substantial white-painted building on a corner site in the centre of High Bentham. Spacious and tastefully updated, the former coaching inn is a popular local meeting place, a spot where young and old alike can relax and enjoy themselves. Lee Ellis, who has been the tenant for two years, is also the chef, and his hearty home cooking has attracted a loyal band of regulars.

Food is served every session except Sunday evening and all Monday unless it is a Bank Holiday Monday. Special offers include two meals at a reduced price; children are welcome in the bar until 9 o'clock. This is a Thwaites pub, and Thwaites provides the two real ales and a smooth bitter, and other thirst-quenchers include four draught lagers and Aston Manor cider. The Black Bull is ideally placed for exploring the dramatic countryside to the north and south, and on the first and second floors are four excellent en suite bedrooms - a single, two doubles and a family room - all with Sky TV. They can be let on a room only or Bed & Breakfast basis, and Lee offers special deals for extended stays. The usual diversions of pool, darts, dominoes, fruit machine and juke box are on hand in the bar, and a function room with seats for up to 50 is available for hire. Wednesday night is quiz night, and there's live entertainment most weekends.

The historic sights of Hornby are a short drive away towards Lancaster, the Yorkshire Dales National Park lies to the north, while the road south leads directly from the inn to the Forest of Bowland, with its majestic moors and fells, and down to Slaidburn.

Opening Hours: All day, every day.

Food: Bar meals.

Credit Cards: Planned.

Accommodation: 4 en suite rooms.

Entertainment: Quiz Wednesday.

Local Places of Interest/Activities: Hornby 4 miles, Lancaster 9 miles, Yorkshire Dales National Park, Forest of Bowland.

Black Bull Inn

23

47a Church Street,
Ribchester,
Lancashire
PR3 3YE
Tel: 01254 878291

Directions:
Ribchester is located on the B6245 7 miles southwest of Clitheroe; 4 miles northwest of Blackburn (A666 then B6245).

The Black Bull is a handsome old stone building on a prominent corner site in the centre of historic Ribchester. A coaching stop in earlier days, it has an excellent atmosphere, a good deal of period charm and friendly, hospitable tenants in Linda and Michael Cairns, a Lancashire couple who came here in June of Millennium year. In the comfortable, relaxing bars, a good selection of food is served lunchtime and evening and all day Saturday, Sunday and Bank Holidays. The exception is Monday, when the pub opens at 6pm and no food is served unless it's a Bank Holiday.

Linda does the cooking, and among many popular dishes her gammon platters have a particularly strong following. Booking are not always necessary, and children are always very welcome - they have their own special play area in the beer garden, where the summer barbecues bring in a good crowd. Thwaites Brewery provides two real ales, and other drinks include a new cider called Kingstone Press. The usual pub games (pool, darts, cards, dominoes) are played in the bar, and there's live entertainment on Saturday evening; Tuesday is quiz night. The tenants plan to introduce overnight accommodation in an adjoining barn, which when renovations are complete will provide budget accommodation for up to 26 guests.

Ribchester, on the banks of the River Ribble, is famous for its Roman Fort, Bremetannacum, which has a museum with many excavated items on display. Also well worth a visit is the ancient Church of St Wilfrid.

Opening Hours: Lunchtime and evening; all day Saturday, Sunday & Bank Holidays. Closed until 6pm Monday except for Bank Holidays.

Food: Bar meals.

Credit Cards: All the major cards.

Accommodation: Budget rooms planned.

Facilities: Car Park, beer garden.

Entertainment: Quiz Tuesday, live music Saturday.

Local Places of Interest/Activities: Ribchester Roman Fort, Clitheroe Castle, Forest of Bowland.

24   The Blue Anchor Hotel

68 Main Street,
Bolton-le-Sands,
Carnforth,
Lancashire
LA5 8DN
Tel: 01524 823241
Fax: 01524 824745

Directions:
From Carnforth take
the A6 south for 2
miles. The hotel is
on the main street of
the village.

On the main street of a village halfway between Carnforth and Morecambe, the **Blue Anchor** is a striking stone building dating back to the 18th century. Highly recommended locally and further afield for food, drink and accommodation, the hotel is run by tenants Ian Burrows and Rachel and Stanley Whittle, and the welcoming atmosphere they generate makes every visit a pleasure.

The range of food is extensive, from snacks served at the bar to a full à la carte selection in the upstairs restaurant; service hours for food are 12 to 2 and 6 to 8.30, Sunday 12 to 7, and booking is definitely advisable at the weekend. The healthy coastal air can create quite a thirst, and the Blue Anchor offers relief in the shape of four real ales (Tetleys, Boddingtons, Jennings and a guest) and a good range of other beers and lagers. The Blue Anchor has an award-winning beer garden and a car park that's available to residents. A jumbo quiz starts at 9.30 every Wednesday evening, and on the first Sunday of the month there's live entertainment from 9pm.

For anyone wanting to explore the Lancashire coastal stretch this is an ideal to drop anchor, and the four guest bedrooms, all en suite, provide comfortable, characterful accommodation. The rooms are let on a Bed & Breakfast basis, with special deals for stays of more than four nights. A long stay is certainly needed to do justice to all the area has to offer: Lancaster and the twin towns of Morecambe and Heysham to the south; to the north, Carnforth with its steam railway centre - the station was the setting for the classic 1940s weepie *Brief Encounter*; and, reaching westward across to Cumbria, the vast, flat tidal plain of Morecambe Bay, home to many varieties of marine life and an important habitat for birds.

Opening Hours: All day, every day.

Food: Bar meals and à la carte.

Credit Cards: Diners, Mastercard, Visa.

Accommodation: 4 en suite rooms.

Facilities: Car Park for residents, beer garden.

Entertainment: Quiz Wednesday, live show first Sunday of the month.

Local Places of Interest/Activities: Morecambe Bay, Morecambe, Heysham, Lancaster, Carnforth.

The Bridge Inn

25

Lower Tatham,
by Lancaster,
Lancashire
LA2 8NL
Tel: 01524 221326

Directions:

From Lancaster, or from the M6 (J34), take the A683 and then a right fork on to the B6480. Lower Tatham is about 2¾ miles along this road.

Two linked buildings, one dating from 1642, the other from 1744, make up this grand old inn, which in coaching days was called the Bridge End. The immaculate white-painted, slate-roofed facade promises a wealth of character within, and that's exactly what the visitor will find in the bar, the snug, the non-smoking main restaurant area (called Margaret's after a one-time licensee) and the upstairs dining area. Also upstairs are two very comfortable guest bedrooms - both doubles - which are let on a Bed & Breakfast basis.

The pub is run with notable flair and style by Peter and Pat Hunter and their cousin Dot, local people who are fortunate to have the services of Alan, a first-rate chef. His dishes are served lunchtime and evening and all day on Sunday, and booking is essential at the weekend. The printed menu and the board of daily specials provide an excellent choice, and favourites among the many home-cooked delights include chicken medley, shoulder of lamb and a particularly good game pie. The last Friday of every month is curry night - always guaranteed to bring in a good crowd. The inn has a lovely secluded beer garden offering splendid views, and among other amenities are an adjacent off-road car park and a caravan park with space for five vans, plus electric hook-up, a disposal area and running water - caravanners can use the inn's toilet facilities.

This is wonderful walking country, and in the vicinity are several places of interest. The neighbouring village has more than its fair share: an ancient stone bridge, the motte and bailey Castle Stede, Hornby Castle (famously painted by Turner) and the 13th century church of St Mary of Antioch. The Bridge is an ideal base for exploring these sights and for venturing further afield - perhaps up to the Yorkshire Dale National Park or down to the Forest of Bowland.

Opening Hours: Lunchtime and evening; all day Friday-Monday.

Food: A la carte menu, bar meals and specials board.

Credit Cards: Planned.

Accommodation: 2 rooms.

Facilities: Car Park, caravan park, bowling green planned.

Entertainment: None.

Local Places of Interest/Activities: Forest of Bowland, Yorkshire Dales National Park, Hornby 1 mile, Lancaster 5 miles.

26   The Coach & Horses

20 Main Street,
Bolton by Bowland,
Clitheroe,
Lancashire
BB7 4NW
Tel: 01200 447202

Directions:

From Clitheroe take the
A59 north to Sawley,
then left on to a minor
road signposted Bolton
by Bowland.

Built in 1800 on the site of an old inn called The Windmill, the **Coach & Horses** combines the charm of a country inn with the comfort of a small hotel and a quality of cooking that would be the envy of many a formal restaurant. All in all, a great place to tarry awhile for a drink, a meal or an overnight stay. Wooden floors, beams, hop bines and pictures and prints of bygone local scenes bring abundant character to the bars, and there's plenty of comfortable seating including a 40-cover dining room.

The Coach & Horses is in the safe hands of Ailsa and Midge, a delightful couple who took over the lease in the autumn of 1999. They both cook, and their menu, available lunchtime (not Tuesday) and evening and all day Sunday, is far more extensive and interesting than in most inns; making a decision on what to order is a pleasant problem, since everything sounds so appetising - and results on the plate do not disappoint. To start, perhaps country paté flavoured with Cointreau, Thai fish cakes with a sweet chilli sauce or deep-fried jalapeno peppers filled with cream cheese; then a pasta bowl, a traditional favourite (fish & chips, a steak, sausage & mash, the day's excellent pie) or something more out of the ordinary such as duck breast with garlic, honey and soy sauce, flamed with crème de cassis, venison in red wine, or, for vegetarians, ratatouille with a cheese and breadcrumb topping. Even the sandwiches are a bit special - smoked bacon with melted cheese, chargrilled chicken breast with lettuce and pesto mayonnaise - and, accompanied by a salad garnish and a few chips, make a first-class snack or quick meal. The themed food nights are always very popular and must be booked in advance. Three quality rooms, all en suite with bath and shower, provide quiet, comfortable Bed & Breakfast accommodation, and there are discounts to the tariff for stays of three days or more. The rooms overlook the village green, with its stocks and whipping post as reminders of harsher days.

The village stands near the River Ribble on the southern edge of the Forest of Bowland, a paradise for walkers and lovers of the countryside. The village church, with its famous Pudsey tomb showing Sir Ralph Pudsey with his three wives and 25 children, is well worth a visit, as are the many attractive neighbouring villages (Downham, Rimington, Sawley with its historic Abbey) and nearby Clitheroe Castle and Museum.

Opening Hours: Lunchtime (not Tuesday) and evening; all day Saturday, Sunday and Bank Holidays.

Food: Bar and restaurant meals.

Credit Cards: Diners, Mastercard, Visa.

Accommodation: 3 en suite rooms

Facilities: Car Park, beer garden.

Entertainment: None.

Local Places of Interest/Activities: Forest of Bowland, Sawley Abbey, Clitheroe.

The Derby Arms | 27

Carrs Green,
Inskip,
Nr. Preston,
Lancashire
PR4 0TJ
Tel: 01772 690326

Directions:

From Preston, A6 to Broughton, turn left on to the B5269 to Inskip; from Blackpool, B5266 to Singleton then B5269.

Graham and Niki Hough welcome visitors to the **Derby Arms**, which stands on a prominent corner site on the B5269 road 8 miles east of Blackpool. The setting is delightfully rural, and the pub, a handsome white-painted building with hanging baskets adorning the front and sides, is an ideal spot to pause for a drink and a meal in a friendly, relaxed atmosphere.

Graham's home cooking, available every day except Wednesday, covers an excellent choice, and the curries and the steak & ale pie are among the favourites. Children have their own special menu, and a traditional Sunday lunch is also offered. Three real ales are on tap, along with a range of popular beers and lagers and a good selection of wines. The non-smoking restaurant has seats for 32, and besides the main bar the Derby Arms has a comfortable lounge, a games room and a function room. An interesting feature in the bar is the illustrated story of the time when this was a mecca for car enthusiasts, with a 1928 Lagonda on the roof and beer drawn through mini-petrol pumps. A singer (person, not car) takes the stage on the first Saturday of the month, and there's a quiz on Wednesdays in winter. At the back of the pub are a beer garden and large car park.

The surrounding area, known as The Fylde, is a great place for walking, and it's but a short drive to Blackpool with its myriad family attractions; even closer are several charming villages, including St Michael's on Wyre, Churchtown and Woodplumpton: all three have interesting churches that are well worth a detour.

Opening Hours: Lunchtime and evening; all day Sat & Sun.

Food: Bar meals.

Credit Cards: Mastercard, Visa, Debit cards (cash back available)

Accommodation: None.

Facilities: Car Park, beer garden, function room.

Entertainment: Singer first Sat of the month.

Local Places of Interest/Activities: Blackpool 8 miles, St Michael on Wyre, Churchtown, Woodplumpton.

Internet/Website:
e-mail: derbyarms@supanet.com

28 The Eagle & Child

3 High Street,
Garstang,
Lancashire
PR3 1EA
Tel: 01995 602139

Directions:

From Preston take the A6 north (7 miles); from Lancaster take the A6 south (9 miles); from Blackpool (12 miles) A586 then A6. The pub stands just off the main road.

When Lorraine and Paul Gibbins took over the lease at the end of 1998 they were maintaining the family connection at the **Eagle & Child**. Lorraine's parents Ian and Mary had run it for the previous ten years, building up its fine reputation as one of the friendliest and most popular local meeting places. Once a posting inn, the premises have been sympathetically updated, and the bars combine traditional and modern elements to stylish, relaxing effect.

Three real ales - Theakstons, Old Speckled Hen and Barnsley Bitter - are always on tap, and from 11am to 2pm food is served Monday to Saturday (and in the evening to residents). Lorraine's regular menu, supplemented by daily specials, offers a good choice, and among the highlights are very moreish home-made chips, a choice of four curries and some very hearty lamb dishes - steaks marinated in rosemary and garlic, and mint-marinated lamb Henry. Children are welcome, and the lounge is declared a no-smoking zone when food is being served. As well as the good atmosphere, the food and the drink, the Eagle & Child also provides very comfortable overnight accommodation in four upstairs letting bedrooms - a twin, a double and two family rooms, all with en suite facilities. The rooms are let on a Bed & Breakfast or Dinner, Bed & Breakfast basis, with discounts for extended stays. Behind the inn are a beer garden and plenty of parking space. In-house entertainment includes a Sunday disco and, every other Thursday, a session of Play Your Cards Right.

Garstang is an ancient, picturesque town with a leisure centre, a Discovery Centre and a bustling Thursday market.

Opening Hours: All day, every day.

Food: Bar meals Mon-Sat lunch; evening meals residents only.

Credit Cards: None.

Accommodation: 4 en suite rooms.

Facilities: Car Park, beer garden.

Entertainment: Disco Sunday, Play Your Cards Right every other Thursday.

Local Places of Interest/Activities: Preston, Blackpool, Lancaster, Barton Grange Garden Centre 5 miles, Greenhalgh Castle 1 mile.

The Golden Ball Hotel   29

6 School Lane,
Pilling,
Nr. Preston,
Lancashire
PR3 6AA
Tel: 01253 790212

Directions:
From Blackpool take
the A586 then A588.

One of the social hubs of the scattered village of Pilling, the **Golden Ball Hotel** was built in 1904. Behind its redbrick facade the style is grandly Victorian, with large rooms, high ceilings, exuberant wallpaper and a long panelled bar counter. It's run by Billy Whiteside and his daughters, and they also manage another pub in the village. Billy's parents ran the Golden Ball from 1968 to 1978, so there's a strong family link.

Excellent food, with plenty of choice, is served lunchtime and evening, and the traditional Sunday lunch with a choice of roasts is particularly popular. This is a Thwaites pub, with Cask Mild and Smooth on tap; other choices for quenching thirsts include Carlsberg Export and Kingswood Press cider. A function room is available for parties or meetings, and outside is a beer garden where children can play in safety, and a fine bowling green. The family has plans to add to the amenities of the Golden Ball by once more making it a hotel - five guest bedrooms will come on stream, some with en suite facilities and four-poster beds.

Fleetwood and Blackpool are an easy drive away, while even closer there's excellent walking, both coastal and country, and some delightful villages to explore - Pilling itself, said to be the second largest village in England; Pressall, once an important salt-mining centre; and Knott End-on-Sea, a quiet holiday resort on the Wyre estuary. The Golden Ball is closed Monday to Wednesday in the daytime.

Opening Hours: Mon-Wed evenings; Thurs & Fri lunchtime and evening; Sat & Sun all day.

Food: Bar meals.

Credit Cards: None.

Accommodation: 5 rooms planned.

Facilities: Car Park, beer garden, children's play area, bowling green.

Entertainment: None.

Local Places of Interest/Activities:
Fleetwood 4 miles, Blackpool 7 miles, walking, fishing, sailing.

30   Hark to Bounty

Slaidburn,
Nr. Clitheroe,
Lancashire
BB7 3EP
Tel: 01200 446246
Fax: 01200 446361

Directions:
Slaidburn is about 9 miles north of Clitheroe on the B6478.

The very name '**Hark to Bounty**' conjures up romance, history and atmosphere, and this famous old inn has since the 13th century, been the focal point of a pretty stone-built village in the heart of the Forest of Bowland. Until 1875 it was known as The Dog, but one day the village squire, who was also the village parson, took a break at the inn from hunting with his pack of hounds. The drinking was disturbed by loud braying from the hounds, and amid the din the squire could hear his favourite hound, which made him call out: 'Hark to Bounty'.

So 'The Dog' became 'Hark to Bounty' and 125 years on the inn continues its tradition of offering the best of hospitality. The locality provides some of the best walking in the whole county, and ramblers' thirsts can be assuaged in the inn's splendid bars by a good selection of ales including the excellent Theakstons brews. The food here is also of a very high quality, and the 50-seat restaurant is a cosy, country-style setting in which to relax over a leisurely meal.

Hark to Bounty offers characterful accommodation in nine guest bedrooms, all with private facilities. They range from a single room to a family room with a double and two single beds, and all have tv and tea-making kit. The oak-beamed lounge bar is a popular meeting place for both local patrons and visitors, and the residents' lounge can double as a small meeting room for up to 20 people. As many as 100 can be accommodated in the Old Courtroom, which was used by travelling justices from the 14th century right up until 1937. Many fine features have been preserved, notably the jury benches, the judge's box and a magnificent 17th oak screen. The Court records may be seen in the County Archives at Preston and in the Archives of nearby Clitheroe Castle.

Opening Hours: Lunchtime and evening; all day Sunday.

Food: Bar and restaurant meals.

Credit Cards: Mastercard, Visa.

Accommodation: Nine en suite bedrooms.

Facilities: Car Park, function room for up to 100.

Local Places of Interest/Activities: Clitheroe 9 miles, country walks (Forest of Bowland, Whitendale Valley, Stocks Reservoir).

Internet/Website:
e-mail: manager@hark-to-bounty.co.uk
website: www.hark-to-bounty.co.uk

Higher Buck Inn

The Square,
Waddington,
Clitheroe,
Lancashire
BB7 3HZ
Tel: 01200 423226

Directions:

1½ miles north of Clitheroe on the B6478 road that runs up to the A682.

Waddington is one of the area's best-known villages and its attractive Coronation Gardens have played a starring role on many a postcard and even on the lids of biscuit tins. On the square at Waddington stands **Higher Buck Inn**, built in the early 19th century on the site of a much earlier hostelry. It was formerly called The Buck and perhaps acquired the 'Higher' from its prominent position overlooking the picturesque village.

Decorated and furnished in a style befitting its age, the bar is very cosy and comfortable, an ideal spot for unwinding with a glass or two of one of Thwaites excellent brews or something from the range of draught lagers. It's also a good place to tarry longer for a lunchtime or evening meal, and from the printed menu and daily specials there's something to please everyone - the home-made pies are favourites with many of the regular patrons. Stephen Pacey, who has been the tenant here since April 2001, has plans to develop the beer garden, which will add another aspect to the amenities; there's plenty of off-road parking space at the rear of the pub. Higher Buck is closed on Mondays except for Bank Holidays and is otherwise open lunchtime and evening and all day Saturday and Sunday.

The area around Waddington is great for rambling and serious walking, with forests and hills in abundance - Easington Fell (1300') and Pendle Hill (1800') are among the most challenging. Also within easy reach are the 13th century Sawley Abbey and the old stone town of Clitheroe in the Ribble Valley; the Castle and its museum are well worth a visit.

Opening Hours: Lunchtime and evening; all day Sat & Sun. Closed Monday except Bank Holidays.

Food: Bar meals.

Credit Cards: Diners, Mastercard, Visa.

Accommodation: None.

Facilities: Car Park.

Local Places of Interest/Activities:
Clitheroe 1½ miles, Sawley Abbey 2 miles, Hurst Green (Stonyhurst College) 4 miles, Pendle Hill, Forest of Bowland.

32 The Kings Arms Hotel

Main Street,
Burton-in-Kendal,
Carnforth,
Lancashire LA6 1LR
Tel: 01524 781409

Directions:

Burton-in-Kendal lies 4 miles north of Carnforth and 6 miles south of Kendal, on the A6070; also close to the M6, junction 35 or 36.

The Royal coat of arms is emblazoned on the sign outside the **Kings Arms**, which stands at the heart of a village on the A6070, with easy access from the M6 (junction 35 or 36). The inn has a history that traces back as far as the 16th century, and it remains a very inviting place to pause for a drink, to linger over a meal or to establish a base for exploring a part of the world that is rich in historical and scenic interest. The records show that the poet Keats stayed at the Kings Arms.

Part of the building was once a cobbler's shop, and, beautifully renovated and refurbished, it opened in November 2000 as a delightful, intimate restaurant. In this non-smoking section an excellent à la carte menu is served lunchtime and evening (booking needed on Saturday night), while in the bar an equally varied bill of fare is offered. Baguettes with tempting fillings such as tuna and sweetcorn mayonnaise or grilled rumpsteak & fried onions are served with chips to provide a first-rate, satisfying light meal, and other choices run from filled jacket potatoes and giant Yorkshire puddings with various fillings to braised liver with mash and onion gravy. Five different brews will keep real ale aficionados happy, and there's a good selection of draught lagers, cider and stout. The guest accommodation comprises six bedrooms, all en suite. The pub has a secluded beer garden and off-road parking space. Among the many places to visit within an easy drive are the lovely Lune Valley; Leighton Hall, one of the finest houses in the county; the quiet coastal village of Silverdale; and the RSPB sanctuary of Leighton Moss, a major breeding centre for bitterns.

Opening Hours: Lunchtime and evening; all day Fri, Sat & Sun.

Food: Bar and à la carte menus.

Credit Cards: Diners, Mastercard, Visa.

Accommodation: 6 en suite rooms. Pets welcome

Facilities: Car Park, beer garden.

Entertainment: None.

Local Places of Interest: Lune Valley, Leighton Hall, Leighton Moss RSPB, Carnforth (Railway Centre) 4 miles.

The Lord Ashton | 33

36 North Road, Lancaster,
Lancashire LA1 1NY
Tel: 01524 841185

Directions:
A central site in North Road, Lancaster.

Fine ales and good food are the selling points of the **Lord Ashton**, which stands close to the centre of the historic county capital. On a corner site, it presents a cheerful white front to the world on the main street (and a blind brick wall in the cul-de-sac round the corner) and inside it's small, cosy and very inviting, with loads of atmosphere. Formerly the Station Hotel, it was renamed in 1991 after the renowned Lord Ashton of Lancaster, the city's most famous son, textile tycoon, benefactor and sometime Liberal MP for the city.

Hughie and Cath McMillan, here since September 2000, have 40 years experience in the trade, and in their short time here have really put the pub back on the map. All the food is prepared and cooked on the premises and can be ordered from 11.30 to 2 Monday to Saturday and from 7 till 9 every day of the week. The pub is open for drinks Sunday from 7, Monday to Thursday lunchtime and evening and all day Friday and Saturday. Parking is available at an adjacent Pay & Display car park.

Lancaster is a fascinating place with plenty to occupy the serious visitor, including the great medieval fortress Lancaster Castle, half a dozen museums, the Lancaster Canal offering boating, fishing and towpath walks of any length you like, and the imposing copper-domed Ashton Memorial, which houses an exhibition of the life and times of Lord Ashton, born James Williamson in 1842 and at one time the city's leading employer in the manufacture of linoleum and textiles. What better place to drink a toast to him than in the bar of the pub that bears his name!

Opening Hours: Lunchtime and evening; all day Fri & Sat, from 7pm Sunday.

Food: Bar meals.

Credit Cards: None.

Accommodation: None.

Entertainment: None.

Local Places of Interest/Activities: All the historic buildings, museums and amenities of Lancaster; Morecambe, Heysham.

34

The Old Oak

111 Preston Road,
Longridge,
Lancashire
PR3 3BA
Tel: 01772 783648

Directions:

From Preston (4 miles) or Clitheroe (10 miles), take the B6243 to Longridge.

Locals and visitors are united in their praise of the excellent hospitality provided at this fine little 18th century inn on the Preston Road. Nigel and Irene Maloney have really stamped their personalities on the place since their arrival three years ago in what is a very successful first venture into the licensed trade.

This is one of the top places in the county for real ales, with at least five always on tap. Theakstons Bitter, Theakstons Mild and Charles Wells Bombardier are the regulars, with two frequently changing guests - in fact you could come here every night for a week and have a different real ale every night. And if you suddenly think you've seen a rabbit, you probably have - it will be Thumper, now installed as one of the family at the Old Oak. Irene is the cook, and a blackboard announces her dishes of the day, which are served Tuesday to Saturday from noon to 2.30 and from noon to 4 o'clock on Sunday. Liver & onions is a great favourite with the regular patrons; children are welcome, and during the hours of food service certain areas of the pub are designated non-smoking. The pub has off-road parking spaces at the front and small beer garden at the back where barbecues are sometimes held.

Quiz night is the first Thursday of each month, and the Old Oak is also host to rather more unusual events including the annual Giant Onion Competition (judged in September) and an annual pie-baking competition that takes place on the Saturday before Good Friday. Round-the-year entertainment is provided in the bar by pool, darts, a juke box and a fruit machine.

Longridge lies at the foot of Longridge Fell, which offers splendid walks and superb views. Longridge was at one time an important source of building stone, producing the materials for several of Preston's civic buildings and the docks at Liverpool.

Opening Hours: All day, every day.

Food: Bar meals.

Credit Cards: None.

Accommodation: None.

Facilities: Car Park, beer garden.

Entertainment: Quiz first Thursday in the month.

Local Places of Interest/Activities: Preston 4 miles, Clitheroe 10 miles, Goosnargh (Chingle Hall medieval haunted manor house) 2 miles, Ribchester (Roman Fort & Museum, 13th century St Wilfrid's Church) 2 miles.

The Plough at Eaves
35

Eaves Lane, Woodplumpton, Preston, Lancashire PR4 0BJ
Tel: 01772 690233

Directions:

From Preston, take the A6 to Broughton then the B5269 to Woodplumpton. Look for the signs to Eaves and follow them for 1½ miles into the countryside. Alternatively, turn first left off the A6 at Station Lane; the Plough is 2 miles along this road on the left.

A real hidden gem, with a history going back to 1645. **The Plough** is a low, white-painted building with a two-storey stone neighbour; inside, it's all gnarled black beams, ornamental plates and horse brasses, a roaring fire in winter, roundback chairs and banquettes with attractive tapestry-style upholstery, a non-smoking dining area with chairs set at immaculate white-clothed tables.

The main ales are from Thwaites Brewery, and the cooking is top-notch. From the abundant choice, highlights include the Plough Whale, a huge fillet of haddock cooked in a special batter and served with chips and mushy peas; lamb marinated with mint and herbs; barbecued pork ribs; and mussels and lobster supplied, like the haddock, by an excellent fishmonger in Blackburn. Service times for food are Wednesday to Saturday lunchtimes, Monday to Saturday evenings and all day Sunday; booking is rcommended on Saturday. The Plough has areas for sitting outside at the front, side and rear, and there's a place for children to play and good off-road parking. Wednesday is quiz night.

The Plough, which is located on an old drovers' road, is steeped in history, as is the area around it: Cromwell fought a major battle nearby, and there are several picturesque villages to explore. Woodplumpton itself is a really delightful place centred round the Church of St Anne. An oddity in the churchyard is a huge boulder said to have been placed over the grave of a local witch called Meg to make sure she stayed firmly underground.

Opening Hours: Lunchtime and evening; all day Sat & Sun. Closed Mon & Tues lunchtime except Bank Holiday Mondays.

Food: Bar meals.

Credit Cards: All the major cards.

Accommodation: None.

Facilities: Car Park, beer garden.

Entertainment: Quiz Wednesday.

Local Places of Interest/Activities: Preston 4 miles, Woodplumpton.

36 The Plough at Galgate

Main Road,
Galgate,
Lancaster,
Lancashire
LA2 0LQ
Tel: 01524 751337

Directions:

The pub is located near the railway bridge on the main A6 at Galgate, four miles south of Lancaster.

South of Lancaster on the banks of the River Conder, Galgate still has some of its original mills, but they are no longer engaged on the purpose for which they were built. Not so **The Plough**, which began dispensing hospitality in the 17th century and continues to do so to this day.

The present leaseholder is Susan Humphries, who came here at the end of 1999, bringing with her nearly 20 years' experience in the licensed trade. The inn, painted white, with black for door and window surrounds, has a particularly warm and welcoming interior, with beams, chairs you can really relax in, horse brasses, copper pans, drinking pots and period prints contributing to the traditional look. The real ale is Boddingtons, with Worthington and Tetley's Creamflow among the kegs, and a refreshing glass or two can accompany something chosen from the chalkboard menu. The food, all prepared to order by Jeanette, is served from noon right through to 8.30pm daily, and the choice runs from light snacks to steaks, with plenty in between.

The pub, which is open all day, every day, stands right on the A6 south of Lancaster and very close to junction 33 of the M6. To the west of Galgate lies the sailing centre of Glasson, on the Lune estuary, while to the east stretches the magnificent open countryside of the ancient Forest of Bowland, with miles of wonderful walks and unsurpassed views. And Lancaster itself, just four miles up the road, is a city filled with history and a must for any visitor to the area.

Opening Hours: All day, every day.

Food: Bar meals served all day.

Credit Cards: Planned.

Accommodation: Planned.

Facilities: Car Park.

Entertainment: None.

Local Places of Interest/Activities: Lancaster 4 miles, Glasson 2 miles, coastal and country walks.

The Plough Hotel 37

2 Lytham Road,
Freckleton,
Lancashire
PR4 1XA
Tel: 01772 632345

Directions:

From Preston (5
miles) A583 then
A584. From Black-
pool (9 miles) A584.

Ernie (James) Berry, former professional footballer, and his wife Barbara hold the lease at **The Plough**, which stands off the A584 on the road that leads to Lytham St Anne's. Behind its mid-Victorian redbrick frontage, the bars are very roomy and comfortable, with a strong traditional appeal. There's an unusual stained-glass feature above the bar counter, and one of the upper-floor windows depicts two white shire horses at work pulling a plough.

Food is served here very lunchtime, with evening meals available by special arrange-ment. Baguettes, with generous fillings such as tuna & cheese melt or hot steak & onions, are very popular choices for a satisfying quick snack, while main courses run from lasagne (meat or vegetarian) to chicken and mushroom pie, pork chop with stuffing and apple sauce, deep-fried scampi and stir-fried beef in a ginger and oyster sauce. Children are wel-come in the pub until 8 o'clock. All the usual pub games and diversions are available - pool, darts, pinball and quiz machines, Sky TV - and the weekly quiz starts at 10 o'clock every Wednesday evening. Happy Hour, with reduced prices on beer and alcopops, is from 5 to 7 Monday to Friday. The three real ales include Plough Ale, brewed specially for the pub by the Moorhouse Brewery at Burnley, another of the lesser-known offerings is the Pheasant Plucker cider, which is best ordered when sober. The pub has ample car parking space and a patio where barbecues are held in the summer.

There's excellent walking with splendid views in and around the village, which stretches along the northern bank of the River Ribble. Several picturesque villages lie nearby, and it's only a very short drive west along the A584 to Lytham St Anne's, whose numerous attrac-tions include a promenade and pier, a fine old windmill, a nature reserve, country park and museums devoted to lifeboats, railways and toys. And Royal Lytham & St Anne's Golf Course is one of the top links courses in the country.

Opening Hours: All day, every day.

Food: Bar meals lunchtime.

Credit Cards: None.

Accommodation: None.

Facilities: Car Park, patio

Entertainment: Quiz Wednesday.

Local Places of Interest/Activities: Lytham St Anne's 3 miles, Blackpool 9 miles, Preston 5 miles.

38   The Ranch House

Head Dyke Lane, Preesall,
Poulton-le-Fylde, Lancashire FY6 0PG
Tel: 01253 790621

Directions:
From Blackpool, 8 miles north on the
A586, then the A588.

A long, low 1960s building set back from the main A588, with plenty of off-road car parking space, a bowling green, an extensive children's play area and a toddlers' play area in the enclosed garden. **The Ranch House** is in the excellent keeping of experienced publicans Kenny and Susan Moore, who previously managed a pub in Cheshire.

The interior of the Ranch House is smart, spacious and extra comfortable, with a traditional feel that belies the modern frontage. The range of drinks served at the intimate bar - note the brass rail and the studded leather counter front - includes Tetleys and a guest real ale, Tetleys Smooth, Caffreys, Theakstons Keg Mild and a regularly changing draught cider. There are seats for up to 150 in two separate dining rooms, where a very wide variety of dishes is served lunchtime and evening Monday to Saturday and all day from noon to 8 o'clock on Sunday. The main menu runs from hot and cold sandwiches and light bites/starters to curries, fish specials, steaks, lamb cutlets, beef stroganoff and chicken and ham pancake in a cream and cheddar sauce. Roast meats are the centrepiece of the Sunday menu, and there's a '2001 Special' three-course menu; a well-priced senior citizens menu is available Monday to Saturday. Happy Hour on all beers is from 5 to 7 Thursday and Friday, and the weekend fun and games start at 9 o'clock on Thursday evening with a karaoke session; Friday is disco night and there's live entertainment on Saturday.

Preesall, once a salt-mining centre, is a very pleasant place to walk around, and a short drive away are the lovely little coastal resort of Knott End-on-Sea, the fishing port of Fleetwood, Wyre Estuary Country Park at Thornton and Pilling, said to be the second largest village in Britain.

Opening Hours: Lunchtime and evening; all day Sat & Sun.

Food: Bar meals.

Credit Cards: All the major cards.

Accommodation: None.

Facilities: Car Park, bowling green, garden with children's play areas.

Entertainment: Karaoke Thursday, disco Friday, live show Saturday.

Local Places of Interest/Activities: Knott End-on-Sea, Fleetwood, Blackpool.

The Travellers Rest

90 Beach Road, Cleveleys,
Lancashire FY5 1EH
Tel: 01253 853060

Directions:
Cleveleys is situated 5 miles north of
Blackpool on the A584.

Close to the seafront at Cleveleys, the **Travellers Rest** started life as the Hazel Grove residential hotel. A large redbrick building on a corner site, the inn is imposing from the outside and even more impressive within. Christine and John, who took over the lease in 2000, are breathing new life into the place, and the bars are filled with interesting and eyecatching features including pot plants, lovely fireplaces, masses of highly polished wood, lots of stained glass and all kinds of objects and memorabilia. The leaseholders' ambitious plans include the creation of a number of themed areas; the first to be completed is the splendid Egyptian section with authentic prints and artefacts.

Food is served every day from noon till 6 or 7 in the evening, and the menus cover a very wide choice. Everything is home-made, and the favourites with the regular patrons include steaks, curries, pasta dishes and Chinese specialities. Children are welcome, and the dining area includes some non-smoking tables. Two big screen TV's, pool and snooker tables, table football and a juke box provide permanent in-house entertainment, and a music quiz fills a regular Thursday evening slot. The inn, which has its own car park at the back, is just a short walk from the beach in the popular seaside resort of Cleveleys.

Quiter than its famous neighbour to the south (Blackpool), it is also more pleasing architecturally: this is not too surprising, as much of the town's growth happened after an architectural competition held in 1906, in which no less a figure than Sir Edwin Lutyens was involved. There's plenty to pass the time here, and lots more to see in the vicinity, including the fishing port of Fleetwood (where the Fisherman's Friend throat lozenge was invented) and the Wyre Estuary Country Park, where waymarked trails run through the habitats of numerous plants, insects and birds.

Opening Hours: All day, every day.

Food: Bar meals (not Tuesday).

Credit Cards: None - cheques welcomed with bankers card

Accommodation: None.

Facilities: Car Park, Full disabled facilities

Entertainment: Quiz Thursday, regular themed party nights, Karaoke

Local Places of Interest/Activities: Blackpool, Fleetwood, Wyre Estuary, seafront trams.

The Hidden Inns of Lancashire and Cheshire

2 East Lancashire

PLACES OF INTEREST:

PUBS AND INNS:

The Hidden Inns of Lancashire and Cheshire

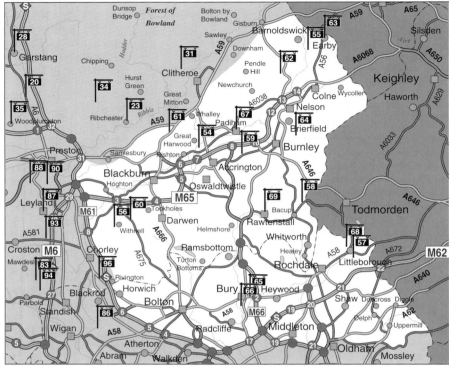

© MAPS IN MINUTES ™ 2001 © Crown Copyright, Ordnance Survey 2001

54 The Albion Alehouse, Clayton-le-Moors	**62** The Moorcock Inn, Blacko, nr Nelson
55 The Anchor Inn, Salterforth	**63** The Red Lion, Earby
56 The Cricketers, Brinscall, nr Chorley	**64** Roggerham Gate Inn, Briercliffe
57 Fishermans Inn, Bury	**65** The Seven Stars, Bury
58 The Flowers Inn, Bacup	**66** The Swan & Cemetery, Bury
59 The Hapton Inn, Hapton, nr Burnley	**67** Whalley Range Inn, Padiham
60 The Hare & Hounds, Abbey Village	**68** The Wheatsheaf, Littleborough
61 The Lord Nelson, Langho, nr Blackburn	**69** The Whitchaff Inn, Rawtenstall

Please note all references refer to page numbers

East Lancashire

Although during medieval times both the Forest of Pendle and the Forest of Rossendale were royal hunting grounds, these both relatively treeless areas have, since hunting ceased, developed along very different lines. Pendle, with the famous hill at its centre, is still an isolated stretch of moorland with few roads traversing the scene. Surrounding the higher ground are a series of untouched villages which, though they saw some industrialisation with the expansion of the textile industry, have still remained small. To the southwest of Pendle Hill lies Whalley, a picturesque village, save for the giant railway viaduct, that is home to one of the best preserved abbeys in the country. The southern edge of the Pendle area is centred around the valley of Colne Water and here are the famous textile towns of Burnley, Nelson, and Colne.

Further south, the larger area, the Forest of Rossendale saw the establishment of no real settlements until the 1400s, when the Crown leased off parts of the forest, and the early 1500s, when the final clearance and deforestation began. During the course of the 18th century, important advances in textile technology brought the introduction of water-powered mills to Rossendale. At this time cotton was also being imported and took over from the traditional woollen cloth manufacture. During the second half of the 19th century the industrial prosperity was so great that Rossendale came known as the Golden Valley. With Blackburn, one of the area's oldest settlements, in the north and Rawtenstall, Darwen, and Bacup in the centre of what was the forest, the whole region was a hive of activity making and finishing the cloth with others providing the necessary support. However, Rossendale, though provided with a much better road system, still offers tremendous opportunities for outdoor leisure and recreation as well, of course, as a fascinating industrial history.

The area of the county, to the north of Manchester and west of the Pennines, is, perhaps, everyone's idea of the county of Lancashire. A region dominated by cotton, East Lancashire has risen and fallen with the fluctuations in the trade over the years but, behind the dark, satanic mills is a population full of humour and wit as well as some splendid countryside. Before the Industrial Revolution this was a sparsely populated region of remote hillside farms and cottages that relied, chiefly, on sheep farming and the wool trade. Many of the settlements date back to before the Norman Conquest and, though little may have survived the rapid building of the 19th century, there are three surprisingly wonderful ancient houses to be seen here: Smithills Hall and Hall-i'-th'-Wood at Bolton and Turton Tower, just to the north. However, there is no escaping the textile industry. Lancashire's ideal climate for cotton spinning and weaving - damp so that the yarn does not break - made it the obvious choice for the building of the mills. There are numerous valleys with fast flowing rivers and streams and then the development of the extensive coalfields around Wigan supplied the fuel to feed the power hungry machinery. There are many illustrations in the region of the harsh working conditions the labourers had to endure and the grime that covered much of the area. However, now that much of this has been cleaned up, the rivers running once again fast, clear, and supporting wildlife, the lasting legacy of those days is the splendid Victorian architecture of which every town has at least one example.

PLACES OF INTEREST

ACCRINGTON

This attractive Victorian market town, as is typical in the area, expanded as a result of the increase in the textile industry of the 18th and 19th centuries. The town is the home of the **Haworth Art Gallery**, one of the most attractive in the country, set in beautiful parkland

44

and housing the largest collection of Tiffany glass - there are 130 pieces - in Europe. The collection was presented to the town by Joseph Briggs, an Accrington man, who went to New York to work with Louis Tiffany for nearly 40 years. Briggs joined the studio in 1890 and rose through the company ranks to become the manager of the Mosaic department before, finally, becoming Tiffany's personal assistant. After the First World War, the fashion for Tiffany glassware waned and, during the economic depression of the 1920s, Briggs was given the sad job of selling off the remainder of the Tiffany stock. Returning to his native Accrington in 1933 with his collection of glass, Briggs gave half to the town and distributed the remainder amongst his family.

BACUP

Built in the 19th century for the sole purpose of cotton manufacture, Bacup remains one of the best examples of a textile town in England even though it suffered more than most when the mills began to close. Any stroll through the town centre will reveal carefully restored shops and houses, with the grander homes of the mill owners and the elegant civic buildings acting as a reminder of the town's more prosperous times. An excellent time to visit the town in during the Easter weekend when the town's famous troop of Morris Dancers take to the streets. Known as the Coconut Dancers, their costume is unique and involves wearing halved coconut husks strapped to their knees and blackening their faces. Maintaining that the correct name is Moorish, not Morris, Dancers, the tradition is thought to go back to the times of the Crusades.

BLACKBURN

The largest town in East Lancashire, Blackburn is notable for its modern shopping malls, its celebrated three day market, its modern cathedral, and Thwaites Brewery, one of the biggest independent brewers of real ale in the north of England. Hard though it may be to imagine today, at the height of the textile industry, Blackburn was the biggest weaving town in the world. In 1931, it received arguably its most influential visitor when Mahatma Gandhi toured the area on a study trip of Lancashire's textile manufacture. Examples of the early

machines, including James Hargreaves' Spinning Jenny and his carding machine, invented in 1760, can be seen at the **Lewis Textile Museum**, which is dedicated to the industry. **Blacjburn's Museum and Art Gallery** has among its treasures several paintings by Turner, the Hart collection of medieval manuscripts, and the finest collection of Eastern European icons in Britain. Mentioned in the Domesday Book, the town was originally an agricultural community before the production of first woollen and then cotton cloth took over.

Much of the town seen today was built on the prosperity brought by the cotton trade and, on the dome of St John's Church, can be seen a weathervane in the shape of a weaving shuttle. However, the town's prominence as a centre for the surrounding community has not been lost as, in 1926, the Diocese of Blackburn was created and the Gothic St Mary's Church, built in 1826, became the Cathedral of the Bishop of Blackburn. Although Blackburn no longer has a manor house, Witton House has long since been demolished, the grounds have been turned into an excellent local amenity. Witton Country Park contains nature trials through woodlands up on to heather covered hill tops, all that remains of Witton House's once extensive grouse shoots.

BOLTON

Synonymous with the Lancashire textile industry, Bolton is also an ancient town that predates its expansion due to cotton by many centuries. First settled during the Bronze Age, by the time of the Civil War, this was a market town supporting the surrounding villages. The town saw one of the bloodiest episodes of the war when James Stanley, Earl of Derby, was brought back here by Cromwell's troops after the Royalists had been defeated. In a savage act of revenge for the massacre his army had brought on the town early in the troubles, Stanley was executed and his severed head and body, in separate caskets, were taken back to the family burial place at Ormskirk. Whilst in captivity in the town, Stanley was kept prisoner at Ye Olde Man and Scythe Inn which, dating from 1251, is still standing in Churchgate today. Dating back to the 14th century, Smithills Hall is an impressive building that is situated on an easily defended hill. Brought by the Bolton Corporation in the late 1930s, the hall has been beautifully restored and, as well as seeing one of the

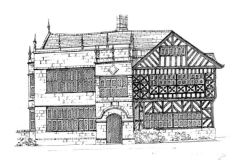

Hall-i'-th'-Wood

oldest and best preserved fortified manor houses in the county, visitors can also wander along the hall's wooded nature trail.

Bolton is indeed fortunate as, also on the northern side of the town, is **Hall-i'-th'-Wood**, its second splendid half-timbered house. Dating back to the late 15th century, the house was extended, in stone, in 1591 and again, in 1648, by its then owner, Alexander Norris, a prominent Puritan. A fine example of a wealthy merchant's house, it was saved from dereliction by Lord Leverhulme in 1900 and has been restored and furnished with displays of fine furniture and interesting items of local importance. However, the hall has a second claim to fame as, for a number of years, Samuel Crompton was one of several tenants here. The inventor, in 1799, of the spinning mule, Crompton's machine was an important factor in the industrialisation of the country's textile industry. Naturally, the hall too has a replica of Crompton's mule on display.

The centre of Bolton is a lasting tribute to the wealth and prosperity generated by the spinning of high quality yarn for which the town was famous. The town hall, opened in 1873, is typical of the classical style buildings that the Victorian town fathers had built. The hall is still the town's central point and is it now surrounded by the recently refurbished pedestrianised shopping malls, market hall, and the celebrated Octagon Theatre. The town's excellent Museum and Art Gallery is also well worth a visit as not only are there collections of natural history, geology, and Egyptian antiques here but also some fine 18th and 19th century English water colours and some contemporary British paintings and graphics.

BRIERFIELD

45

This industrial town has magnificent views of Pendle Hill as it lies on a steep slope at the bottom of which is an attractive Quaker Bridge over Pendle Water. At the beginning of the 19th century, coal was discovered in the area and, within a few years, three pits had opened, thus sealing Brierfield's fate as a place of industry. The laying of turnpike roads, followed by the opening of the Leeds and Liverpool Canal, gave the growing village a further boost and, by 1833, a handloom weaving business was also flourishing here. The humid climate and expanding transport system made Brierfield an ideal place for the burgeoning cotton industry, which had become the main source of employment here by the end of the 19th century.

BURNLEY

A cotton town that is rich in history as well as being the largest town in this area of East Lancashire. Incorporating some 50 square miles, the town offers visitors a wealth of contrasts, from some of the best preserved industrial landscapes in Britain to the magnificent, untouched moorlands just to the east. First established at the beginning of the 9th century, the town nestles in a basin between the River Calder and the River Brun, from which it takes its name. With the Industrial Revolution and the building of the Leeds and Liverpool Canal, Burnley not only expanded but grew in stature until, by the end of the 19th century, it was the world's leading producer of cotton cloth.

A walk along the towpath of the canal, through an area known as the Weavers' Triangle, is like taking a step back in time. This is an area of spinning mills and weaving sheds; foundries where steam engines and looms were made; canal-side warehouses; domestic buildings, including a unique row of workers' cottages; and a Victorian school house. **The Weavers' Triangle Visitors Centre** is housed in the former wharfemaster's house and canal toll office. The centre is open to the public on several afternoons a week during the summer months and on most bank holidays.

The history of Burnley can also be explored by boat along the Leeds and Liverpool Canal. This famous waterway leaves the Weavers' Triangle via a huge embankment which carries the canal across the town. Known as the 'straight

46

mile', it is in fact less than that but no less exciting and, at 60 feet above the ground, it is one of the most impressive features of the canal's length. Situated on the Todmorden Road on the outskirts of Burnley, the **Towneley Hall Art Gallery and Museum**. The home of the Towneley family since the 14th century, right up until 1902, parts of the present building date from the 15th century. Visitors can not only view the art collections, the Whalley Abbey Vestments, and the museum of local crafts and industries, but also take in a tour of the house. The kitchens, with their open fires, the servants' hall, and the fascinating family rooms are all on display. The grounds too are open to visitors and there are facilities for golf, tennis, bowls, and other outdoor pursuits.

Two other interesting places to visit whilst in Burnley are the **Burnley Heritage Centre**, where memorabilia from the town's past on display includes old photographs, a Lancashire loom, and a replica 1930s kitchen and living room. The Stables Museum, open at the weekends, is one of the town's newest attractions and can be found at the wharf. Run by the Horses and Ponies Protection Association, the museum is a must for horse lovers and the exhibitions include information of the rescue and care of neglected horses, ponies, and donkeys as well as a display of the life of the canal horse.

BURY

Looking at Bury today it seems hard to imagine that, at one time, this typical Lancashire mill town had a castle. A settlement probably existed here in the Bronze Age and there is certainly evidence that the Romans passed through this area. By the 12th century, the town was the manor of the Norman de Bury family and, in the mid-14th century, the land came under the ownership of the Pilkingtons. Though the age of the castle is not known, its site is now covered by a 19th-century drill hall, it was dismantled following the Battle of Bosworth in 1485 where Henry VII defeated Richard III. Unlucky Thomas Pilkington had backed the wrong side. It is certainly people rather than buildings for which the town is famous.

Apart from the hapless Thomas Pilkington, whose family, centuries later, made a fortune in glass at St Helens, both the Peel family and John Kay helped to shape the town's future.

John Kay was the inventor of the flying shuttle, which although transforming the life of the weaver, did nothing towards creating personal wealth for Kay. With no head for business, Kay moved to France, died penniless, and lies buried in an unmarked grave. Before Robert Peel Senior opened his Ground Calico Printing Works in 1770, this small market town lay amid green and fertile land. However, the opening of the works along with the subsequent mills, print and bleach works so dominated this part of the Irwell Valley that not only did they transform the landscape but also heavily pollute the river.

At the height of the valley's production it was said that anyone falling into the river would dissolve before they had a chance to drown. Today, thankfully, the valley towns are once again clean and the river clear and fast flowing. With the family fortune gleaned from these prosperous mills, Robert Peel, born in the town in 1788, was able to fund his illustrious career in politics. Famous for the repeal of the Corn Laws, Robert Peel was also at the forefront of the setting up of the modern police force - hence their nickname 'Bobbies'. In the Bury's market square is a bronze statue to the town's most famous son. Bury's Art Gallery and Museum, home to the renowned Thomas Wrighley collection of Victorian oil paintings and water col-

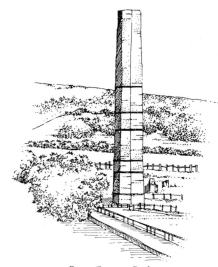

Burrs Country Park

ours, also hosts a lively programme of temporary exhibitions and the museum features a cobbled street of reconstructed shops and dwellings from Bury's past. The history of Lancashire's famous regiment, from its foundation in 1688, is displayed in the Lancashire Fusiliers Museum. On the outskirts of the town lies Burrs Country Park which, as well as offering a wide range of activities, also has an interesting industrial trail around this historic mill site.

Colne

Before the Industrial Revolution turned this area into a valley devoted to the production of cotton cloth, Colne was a small market town that specialised in wool. Unfortunately, there are few reminders to the days before industrialisation but St Batholomew's Church, founded in 1122, is still here and contains some interesting interior decorations and furnishings. In the centre of the town, next to the War Memorial is another memorial. The statue is of Lawrence Hartley, the bandmaster on the ill-fated Titanic who, heroically, stayed at his post with his musicians and played *Nearer my God to Thee* as the liner sank beneath the waves of the icy Atlantic in 1912. Colne is also the unlikely home of the British in India Museum, where exhibits covering many aspects of the British rule over the subcontinent, from the 17th century until 1947, can be seen.

Darwen

Visitors to the town may be forgiven for thinking they have been here before as Darwen will be familiar to all viewers of the BBC series *Hetty Wainthropp Investigates*, which stars Patricia Routledge. Dominating the town from the west and situated high on Darwen Moor, is **Darwen Tower**, built to commemorate the Diamond Jubilee of Queen Victoria in 1897. The view from the top of the tower, which is always open, is enhanced by the height of the hill on which it stands (1,225 feet) and with the help of the plaques at the top much of the Lancashire landscape, and beyond, can be seen. A striking landmark, very visible from the tower, and in the heart of Darwen is the chimney of the India Mill. Constructed out of hand-made bricks, it was built to resemble the campanile in St Mark's Square, Venice. To the west of Darwen lies **Sunnyhurst Wood** and visitor centre in the valley of a gentle brook that originates on Darwen Moor to the south. Acquired by public subscription in 1902, to commemorate the coronation of Edward VII, this area of woodland, covering some 85 acres, is rich in both bird and plant life. The visitor centre, housed in an old keeper's cottage, has an ever changing exhibition and there

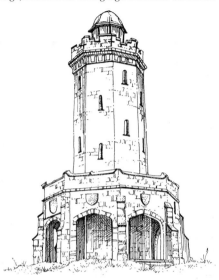

Darwen Tower

is also the Olde England Kiosk, built in 1912, which serves all manner of refreshments.

Delph

Taking its name from the old English for quarry, this is probably a reference to the bakestone quarries found to the north of the village. Also close by, and high on a hill above the village, lies Castleshaw, one of a series of forts the Romans built on their military road between Chester and York. The banks and ditches give visitors an excellent indication of the scale of the fort and many of the items found during recent excavations are on show in the Saddleworth Museum.

Diggle

Above the village, on Diggle Moor, lies Brun Clough Farm where, it is said, the cries of child slaves who were ill treated in the early days of

48

the textile mills can still be heard coming from the out-houses. Part of the Oldham Way footpath, a 30 mile scenic walk through the countryside on the edge of the Peak District National Park, crosses the moorland. Much of the village itself is a conservation area, where the pre-industrial weaving community has been preserved along with some of the traditional skills. However, Diggle Mill, which used to operate the second largest waterwheel in the country, no longer exists. The Huddersfield Narrow Canal, completed in 1811, is one of the three canals that crossed the difficult terrain of the Pennines and joined Lancashire with Yorkshire. The entrance to the Standedge Canal Tunnel, the longest and highest canal tunnel in Britain, lies in the village. The last cargo boat passed through the tunnel in 1921 and following a long period of closure, it has now been re-opened.

DOBCROSS

This attractive Pennine village, once the commercial heart of the district of Saddleworth, retains many of its original weavers' cottages, clothiers, and merchants' houses, and little has changed around the village square in the last 200 years. Used as the location for the film, Yanks, Dobcross is also famous as the birthplace of the giant Platt Brothers Textile Machinery business which was, in the latter part of the 19th century, the largest such machine manufacturing firm in the world.

EARBY

The town lies almost on the county border with Yorkshire and here can be found the **Earby Mines Museum** housed in the old Grammar School building. With the largest collection of lead mining tools and equipment used in the Yorkshire Dales on display, there is much to see, including examples of the minerals extracted, a lead crushing mill, and other working models.

GREAT HARWOOD

Before the Industrial Revolution, this was a quiet village of farms and cottages nestling between two streams. It had long been famous for its fine woollen cloth, when at the beginning of the 19th century cotton handloom weaving and then, by the 1850s, the introduction of the factory system and the cotton mills took over.

Only one mill remains, but at the industry's height, the town supported 22 mills. Not surprisingly, Great Harwood's most famous son was very much linked with cotton. In 1850, John Mercer, an industrial chemist, developed the technique of processing cotton to give it a sheen and the technique, mercerisation, is still used today. The free-standing clock tower found in the Town Square was erected in 1903 to commemorate Mercer's contribution to the life of his home town.

HEALEY

Lying in the valley of the River Spodden, this old village, now almost engulfed by the outer reaches of Rochdale, is an area rich in wildlife as well as folklore. Nearby is **Robin Hood's Well**, one of a number of springs feeding the river. Here, it is said, sometime in the 12th century the Earl of Huntington was lured to the well by a witch pretending to be his nursemaid. Once at the well, the witch told the young man that he would never inherit his earldom unless he had her magic ring as a means of identification. Gazing into the well, Robin got such a fright that he fainted and the witch took off on her broomstick. Emerging from the well, the King of the Fairies gave the lad his own ring and told him to go up into Healey Dell and interrupt the witches while they were hatching their next spell. Doing as he was instructed, Robin entered the coven and threw the ring into their cauldron, whereupon there was a great flash of light and the witches were reduced to evil looking fairies destined to live forever in the Fairy chapel. Opened in 1972, **Healey Dell Nature Reserve** does not promise visitors sightings of either witches or fairies but there is a wealth of wildlife to be discovered along the nature trails. This is an ancient area which has only been interrupted by the construction of the commercially nonviable Rochdale to Bacup railway in the late 19th century. The oak and birch woodland on the northern river bank is all that remains of a prehistoric forest, whilst the owners of Healey Hall made some impact, likely has changed here for centuries.

HELMSHORE

This small town still retains much evidence of the early Lancashire cotton industry and, housed in an old cotton mill, is the Museum of the Lancashire Textile Industry, **Higher Mill Museum**. The building, which dates from 1789, was one of the first fulling mills to be built in the Rossendale area.

HOGHTON

Originally a collection of hamlets with handloom weavers' cottages, the village was, during the 17th century, a place of unlawful Catholicism. Arrowsmith House was the place where Edmund Arrowsmith said his last mass before being captured and sentenced to death for being a Catholic priest and a Jesuit. It is however, today, best known as the home of Lancashire's only true baronial residence, Hoghton Tower, which dates from 1565. The de Hoghton family have owned the land in this area since the time of the Norman Conquest and the house was built in a style in keeping with their social position and importance. The famous banqueting hall, on the ground floor, is where James I is said to have knighted the Sir Loin of Beef in 1617. The name of the house is though a little misleading as the tower was blown up by Cromwell's troops in 1643 when they over ran the Royalist garrison stationed here. Another famous visitor, who caused less disruption, was William Shakespeare, who came to perform with William Hoghton's troupe of players. As well as the famous banqueting hall, other rooms open to the public include the beautifully preserved ballroom, the King's bedchamber, and the audience chamber. The grounds, too, are well worth a visit and are as perfectly preserved as the house.

HORWICH

Before the town developed as a centre for the building of steam engines, in the mid-19th century, Horwich was supported by the coal mines and quarries that lay between here and Bolton. In the late 18th century, a local farmer cut some steps down to the Dean Brook, on the town's southeastern boundary, to make the carrying of the coal to the developing textiles mills, by the stream, easier. By the mid-19th century, the company, Gardener and Bazley, had built Dean Mills in the valley, along with a purpose-built village, later to become Barrow Bridge, for the mill workers and their families. The workers' village was the inspiration for Benjamin Disraeli's famous novel *Coningsby*.

LITTLEBOROUGH

Little more than a suburb of Rochdale today, this small town lies on the main route between Lancashire and Yorkshire first laid down by the Romans. The road takes in Blackstone Edge and here are some of the best preserved parts of the Roman structure. At the summit is a medieval cross, the Aigin Stone, which offers spectacular views over Lancashire right to the coast.

NELSON

This town, along with its neighbour, Colne, and Burnley are now inseparable as they share the same valley running along the length of Colne Water. Nelson is a modern textile town which takes its name from the hotel, The Lord Nelson, which stands by the railway line running along the valley bottom. However, although the town itself might have been the product of the Industrial Age, two of its suburbs, Little and Great Marsden, have been here for centuries. Here, above Nelson, also lies Marsden Park, and once Marsden Hall, the home of the de Walton family until their line died out in 1912. Acquired by the local authority, much of the hall was demolished whilst the parkland was developed.

NEWCHURCH

This charming Pendle village was named after John Bird, Bishop of Chester, consecrated a new church here in 1544. Earlier, during the Middle Ages, Newchurch was a cow and deer rearing centre, as well as part of the old hunting forest of Pendle but, by the reign of Elizabeth I, the area was becoming deforested and farming was beginning to take over as the primary source of income. Newchurch did not escape from stories of witchcraft that surrounded the notorious Pendle Witches trial in the 17th century,

Newchurch

and many ghostly tales and shadowy traditions are said to associated with the village. Though those times were a frightening experience for anyone living in the area, by the 18th century the witch hunts were over and the village grew rapidly as part of the expanding textile industry, first with handloom weavers and then with the construction of a factory for washing and dyeing wool.

OSWALDTWISTLE

This typical Lancashire textile town could be considered to be at the heart of the industry since it was whilst staying here, at what is now Stanhill Post Office, that James Hargreaves invented his famous 'Spinning Jenny' in 1764. Although he was forced to leave the area after, sometimes violent, opposition to his machine from local hand spinners, the town's prosperity is largely due to textiles and, in particular, calico printing. However, Oswaldtwistle is a much older settlement than its rows of Victorian terraced houses would suggest as the name means the boundary of the kingdom of Oswald, who was a 7th century Northumbrian king.

PADIHAM

Padiham, a charming little town of narrow winding lanes and cobbled alleyways, still retains characteristics typical of the early days of the Industrial Revolution. However, there was a settlement here long before the Norman Conquest and Padiham was also the market town for the western slopes of Pendle. Padiham is also the home of **Gawthorpe Hall**, which lies to the east of the town. A splendid 17th century house, it was restored with a flourish of Victo-

rian elegance during the 1850s by Sir Charles Barry. Although Gawthorpe Hall had been the home of the Shuttleworth family since the early 15th century, work on the construction of the present hall only started in 1600. The Hall is open to the public, and the beautiful period furnishings are enhanced by the ornately decorated ceilings and the original wood panelled walls, which also provide the perfect setting for the nationally important **Kay-Shuttleworth Needlework and Lace Collection**.

PENDLE HILL

A constant feature of the skyline in this part of Lancashire, this great whaleback mountain lends into name to the ancient hunting ground and region it still dominates. The hill, and the surrounding tiny villages, have a rich history and, due to the isolation, there are also many legends: none more well known than the tragic story of the **Pendle Witches**. The infamous

View from Pendle Hill

witches were, in the main, old women who dabbled with plants and herbs, knowing which could heal and which, when ingested, would spell certain death. The early 17th century was a time of superstition and fear and, in 1612, several of the women were imprisoned in Lancaster Castle as a result of their seemingly evil practices. At the trial, chilling accounts of witchcraft came to light as families and neighbours accused each other of wrongdoing. Later that year, on August 10th, ten women and one of their sons were found guilty of witchcraft and were hanged in front of huge crowds. Though, as a rule, witches tended to come form the poorer elements of society, one of the women, Alice Nutter, was said to be rich, with a sizeable estate. A few years later, in 1633, there

Gawthorpe Hall

were further trials and, while some of the accused died in prison, four prisoners were taken to London and put on show. To the west of the hill's summit lies Apronfull Hill, a Bronze Age burial site that is said to be the place from which the Devil threw stones at Clitheroe Castle, creating what is known as the Devil's window. Something of this old, dark tragedy still broods over Pendle and many memories and places which hard back to those grim days remain. Those interested in finding out more about the trials should visit the **Pendle Heritage Centre** at Barrowford, to the southeast of the hill. Historically, witches aside, the hill was one of the many beacon hills throughout the country that, forming a chain, were lit in times of national crisis, such as the sighting of the Spanish Armada.

RAMSBOTTOM

At one end of the East Lancashire Railway, this picturesque village overlooking the Irwell Valley is well worth visiting. However, one of best views of the village and, indeed, the surrounding area, can be found from **Peel Tower**, which dominates the skyline. Built in 1852 to commemorate the life of the area's most famous son, Sir Robert Peel, the tower is some 128 feet high. Now restored, the tower itself is occasionally open to the public.

RAWTENSTALL

The town first developed as a centre of the woollen cloth trade with the work being undertaken by hand workers in their own homes before steam-powered mills were introduced in the early 19th century. The introduction of the cotton industry to the town happened at around the same time. Lower Mill, now a ruin, was opened in 1840 by the Whitehead brothers who were some of the area's first manufacturing pioneers. The Weaver's Cottage, purpose built for a home weaver, is one of the last buildings remaining of its kind and it is open to visitors at weekends during the summer. Also in the town, and housed in a former Victorian mill owner's house called Oakhill, is the **Rossendale Museum**. Naturally, the area's industrial heritage is given a prominent position but collections of the region's natural history, fine art and furniture, and ceramics are on display too. At one end of the town stands a new railway station which marks the end of a very old railway line - the East Lancashire Railway. Opened in 1846

and run commercially until 1980, when the last coal train drew into Rawtenstall, the line is now in the hands of the East Lancashire Railway Preservation Society. The steam-hauled passenger service (running at weekends with additional summer services) offers an exhilarating 17 mile round trip along the River Irwell between Rawtenstall and Bury, via Ramsbottom.

RISHTON

Originally a Saxon settlement, the name means the fortified village or dwelling place amid the rushes, and, during the Middle Ages, the village grew in importance as an early textile centre with the operation of its fulling mill. By the 17th century, Rishton had gained a name for the manufacture of linen cloth and in 1766 it became the first village to weave calico. As the Industrial Revolution advanced, the industry moved from the weavers' homes into newly built mills. The manor of Rishton, once owned by the Petre family, was part of the larger estate of Clayton-le-Moors and the manor house, Dunkenhalgh Hall, is said to have been named after a Scottish raider called Duncan who made his home here. Elizabethan in origin, the hall is now a private hotel.

ROCHDALE

Lying in a shallow valley formed by the little River Roch, the town is surrounded, to the north and east, by the slopes of the Pennines that are often snow covered in winter. With its origins in medieval times, the town, like so many others in Lancashire, expanded with the booming cotton industry and its Town Hall rivals that of

Peoneers' Co-operative Museum

52

Manchester in style if not in size. However, it is not textiles for which Rochdale is famous but as its role as the birthplace of the Co-operative Movement. In carefully restored Toad Lane, to the north of the town centre, is the world's first Co-op shop, the Rochdale Pioneers. The Co-op movement now represents a staggering 700 million members in 90 countries around the world and the celebration of its 150th anniversary in 1994 focused on attention on Rochdale and the **Pioneers' Co-operative Museum**. The town has some other famous sons and daughters and these include the famous 19th century political thinker, John Bright, the celebrated singer Gracie Fields, and Cyril Smith, its former longstanding Liberal Member of Parliament. The beginning of the 19th century also saw the birth of the **Rochdale Canal**, a brave piece of civil engineering that traversed the Pennines to link the River Mersey with the Calder and Hebble Navigation. Some 33 miles in length and with 92 locks, it must be one of toughest canals ever built and, though the towpath can still be walked, the last commercial boat passed through the locks in 1937. Officially abandoned in 1952, some sections of the canal have been restored. Between Rochdale and Littleborough lies Hollingworth Lake, originally built as a supply reservoir for the canal, but for many years a popular area for recreation known colloquially as 'the Weavers' Seaport', as cotton workers unable to enjoy a trip to the seaside can here. Now part of the Hollingworth Lake Country Park and with a fine visitor centre, there are a number of pleasant walks around its shores.

TOCKHOLES

This interesting textile village was once an isolated centre of nonconformism and, next to a row of cottages, can be found the United Reformed Chapel, founded in 1662, though it has been rebuilt twice, in 1710 and in 1880. The Parish Church also has some unusual features and as well as the unique lance-shaped windows, there is an outdoor pulpit dating from the days when the whole congregation could not fit inside the building. Close to the pulpit is the grave of John Osbaldeston, the inventor of the weft fork, a gadget that allowed power looms to weaving intricate patterns. Just to the south of the village lies **Roddlesworth Nature Trail**, a path that follows the line of an old coach

drive. Along the trail, for which details can be obtained at the information centre, can be found the ruins of Hollinshead Hall. Built in the 18th century and once very grand, the ruins were tidied up in the early 1990s but, fortunately, the wishing well has withstood the ravishes of time and neglect. Reminiscent of a small Georgian chapel, the well inside dates back to medieval times when its waters were thought to cure eye complaints.

TURTON BOTTOMS

Turton Tower is another fine example of a half-timbered house, similar to those in Bolton. Built around an early 15th century pele tower, constructed as a defence against Scottish raiders, this superb Tudor house was used as a farmhouse in the 18th century and today it is a wonderful museum. As well as the collections of armour, visitors can view the Tudor and Victorian furniture that is also on display.

UPPERMILL

Of the villages that make up the district of Saddleworth, Uppermill is the most central. It is certainly home to the area's oldest building, Saddleworth Parish Church, which was originally built in the 12th century by the Stapletons as their family chapel. Extended over the years, it has several interesting features including a gravestone to commemorate the Bill-o-Jacks murders. In 1832, the people of Saddleworth were stunned to learn that the landlord of the Moorcock Inn and his son had been bludgeoned to death. Several thousand people turned out for the funeral but the case was never solved. Housed in an old mill building on the banks of the Huddersfield Canal, the **Saddleworth Museum** tells the story of this once isolated area and there is a reconstruction of an 18th century weaver's cottage as well as a collection of woollen textile machinery, local history gallery, and local art exhibitions. Also here is the Brownhill Visitor Centre, which has not only information on the northern section of the Tame Valley but also exhibitions on local wildlife and the area's history.

WHALLEY

The centuries have done little to change the charm and character of Whalley. Although it is now somewhat dominated by the 49-arch railway viaduct, Whalley has a much older history which dates back to the 13th century and the time when **Whalley Abbey** was founded by Cistercian monks. In fact, Whalley was not the monks' first choice as they had already set up a religious house at Stanlow, on the banks of the River Mersey and now under a huge oil refinery, in 1172. Seeking somewhere with less harsh and more fertile land, the monks moved to Whalley in 1296 but their attempts to build were hampered as Sawley Abbey felt threatened by the competition for the donations of land and goods expected from the local population. Building finally began in 1310 and by 1400 the imposing and impressive abbey had taken shape. The demise of the abbey came, as it did to all religious houses, under Henry VIII, but Whalley's abbot, joining forces with the abbot of Sawley, took part in the Pilgrimage of Grace in an attempt to save their houses. This failed and the abbots were both executed. Now owned and cared for by the Diocese of Blackburn, Whalley Abbey is one of the best preserved such places in the country and its future secure as it also acts as a conference centre. Whalley's Parish Church, dating from the 13th century, is also well worth a visit. Built on the site of an older place of worship, the churchyard is home to three ancient crosses and the church itself contains a set of the some of the finest choir stalls anywhere. They were brought here from the abbey after the Dissolution and though they are not elaborate there are some intriguing carvings on the lower portions.

WHITWORTH

This pleasant town of cottages and farms lies on Pennine moorland above Rochdale. Between here and Bacup, a distance of only seven miles, the railway line, another feat of Victorian engineering, climbs over 500 feet. Not surprisingly, there were various problems during its construction, such as frequent landslides, but once constructed this was a picturesque line with attractive station houses with neat well tendered gardens along the route. The line, like so many, fell to the extensive railway cuts of the 1960s.

WITHNELL FOLD

Although this village is only a short and pleasant walk, crossing the Leeds and Liverpool Canal, from its neighbour Brindle, it is a very different place indeed. An industrial village, dominate by a huge chimney, Withnell Fold does, however, have its own claim to fame. The mill, built in 1844 overlooking the canal, became the world's biggest exporter of high-quality banknote paper.

WYCOLLER

This hamlet lies amidst the moorlands that rise to the east of the textile towns of the Colne valley and up to the bleak summits of the Pennines. Now almost deserted, it was once a thriving place as an important centre for the wool trade and as a handloom weavers' settlement but it lost most of its inhabitants to the new factories in the west. Fortunately, the place has been saved by the creation of a Wycoller Country Park, surrounding the village, and many of the buildings have been restored. There is also a delightful old hump-backed packhorse bridge crossing a stream and, above the village, a single slab gritstone bridge, Clam Bridge, that is thought to date from the Iron Age. Now a ruin, Wycoller Hall as the inspiration for Ferndean Manor in Charlotte Brontë's Jane Eyre: Wycoller was one of the villages to which the sisters walked from their house at Haworth.

Whalley Abbey

54   The Albion Alehouse

243 Whalley Road,
Clayton-le-Moors,
Accrington,
Lancashire
BB5 5HD
Tel: 01254 238585

Directions:

Clayton-le-Moors is located 2 miles east of Blackburn on the A678, very close to junction 7 of the M65.

Standing on the banks of the Leeds & Liverpool Canal, the **Albion**, a sturdy stone building, dates from the same period as the canal (late 18th century) and was formerly a tea room. Known for a time as The Narrowboat, the Albion is a mecca for real ale enthusiasts, with excellent brews from the Rossendale Brewing Company. A minimum of five ales from the brewery are always available at the bar, plus porter, stout, a wheat beer and a regularly changing traditional cider.

John Burke, the licensee and from October 2001 the owner, has the services of an excellent Swiss chef whose menu of British and Continental dishes is available to enjoy in the atmospheric bar up to 10 o'clock in the evening. His dishes range from traditional British favourites such as meat and vegetable pie to halibut with prawns and tomatoes, sirloin steak boscaiola and farfalle with chicken, and there are always main-course options for vegetarians. The Albion is open from 5pm on Monday and Tuesday, and from 3pm on Wednesday, and is open all day from Thursday to Sunday. The weekly quiz starts at 9.30 on Thursday, a live band performs its own pieces on Friday and the inn hosts occasional poetry nights and some important annual events: a play performed by the resident theatre company in the third week in September, a real ale festival in July and a cider festival in October. The Albion has a good selection of books to browse with a pint, and Rachel, who works in the pub, has her artwork on display. Picnic benches are set out on a patio garden that overlooks the canal, where moorings can be arranged with notice.

There's plenty to interest the visitor along the canal and in the nearby town of Blackburn, once the most important weaving town in the world, and Accrington, where the Haworth Art Gallery, set in beautiful parkland, houses the largest collection of Tiffany glass in Europe.

Opening Hours: Mon & Tues from 5, Wed from 3, Thurs-Sun all day.

Food: Bar meals.

Credit Cards: None.

Accommodation: None.

Facilities: Car Park, canalside patio.

Entertainment: Quiz Thursday, live band Friday, annual events (see above).

Local Places of Interest/Activities: Leeds & Liverpool Canal, Blackburn 2 miles, Accrington 1 mile.

The Anchor Inn | 55

Salterforth Lane,
Salterforth,
Barnoldswick,
Lancashire
BB18 5TT
Tel: 01282 813186

Directions:

From Colne, A56 to
Kelbrook then B9383
for about ½ mile.
From Skipton, A59
then A56; take minor
road signposted
Salterforth to the
right at Earby.

Renowned for its fine cask ales and traditional home-cooked food, the **Anchor Inn** would be a fascinating place to visit even without those major attractions. Originally The Travellers Rest, it was built on the old packhorse way, used by drovers and salters, that dropped down from White Moor on its way to Yorkshire. When the Leeds-Liverpool Canal was built at the end of the 18th century the pub found itself positioned below the water level and was therefore subject to severe damp. A new inn was built above the old, originally called the Canal Tavern but subsequently The Anchor. The Travellers Rest became the cellar of the new inn and over the years formed an impressive array of stalactites and stalagmites which visitors to the inn can see on a tour accompanied by the landlord John Stather.

John, who has been here for 10 years, is rightly proud of the inn, not only for its intriguing history but also for the reputation it has earned for being one of the very best places in Lancashire for food and drink. There's always an impressive selection of cask ales and keg beers on offer in the bar (once the landlord's parlour), including the locally brewed Black Cat Mild, Ruddles, Theakstons and Directors. Home baking is the highlight of the cooking, and many a visitor who has enjoyed tucking into a wonderful traditional plate pie is unable to resist rounding things off with a syrup sponge and custard! Booking is advisable, especially on a Sunday, for a table in the 20-cover non-smoking restaurant. Children are always welcome, and at the rear of the inn is a large beer garden with seats for 60 plus swings, a slide and a sand pit.

The Anchor, with its unique history and atmosphere and its outstanding ales and home cooking, is open all day, every day and should be a must on every itinerary in this part of the country.

Opening Hours: All day, every day.

Food: Bar meals (traditional home cooking).

Credit Cards: All the major cards.

Accommodation: None.

Facilities: Car Park, beer garden with

children's play area.

Entertainment: Quiz Thursday.

Local Places of Interest/Activities: This pub, Leeds-Liverpool Canal, Earby Mines Museum.

56

The Cricketers

94 School Lane,
Brinscall,
Chorley,
Lancashire
PR6 8QP
Tel: 01254 830211

Directions:

From Chorley A674 for about 1½ miles; turn right on to minor road signposted Brinscall. From Preston or M65 (J3) take A675; turn right at Abbey Village on to minor road through Withnell to Brinscall.

Small, cosy and atmospheric, the stone-built **Cricketers** stands in a row of old houses in the village of Brinscall, easily reached from the A674, A675 or M65 (J3). For the past ten years the inn has been in the safe hands of Tina (who was born in the village) and Leslie Nash.

Leslie is also the chef, and a very good one, too. His dishes, which typically range from garlic mushrooms to burger barm, chilli, sweet & sour pork, steaks, roast of the day and beef in red wine, are served lunchtime and evening Tuesday to Saturday and from 12 to 6 on Sunday. Twice a month the inn holds special theme nights for which booking is essential. This is a Jennings inn, and that excellent brewery provides a seasonal brew as well as Old Smoothie and a bitter. There's limited parking by the front door and a real surprise at the back - a delightful secluded beer garden that can only be reached through the bars, so it's safe and secure for children to romp in; barbecues are sometimes held here in the summer. A quiz starts every other Sunday at 9 o'clock, and once a month a singer performs on a Saturday evening.

With the proximity of the motorway and other main roads, Preston, Bolton and Chorley are all within a painless drive, while even closer there are several places of interest to visit, including Tockholes, with a fine parish church and a nearby nature trail; Withnell Fold, whose mill was once the world's biggest exporter of high-quality banknote paper; and Darwen with its dominating Diamond Jubilee Tower.

Opening Hours: All day, every day.

Food: Bar meals (not Monday).

Credit Cards: None.

Accommodation: None.

Facilities: Beer garden.

Entertainment: Quiz every other Sunday.

Local Places of Interest/Activities: Chorley, Preston, Bolton, Darwen.

Fishermans Inn 57

**Hollingworth Road, Littleborough,
Lancashire OL15 0AZ
Tel: 01706 378168**

Directions:
From junction 21 of the M62 follow the
signs for Hollingworth Lake Country Park.
The inn is located at the corner of
Hollingworth Road and Lake Road.

First licensed in 1818, when it was known as Clegg Hall, this most welcoming and individual of inns enjoys a superb setting on the banks of Hollingworth Lake. Inside, there's a splendid mix of styles and themes and decor - half-panelling here, exposed brick there, a fascinating collection of musical instruments, framed sheet music and assorted prints, posters, old street signs and other collectibles.

Licensee Christopher Holmes, ably assisted by his father Bill and manageress Beverley, offers outstanding hospitality throughout, and in addition to the roomy bars and dining areas picnic benches are set outside overlooking the lake. Appetising pub food is served from opening time onwards on menus that range from light snacks to burgers, steaks and scampi. The famous Sunday carvery, served from noon to 4 o'clock, offers a choice of at least four roast meats and poultry, with plenty of fresh vegetables, soup to start, home-made desserts and coffee. Three real ales, keg bitters and draught lagers deal with fresh air-generated thirsts, and the bar stays open until 12.45 am. There's plenty of space here, so bookings aren't necessary for parties of fewer than six, but larger groups should make reservations (the largest parties can be catered for in the Weighvers function room with space for up to 120!).

Entertainment in the form of live music, karaoke and quizzes is laid on every night of the week, and Hollingworth Lake Country Park, literally on the doorstep, is one of the region's best known recreation areas. With the hospitality, the good food and drink, the entertainment and the lake, the Fishermans Inn is the perfect place to unwind, within easy distance of Rochdale and Manchester but equally convenient for the wide open spaces of the Pennines.

Opening Hours: All day, every day.

Food: Bar meals.

Credit Cards: All the major cards.

Accommodation: None.

Facilities: Car Park, function room.

Entertainment: Something every night.

Local Places of Interest/Activities:
Hollingworth Lake Country Park, Rochdale 3 miles, Pennine Way.

Internet/Website:
www.fishbythelake.co.uk

58 The Flowers Inn

141 Todmorden Road,
Bacup,
Lancashire
OL13 9UA
Tel: 01706 873931

Directions:

The pub is located
about 1 mile from the
centre of Bacup on the
A681 Todmorden
Road.

After a stroll round the textile town of Bacup, a short drive east will bring the visitor to this pretty former farmhouse on the Todmorden side of the town. The first premises in Bacup to be licensed, it has maintained its position down the years as one of the most popular local meeting places.

The welcome, the hospitality and the good cooking are now in the capable hands of Gerry and Trish Blakely and their family, who became tenants in October 2000. Trish does the cooking, and her steak & kidney pudding, served with a lovely rich gravy, has quickly become established as a favourite. Her menu is available every day from 12 to 3 at lunchtime and from 5 to 8 in the evening. The quality bar meals are complemented by some good beers, including Tetley's Cask and John Smith's Smooth. Evening entertainment at The Flowers includes Who Wants to be a Millionaire on Tuesday, a disco on Friday, disco or karaoke on Saturday and an Irish disco on Sunday. (Easter visitors to Bacup might well encounter different entertainment in the shape of the town's famous Morris Dancers, who call themselves the Coconut Dancers.) A couple of picnic tables are set out on the pretty little lawn at the front of the pub, while to the rear are a beer garden, off-road parking and a site for overnight campers or caravanners.

There's plenty of good walking hereabouts, and attractions within an easy drive include the Rossendale Museum at Rawtenstall and the preserved East Lancashire Railway, which runs from Rawtenstall along the River Irwell to Bury.

Opening Hours: Lunchtime and evening; all day Fri, Sat & Sun.

Food: Bar meals.

Credit Cards: None.

Accommodation: None.

Facilities: Car Park, caravan/camping site.

Entertainment: see above.

Local Places of Interest: Rawtenstall 3 miles, Todmorden 4 miles, Forest of Rossendale.

The Hapton Inn   59

*2 Accrington Road,
Hapton,
Burnley,
Lancashire
BB11 5QL
Tel: 01282 771152*

Directions:

Half a mile from junction 8 of the M65; take the A679 towards Burnley. The inn is about two miles along on the right.

A great place for all the family, with the warmest of welcomes and real hospitality from long-serving leaseholders Carol and Ian Bailey. The handsome greystone building started life as a coaching stop in the 18th century, and the interior has been carefully updated while retaining some of the best original features. The cosy bar and the raftered dining area are home to an eclectic assortment of objects, including plates and earthenware bottles, copper ornaments, old farming implements - even a stuffed bird in a display case high up on a wall. there's good off-road parking at the rear of the pub, along with a beer garden and areas where children can romp in safety.

The Hapton Inn has earned a considerable reputation down the years for the quality and variety of its food, which is served lunchtime and evening Monday to Friday and all day Saturday and Sunday. The dining area has seats for 50, but there's room for upwards of 100 altogether in the pub, including a separate room for children. Hot beef sandwiches are among the favourites for a satisfying quick snack, while among the main courses the chilli con carne and the steak & kidney pie have a strong following. There's an equally good selection of ales, including real ales from Boddingtons, Tetleys, Flowers and Timothy Taylor, plus Trophy Smooth, Tetley Creamflow and a range of popular lagers and ciders. Nostalgia rules at the inn on the second Tuesday of the month, when the local Morris Minor club has its get-together.

The proximity of the M65 makes access east and west very easy, while in the more or less immediate vicinity the attractions include the Leeds & Liverpool Canal, offering towpath walks through lovely countryside and the splendid 17th century Gawthorpe Hall with its period furnishings and the renowned Shuttleworth Collections of needlework and lace.

Opening Hours: Lunchtime and evening; all day Sat, Sun & Bank Holiday Mons.

Food: Bar meals.

Credit Cards: Mastercard, Visa.

Accommodation: None.

Facilities: Car Park, beer garden, children's play areas.

Entertainment: None.

Local Places of Interest/Activities:
Accrington 2 miles, Burnley 2 miles, Leeds & Liverpool Canal, Gawthorpe Hall 2 miles.

60 The Hare & Hounds

Bolton Road,
Abbey Village,
Chorley,
Lancashire
PR6 8DP
Tel: 01254 830334

Directions:

From Preston, take the
A675 to Abbey Village,
about 6 miles.

Wayne and Tracy, a local couple, took their first steps in the licensed trade when they took over the lease of the **Hare & Hounds**. A grand old coaching inn built at the end of the 18th century, it stands in a quiet location by the A675 about halfway between Preston and Bolton; Blackburn is a short distance to the north.

The interior of the inn is cosy and traditional, with pillars and ceiling beams, a welcoming real fire and a display of bygones and memorabilia on the walls. Food and drink both play an important in the success and popularity of the Hare & Hounds: Tracy produces a very varied menu of top-quality pub dishes, which are served at both lunchtime and evening sessions Monday to Friday and from noon right through to 8 o'clock on Saturday, Sunday and Bank Holidays. Everything is fresh and wholesome, but a large number of the regular patrons look no further than Tracy's excellent steak & mushroom pie. Real ale aficionados are also spoilt for choice here, with several varieties coming from the Three Bs Brewery in Blackburn. A fruit machine, quiz machine, darts and table football are on hand to provide entertainment, and there's live music every Saturday from about 9 o'clock.

There are plenty of good thirst-generating walks in the vicinity of the Hare & Hounds, and the neighbouring villages offer plenty for the motorised visitor to see: St James' Church in Brindle, the mill overlooking the Leeds & Liverpool Canal at Withnell Fold, the ruins of Hollinghead Hall just south of Tockholes on the Roddlesworth Nature Trail, and the superb Elizabethan Astley Hall in Chorley.

Opening Hours: Lunchtime and evening; all day Saturday, Sunday and Bank Holidays.

Food: Bar meals.

Credit Cards: None.

Accommodation: None.

Facilities: Off-road car parking.

Entertainment: Live performers Saturday.

Local Places of Interest/Activities: Preston 6 miles, Bolton 6 miles, Blackburn 3 miles.

The Lord Nelson 61

Whalley Old Road,
York Village,
Langho,
Blackburn,
Lancashire
BB6 8DU
Tel: 01254 240261
Fax: 01254 245322

Directions:

From Blackburn, take the A666 road north; turn right up York Lane at a mini-roundabout at Langho, just before the A666 joins the A59.

On a clear day you can see Blackpool Tower from this grand old inn, which stands in an attractive hamlet off the A666, a short distance from Langho, not far from Whalley and an easy drive from Blackburn and Clitheroe. The list of landlords displayed in the bar dates back to 1825, but the inn is much older, and behind the sturdy stone facade there's a wealth of old-world charm, including gnarled beams, two open fireplaces, old prints and pictures and some splendid wood panelling at the brass-railed bar counter.

Paul Fortescue and Tim Pye, here as tenants since January 2001, are lucky to have the services of a really top-class chef in Stefan Zupnyk, whose menus provide a constantly changing selection of dishes distinguished by fine flavours and excellent sauces. He cooks what takes his fancy and will try to cater for special requests, but favourites in his repertoire include roasted ham hocks, minted shoulder of lamb, and succulent beef served on ratatouille. The food, which is complemented by a very fine selection of wines, is served from 12 till 2 and from 6 till 9 Monday to Saturday and from noon right through to 9 o'clock on Sunday. There are seats for 40, and booking is advisable at all times and very necessary at the weekend. A minimum of three hand-pulled cask ales is always at the ready - John Smiths, Theakstons and Marstons Pedigree - along with three draught lagers. Live entertainment takes place monthly on a Saturday, and the inn also holds regular special events such as wine tasting evenings.

There's outside seating to the front and rear of this exceptional pub, from where it's a short drive to several local places of interest: at Whalley, a little way north up the A59, the 14th century Cistercian Abbey is one of the best preserved of its kind in the country, and the Church of St Mary features some of the very finest choir stalls to be found anywhere.

Opening Hours: All day, every day.

Food: Bar and restaurant meals.

Credit Cards: Mastercard, Visa, Switch.

Accommodation: None.

Facilities: Beer Garden

Entertainment: Quiz Tuesday.

Local Places of Interest/Activities: Whalley 3 miles, Blackburn (Textile Museum, Cathedral), Clitheroe (Castle and Museum).

62

The Moorcock Inn

Gisburn Road,
Blacko,
Nelson,
Lancashire
BB9 6NG
Tel: 01282 614186

Directions:

From Nelson take the A682 north, pass through the villages of Barrowford and Blacko. The inn is ¾ mile beyond Blacko on the right.

A place for all the family, easily reached from Nelson or from junction 13 of the M65. There are splendid views in all directions from the inn, which, both inside and out, retains much of the character from its days as a coaching inn and alehouse. The walls of the bar are covered with gleaming brass and copper ornaments, and much of the public area is given over to eating, with smart Windsor chairs set at immaculately laid tables.

Food is big business here, and John Patterson, who took over as tenant with his wife Janet at the beginning of 2001, has been the chef for 18 years. His menu offers plenty of choice and is available lunchtime Monday, lunchtime and evening Tuesday to Friday and all day on Saturday and Sunday. Booking is advisable on Sunday, when the carvery, with a choice of three roasts, is a popular addition to the menu. Children are very welcome, and there are designated no-smoking areas in the eating areas.

The Moorcock has plenty of off-road parking and stands in lovely countryside that's full of interesting places to see and explore. Among the scenic attractions is Pendle Hill, which offers superb views and a rich history. The lead mining museum at Earby is but a short drive away, while to the south, beyond the Forest of Pendle, Gawthorpe Hall should be visited for its beautiful period furnishings and its marvellous collections of lace and needlework.

Opening Hours: Lunchtime and evening; all day Sat & Sun. Closed Mon evening.

Food: Bar meals.

Credit Cards: All the major cards.

Accommodation: None.

Facilities: Car Park.

Entertainment: None.

Local Places of Interest/Activities: Pendle Hill, Barrowford (Pendle Heritage Centre), Nelson, Earby.

The Red Lion — 63

Red Lion Street,
Earby,
Lancashire
BB18 6RD
Tel: 01282 843395

Directions:

Earby stands 10 miles northeast of Burnley on the A56; from Skipton, A59 then A56.

Good food and good ale are served in pleasant, comfortable surroundings at the **Red Lion**, a grand old inn dating back over 250 years. It's very much a family affair, with Julie and Barrie Grave at the helm, assisted by Mum and Dad David and Dorothy; the pub has been in the ownership of the family for 13 years. Prints of Earby in days gone by are an attractive feature in the bar of this inviting free house, where Tetleys Mild and Tetleys Bitter are among the brews on tap.

Julie is in charge in the kitchen, and from her nicely varied menu lasagne (meat or vegetarian), seafood platter and splendid Cumberland sausage are among the favourite choices. Children are welcome, and they even have their own section of the menu. Food is served every day between 12 and 2 at lunchtime and from 8 o'clock to 10 in the evening; the pub is open lunchtime and evening Monday to Thursday and all day at the weekend. Brains here need to be sharpened once a month, when the general knowledge quiz takes place from 9 o'clock on a Tuesday evening. Off-road parking is available on the other side of Red Lion Street (not many pubs have a street named after them, or was it the other way round?).

Almost on the county border with Yorkshire, Earby has a fascinating attraction for visitors in the shape of the Mines Museum, housed in an old grammar school building. Its displays include the largest collection of lead mining tools and equipment used in the Yorkshire Dales, along with examples of the minerals extracted, a lead-crushing mill and other working models.

Opening Hours: Lunchtime and evening; all day Friday to Sunday.

Food: Bar meals.

Credit Cards: None.

Accommodation: None.

Entertainment: Quiz monthly on a Tuesday.

Local Places of Interest/Activities: Earby Mines Museum, Colne 3 miles, Skipton 6 miles.

64 Roggerham Gate Inn

Todmorden Road,
Briercliffe,
Burnley,
Lancashire
BB10 3PQ
Tel: 01282 422039

Directions:

The pub lies east of Burnley, halfway between Worsthorne and Harle Syke on a minor road that can be reached off the A646 south of Burnley; take the road marked Mereclough and Worsthorne.

A handsome, compact, stone-built house dating from 1876 in a picturesque location looking down on Briercliffe. The minor road on which it stands was once the packhorse road between Leeds and Halifax, and the pub's name is thought to derive from the highwaymen (rogues) who once frequented the area.

Tony and Sue Wiaczek bought the inn in 1993, and immediately its fortunes took a turn for the better. They refurbished it from top to toe, restoring its period character and once again making it an inviting place to pull in for a pint and something to eat. Youngers IPA is the resident real ale, and other options include Scotch Bitter and Beamish Black. A log fire warms the bar, and there's a feature range in the non-smoking dining room, where Tony makes sure that there's always a choice of tasty home cooking. Steaks, gammon and sausages are supplied by an excellent local butcher; the Thai red and green curries are winning a place on the list of favourites, and Sue's cheese and onion pie shows just how good a vegetarian dish can be. Tables and chairs are set out on the patio, and the owners have plans to create a beer garden which will make the most of the lovely setting.

Tony can arrange trout fishing on nearby Swinden Reservoir, and there's excellent walking - the Brontë Way, linking Haworth with the Brontës' publishers, runs past the pub. Other nearby attractions include the restored Queen Street Mill, a bird centre at Mereclough and two very grand houses - Towneley Hall with its museum and art gallery, and the National Trust's Gawthorpe Hall, home to a wonderful needlework and lace collection.

Opening Hours: Lunch and evening Monday, all day Tues-Sun.

Food: Bar meals.

Credit Cards: None.

Accommodation: None.

Facilities: Car Park.

Entertainment: None.

Local Places of Interest/Activities: Burnley, Towneley Hall, Queen Street Mill, fishing on Swinden Reservoir.

The Seven Stars | 65

Rochdale Road,
Bury,
Lancashire
BL9 7DB
Tel: 0161 764 7305

Directions:

Turn off the M66 at Junction 2 signed for Bury Town Centre. The pub is the first on Rochdale Road.

The mother-and-daughter team of Carol Siddall and Kelly Rothwell have a warm welcome for one and all at the **Seven Stars**, the first pub on Rochdale Road after leaving junction 2 of the M66 at the Bury Town Centre turn-off. Built as a pair of private houses in the middle of the 19th century and later a coaching inn, the Seven Stars is easy to find on its corner site, and once inside there's no mistaking the relaxed, inviting atmosphere.

Food is served lunchtime from 12 noon until 14.30 Monday to Saturday and from 14.00 until 17.30 on Sundays. Carol's menu runs the gamut of familiar pub fare: soup and sandwiches for a quick snack, salads, jacket potatoes, burgers and main courses such as traditional fish & chips, chicken curry, Cumberland sausage served with a fried egg, gammon steak and the heartily recommended steak & mushroom pie. The day's specials are announced on a board, and to accompany the food is a good choice of beers and lagers. Pool, darts, a juke box, fruit machine and tv are all available in the bar, where Thursday night sees the weekly quiz, there's karaoke every other Saturday and an all-comers knock-out darts competition on Sunday.

The town of Bury, with its busy market place and fine art gallery and museum, is just along the road, while in the other direction lies Rochdale, birthplace of Gracie Fields, John Bright and the Co-op Movement. Its Town Hall, almost as imposing as Manchester's, is well worth a look, and the Rochdale Canal provides pleasant towpath walks.

Opening Hours: All day, every day.

Food: Bar meals.

Credit Cards: Planned.

Accommodation: None.

Facilities: Car Park.

Entertainment: Quiz Thursday, karaoke every other Saturday, darts competition Sunday.

Local Places of Interest/Activities: Bury 1 mile, Rochdale, Manchester.

66   The Swan & Cemetery

406 Manchester Road, Bury,
Lancashire BL9 9NS
Tel: 0161 764 1508
Fax: 0161 764 7311

Directions:
The pub is located on Manchester Road less than a mile from the centre of Bury.

After running pubs in Cheshire, Shropshire and elsewhere in Lancashire since 1990, Geoffrey and Lynne Wallwork arrived here as tenants in the spring of 1999. The inn dates from the middle of the 19th century and owes its unique name to two simple facts: a cemetery stands just across the road, and there's also a small lake, in the grounds of the vicarage of St Peter's, where a colony of swans once lived. The swans have long since gone but the inn has kept its name and a good deal of its original charm and character, with wood featuring strongly in the bars and an assortment of prints, pictures and memorabilia on the walls.

It's a very popular place for food, which is served throughout the bars as well as in the restaurant all day from 11.30 till 9 (from noon on Sunday). The full menu and the board of daily specials offer the visitor plenty of choice, and the Sunday roasts are particularly popular - booking is recommended all day on Sunday and on Friday and Saturday evenings. Children are welcome, and there are some non-smoking areas in the pub. Thwaites Brewery supplies the real ale and there's also a good selection of draught lagers. Picnic benches are arranged neatly on the patio at the front, and there is more open space at the rear, along with good off-road parking space. Gourmet nights are held once a month, there's live entertainment once a month on a Saturday, and quiz night comes round every Thursday.

Bury, a typical Lancashire mill town, has an interesting Art Gallery and Museum with a notable collection of Victorian oils and watercolours; also in Bury is the Lancashire Fusiliers Museum, and standing proudly in the busy market square is a bronze statue of Robert Peel, the town's most famous son.

Opening Hours: All day, every day.

Food: Bar meals served all day.

Credit Cards: Diners, Mastercard, Visa.

Accommodation: None.

Facilities: Car Park.

Entertainment: Quiz Thursday.

Local Places of Interest/Activities: Manchester 4 miles, Bolton 6 miles.

Whalley Range Inn 67

78 Church Street,
Padiham,
Lancashire
BB12 8JQ
Tel: 01282 771842

Directions:
Padiham lies 2 miles
west of Burnley on
the A646.

Jacqueline and Peter Haigh brought with them over 20 years experience in the licensed trade when they took over the lease of **Whalley Range Inn** in the spring of 2001. On Church Street, not far from the centre of town, the inn dates back to the early part of the 19th century and was formerly called the Top Drum and before that the White Horse.

A warm welcome is assured, and there's a really smashing atmosphere in the public rooms. An excellent range of drinks is served at the bar, which features a long, stone-faced counter. Options include two real ales (Theakstons and a guest), Worthington Creamflow and Theakstons Mild. Jacqueline produces a good variety of traditional bar food, which is available from 11 to 2.30 Monday to Thursday and from 11 to 4 Friday and Saturday. Small parties and functions can be catered for and buffets can be prepared on request. The Whalley Range has a very pleasant and secluded beer garden, and there's a car park across the road.

Padiham is a delightful small town of narrow, winding lanes and cobbled alleyways, well worth taking time for a stroll before lunch in the pub. The local grand house is Gawthorpe Hall, a splendid 17th century mansion which contains some beautiful period furnishings and a superb needlework and lace collection. Among other nearby attractions are the Leeds & Liverpool Canal and the Forest of Pendle.

Opening Hours: Lunchtime and evening; all day Friday-Sunday.

Food: Bar meals lunchtime.

Credit Cards: None.

Accommodation: None.

Facilities: Beer garden.

Local Places of Interest/Activities:
Gawthorpe Hall, Forest of Pendle, Burnley 2 miles.

68 The Wheatsheaf

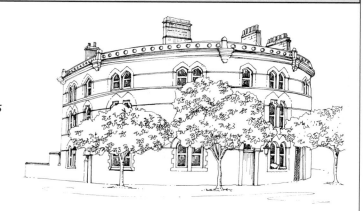

Church Street,
Littleborough,
Lancashire
OL15 8AB
Tel: 01706 377695

Directions:

In the heart of Littleborough, 3 miles northeast of Rochdale on the A58.

The Wheatsheaf, which stands in the centre of the small town of Littleborough, must surely be one of the most unusual and distinctive pubs in the whole country. It occupies half of a massive semi-circular stone structure dating from the end of the 19th century and originally a hotel with stables and a brewery; the building spans three floors, topped by tall chimneys and an ornamental parapet with 'portholes' in the stone.

Sandra Bailey, who has spent her whole life in Littleborough, took over the lease with her daughter Sara in 1993, since when they have been providing a warm welcome for their regular patrons and to visitors from further afield. There's always a good atmosphere in the bar, where three real ales (Boddingtons, Flowers IPA and a guest) are on tap - Happy Hour on beer is from 4 till 6 Monday to Saturday and from 12 till 1 on Sunday. Food is served Sunday lunchtime only, from noon till 3 o'clock. Sandra does the cooking, and her menu comprises three starters then always a choice of roast beef, lamb or pork, along with other splendid home-cooked dishes such as steak & kidney pie, cheese & onion pie, or braised steak; dessert could be apple crumble, profiteroles with chocolate sauce or strawberry short-cake; children can have small portions or their own special dishes, with a free ice cream to finish. The food is very reasonably priced and absolutely delicious. A general knowledge quiz takes place in the bar from 9pm on Thursday, and on Friday the disco revs up at 8 o'clock. The Wheatsheaf has a secluded beer garden and a patio with a secure children's play area. There are also two function rooms, one of them with its own bar.

Littleborough offers easy access to both the metropolis of Greater Manchester and the wide open spaces of the Pennine countryside. Attractions in the immediate vicinity include Hollingworth Lake Country Park, the Rochdale Canal (soon to be re-opened to boats), Healey Dell Nature Reserve and Blackstone Edge, whose summit affords spectacular views over Lancashire right across to the coast.

Opening Hours: All day, every day.

Food: Bar meals Sunday lunch only.

Credit Cards: None.

Accommodation: None.

Facilities: Beer garden, function rooms.

Entertainment: Quiz Thursday, disco Friday.

Local Places of Interest/Activities: Rochdale 3 miles, Rochdale, Pennine Way.

The Whitchaff Inn   69

371 Bury Road,
Townsend Fold,
Rawtenstall,
Rossendale,
Lancashire
BB4 6EH
Tel: 01706 213198

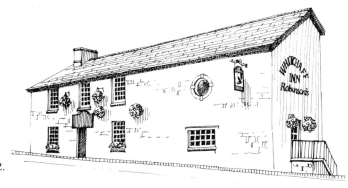

Directions:
Rawtenstall is 7
miles south of
Burnley on the A682.
The inn looks down
on the town on the
Bury Road.

Looking down over Rawtenstall from its lofty position, the **Whitchaff Inn** is a distinctive sight on the Bury Road. Tall and narrow, with a steeply raked slate roof, the stone building dates from 1761. It's been a pub for well over 100 years and used to called the Hare & Hounds; the present unusual name, adopted in the 1970s, is a combination of the shortened names of two of the owners of the day.

   The bars have abundant traditional appeal, with lots of gleaming brass, display plates and Windsor chairs set at neat little tables. Barry and Sue Pilkington, here for six years, have a friendly greeting for one and all, and lovers of good ale are in for a real treat: cask-conditioned Robinson's Best, Fredericks, Hatters Mild and a seasonal guest provide a tempting choice, and some of the ales are secondary-brewed in the pub's cellar. A former stable now houses the atmospheric restaurant, where the printed menus and daily specials offer upwards of 100 dishes, almost all of them home-cooked. Sizzling platters, crispy duck, stir-fries and black pudding are just a few of the specialities, and the four-course Sunday lunch and three-course teatime specials (available up to 8 o'clock) offer particularly good value for money.

   The pub has plenty of off-road parking, and an unusual feature is a Post Office letter box in the wall at the front. Every Thursday at the Whitchaff a quiz is hosted by local personality Fred Fielder from GM Radio. Attractions in Rawtenstall include the Rossendale Museum and the preserved East Lancashire Railway, which runs along the River Irwell to Bury by way of Ramsbottom.

Opening Hours: Lunchtime and evening; all day Saturday and Sunday.

Food: Bar and à la carte menus.

Credit Cards: Mastercard, Visa.

Accommodation: None.

Facilities: Car Park.

Entertainment: Quiz Thursday.

Local Places of Interest/Activities: Burnley 7 miles, Bury 5 miles.

The Hidden Inns of Lancashire and Cheshire

3 West Lancashire

PLACES OF INTEREST:

PUBS AND INNS:

The Hidden Inns of Lancashire and Cheshire

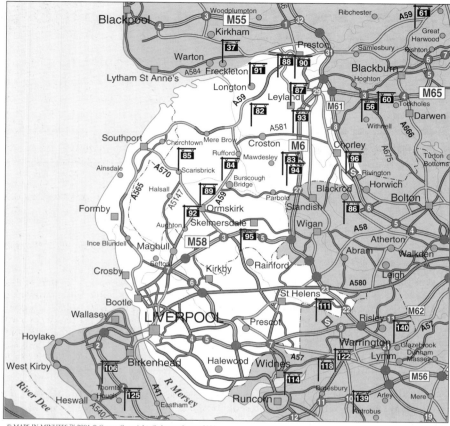

© MAPS IN MINUTES ™ 2001 © Crown Copyright, Ordnance Survey 2001

82 The Blue Anchor, Bretherton	**90** The Railway Hotel, Lostock Hall, nr Preston
83 Brook House, Heskin	**91** The Red Lion, Longton, nr Preston
84 The Farmers Arms, Burscough, nr Ormskirk	**92** Town Green Inn, Aughton, nr Ormskirk
85 Heatons Bridge Inn, Scarisbrick, nr Ormskirk	**93** The Travellers Rest, Euxton
86 Kirkless Hall, New Springs	**94** The Tudor Inn, Wrightington
87 The Original Ship, Bury	**95** The Wheatsheaf Hotel, St Helens
88 The Pear Tree Inn, Penwortham	**96** The White Horse, Heath Charnock, nr Chorley
89 The Plough, Ormskirk	

Please note all references refer to page numbers

West Lancashire

This area of Lancashire, with its sandy coastline and flat fertile farmland, is home to the elegant Victorian seaside resort of Southport, the ancient market towns of Chorley and Ormskirk, and Wigan, another ancient place with a rich industrial past. Following the reorganisation of the county boundaries in the 1970s and the creation of Merseyside, much

Leeds and Liverpool Canal

of the coast and the southwestern area of Lancashire became part of the new county but the individual character and charm of this area has certainly not been lost. As well as offering a step back in time, the broad promenades of Southport, its elegant tree-lined streets, and its superb shopping still makes this one of the most visited towns in this region. Though the silting up of the Ribble estuary, to the north, has caused the sea at this resort to recede, further south, at Ainsdale and Formby, not only is there paddling but also an vast ex-

panse of sand dune and pine forest that is now an important nature reserve. Behind the coast, the flat lands of the West Lancashire plain were once under water, but drainage has provided the old towns and quaint villages with rich fertile land that now produces a wealth of produce all year round and the roadside farm shops are very much a feature of the area. Although there are several rivers flowing across the land, the chief waterway, which is hard to miss, is the Leeds to Liverpool Canal. Linking the port of Liverpool with industrial Leeds and the many textile villages and towns in between, this major navigation changed the lives of many of the people living along its length. However, the section through West Lancashire, passed rural villages, is perhaps one of the more pleasant stretches. There are plenty of charming canal side pubs in the area and walks along the towpath, through the unspoilt countryside, have been popular for many years. There is also, in this section, the wharf at Wigan Pier now a fascinating living museum that brings the canal to life.

PLACES OF INTEREST

AINSDALE

Towards the sea, from the centre of the village, lies what was Ainsdale-on-Sea with its old Lido and the more modern Pontin's holiday village. Between here and Formby, further down the coast, the sand dunes form part of the Ainsdale National Nature Reserve and one of the most extensive dune systems in the country. Breeding in the shallow pools that form in the sand dunes, this is one of the last homes of the endangered natterjack toad. As well as supporting the toads, the salt pools are the natural habitat for a variety of dune plants, including grass of Parnassus and round-leaved wintergreen.

AUGHTON

Agricultural land surrounds a picturesque village dominated by the spire of St Michael's Church. An ancient place, it was mentioned in the Domesday Book; the register of church rectors goes back to 1246 and much of the building's medieval framework remains though its was restored in 1914. Close by lies the Old Hall on a site that has been occupied since Saxon times. The ruins of a 15th century pele tower are visible in the garden and, as well as having a priest's hole, the house is reputed to have been Cromwell's base whilst he was active in the area.

74

BURSCOUGH

Situated on the banks of the Leeds and Liverpool Canal, the village's Parish Church was one of the Million, or Waterloo, Churches built as a thanks to God after the final defeat of Napoleon in 1815. A later addition to the church is the Memorial Window to those of the parish who died for their country during the First World War. Little remains of Burscough Priory, founded in the early 12th century by the Black Canons. Receiving lavish endowments from the local inhabitants, the priory was, at one time, one of the most influential religious houses in Lancashire.

CHORLEY

A bustling and friendly place, Chorley is a charming town that is locally famous for its market that dates back to 1498. Today, there are two markets - the covered market and the open, 'flat iron' market. This peculiar and intriguing name stems from the ancient practice of trading by displaying goods on the grounds without the use of stalls. Dating back to 1360 and standing on the site of a Saxon chapel, the **Church of St Lawrence** is the town's oldest building. The church is said to contain the remains of St Lawrence, brought back from Normandy by Sir Richard Standish, and whether they are his relics or not, during the Middle Ages, the saint's shrine certainly brought pilgrims to the parish. The Civil War also brought visitors to the town only less welcome ones. Following defeat at the nearby Battle of Preston, Royalist troops were twice engaged in battle here by Cromwell's victorious forces.

Though not a happy time for either the Royalist or the town, the skirmishes did place Chorley on the historical map of England. Chorley was the birthplace, in 1819, of Henry Tate. The son of a Unitarian minister, in 1832, Henry was apprenticed to the grocery trade in Liverpool and, by 1855, he had not only set up his own business but also opened a chain of six shops. Selling the shops, Henry entered into the world of the competitive sugar trade and founded the world famous business of Tate & Lyle. Opening a new sugar refinery with the latest machinery from France, Henry cornered the refining business in Britain from which he made his fortune. A great benefactor, Henry not only gave away vast sums of money to worthy causes but also to the art gallery which now bears his name.

However, the jewel in Chorley's crown is undoubtedly **Astley Hall**. Built in the late 16th century and set within some beautiful parkland, the hall is a fine example of an Elizabethan mansion. Extended in 1666, and later in 1825, this is truly a house of history and the rooms, which reflect the passing of the centuries, contain superb items of furniture from 1600 to the Edwardian period. Whether or not Cromwell stayed at the hall following the Battle of Preston is open to debate but his boots are here on display. The hall was given to the borough in 1922 by Reginald Tatton and it was he who insisted that the building should incorporate a memorial to those who had died in World War I. As a result, a small room has been devoted to the local men who fought and died for their country and, along with the display of photographs, there is a Book of Remembrance.

CHURCHTOWN

This charming village, now a small part of Southport, has retained much of its village feel and is certainly worthy of exploration in its own right. Considerably predating the seaside resort, Churchtown is, as its name suggests, centred around its Church of St Cuthbert, where perhaps the monks of Lindisfarne rested here with the relics of their famous saint while fleeing from the Danes. However, it is likely that the village was, for many years, known by the name of North Meols and a chapel of Mele was mentioned in the Domesday Book. Derived from the Norse word 'melr' meaning sand dune, there was certainly a thriving fishing village here in the early 12th century. In 1224, Robert de Coudrey granted the village the right to hold a market, the likely place for which is the cross standing opposite the church in the heart of the village. As the settlement lay on a crossroads and at the start of a route over the sands of the Ribble estuary, it was a place of considerable importance.

It was also here that the tradition in this area of sea bathing began, when, in 1219 St Cuthbert's Eve was declared a fair day, which later became known as Bathing Sunday. There is still plenty to see in this small village. The present Meols Hall dates from the 17th century but its appearance today is largely thanks to the work carried out by the late Colonel Roger Fleetwood-Hesketh in the 1960s. When the Colonel took over the house in the late 1930s, the older and larger part of the hall had been demolished in 1733 and the remaining building was rather nondescript. Taking the gabled bay of the late 17th century, extensions were added to give the house a varied roofline and a three dimensional frontage. The hall is the last home of the Hesketh family, who, at one time, had owned most of the coastal area between Southport and Heysham. Occasionally open to visitors, the hall has a fine art collection and in the entrance hall are three carved chairs that were used in Westminster Abbey for the coronation of Charles II. During World War I, Moels Hall was used as a military hospital. Planned on the site of the old Churchtown Strawberry Gardens in 1874, the Botanic Gardens, restored in 1937, are beautifully maintained and present a superb example of classic Victorian garden design. With magnificent floral displays, a boating lake, wide, twisting paths, and a fernery, little has changed here since the day the gardens were first opened by the Rev Charles Hesketh. Built in 1938, following the gardens' restoration, the Botanic Bowling Pavilion mimics the style of the late Regency architect Decimus Burton. Here too is the Botanic Gardens Museum, with its fine exhibition on local history and its gallery of Victoriana.

CROSTON

This historic village in the heart of rural West Lancashire, has been a centre for local farmers since it was granted a weekly market charter in 1283. Beside the banks of the River Yarrow, a tributary of the River Douglas, much of the village, including the 17th century almshouses and the lovely 15th century church, are part of a conservation area. The strong links with agriculture are still apparent in this area and the open farmland actually extends right into the village centre.

FORMBY

The origins of this small coastal town lie in the time of the Vikings and the name Formby comes from the Norse Fornebei meaning Forni's town. Between the Norman Conquest and the time of the Dissolution in 1536, there were a succession of landowners but, by the mid-16th century, the Formby and Blundell families emerged as the chief owners. Formby Hall, built for William Formby in 1523, occupies a site that was first developed in the 12th century. Today, Formby is perhaps better known as a quiet and desirable residential area and also the home of an important red squirrel sanctuary at the Na-

tional Trust **Freshfield Nature Reserve** and pine forest. Linked with Ainsdale's nature reserve, the two form over 400 acres of dunes and woodland, as well as shoreline, from which there are magnificent views over the Mersey estuary and, on a clear day, the hills of Wales and of Lakeland are also visible.

HALSALL

Halsall is a charming unspoilt village, close to the Leeds and Liverpool Canal, that lies is the heart of the fertile West Lancashire plain. St Cuthbert's Church, which dates from the middle of the 13th century, is one of the oldest churches in the diocese of Liverpool and it remains one of the prettiest in the county. The spire, which was added in the 15th century, rises from a tower that has octagonal upper stages.

INCE BLUNDELL

The village takes part of its name from the Blundell family who have, for centuries, exerted much influence on the village and surrounding area. Ince comes from the Celtic word 'Ynes' which means an island within a watery meadow and it would have perfectly described the village's situation before the surrounding land was drained. The annual candlelight service at the village **Church of the Holy Family** is an ancient custom that appears to be unique to this country. The people of the parish decorate the graves in the cemetery with flowers and candles before holding a service there. Common in Belgium, this custom was brought to the village at the beginning of the 20th century.

LEYLAND

The town is probably best known for its associations with the manufacture of cars and lorries and the **British Commercial Vehicle Museum**, the largest such museum in Europe, is well worth a visit. Housed on the site of the former Leyland South Works, where commercial vehicles were produced for many years, there are many restored vans and lorries on display with exhibits ranging from the horsedrawn era, through steam-powered wagons right up to the present day vans and lorries. Leyland is, however, an ancient settlement and documentary evidence has been found which suggests that the town was a Crown possession in Saxon times and it was owned by Edward the Confes-

76

sor. The village cross marks the centre of the old settlement, around which the town expanded and it is in this area of the Leyland that the older buildings can be seen. Founded in the 11th century, much of the present St Andrew's Church dates from 1220 although there was some restoration work undertaken in the 15th century. The Eagle and Child Inn is almost as old, said to date from around 1230, and it served the needs of travellers journeying along the ancient highway which passed through the town. Whilst not one of the town's oldest buildings, the old Grammar School, parts of which dates from the late 16th century, is hardly modern. Today it is home to the town's Heritage Museum, a fascinating place that describes, through interesting displays and exhibits, the history of this ancient market town.

MAWDESLEY

This quiet village is well worth a visit as it is a past winner of the Best Kept Village of Lancashire award. Surrounded by the farmland of the West Lancashire plain, this rural village was once associated with a thriving basket making industry, founded 150 years ago. Mawdesley Hall, thought to have been erected by William Mawdesley in 1625, has some key architectural features and the village school is certainly worth a second glance.

MERE BROW

Just to the south of the village lies the Wildfowl and Wetlands Trust at **Martin Mere**, over 350 acres of reclaimed marshland which was established in 1976 as a refuge for thousands of wintering wildfowl. Until Martin Mere was drained in the 17th century to provide rich, fertile farmland, the lake was one of the largest in England. Indeed, some believe that it was into Martin Mere that King Arthur's sword, Excalibur, was tossed after the king's death. Today, the stretches of water, mudbanks, and grassland provide homes for many species of birds and, with a network of hides, visitors can observe the birds in their natural habitats. There is also a series of pens, close to the Visitor Centre, where many birds can be seen all year round at closer quarters. It is known particularly for the vast numbers of pink-footed geese which winter here, their number often approaching 20,000; although winter is a busy time at Mar-

tin Mere, a visit in any season is sure to be rewarded. The Visitor Centre caters for everyone and, as well as the shop and café, there is a theatre and a wealth of information regarding the birds found here and the work of the Trust.

ORMSKIRK

The origins of this important market town in the West Lancashire plain date back to the time of the Vikings, when their leader, Orme, first settled the area in AD 840. The town received its first market charter from Edward I in 1286 and the market is still a key event in the region. The partial drainage of Martin Mere, in the late 18th century, to provide more rich, fertile agricultural land, as well as the growth of nearby Liverpool, increased the prosperity of the town. Ormskirk was also touched by the Industrial Revolution and, whilst the traditional farming activities continued, cotton spinning and silk weaving also became important sources of local income. Today, the town has reverted to its traditional past. The **Church of St Peter and St Paul**, in the centre of the town, unusually has both a steeple and a tower. The tower, added in the 16th century, was constructed to take the bells of Burscough Priory after the religious community had been disbanded by Henry VIII. However, the oldest feature found in the church is a stone carving on the outer face of the chancel's east wall that was probably the work of Saxon craftsmen. Ormskirk too has a famous son: a market trader, called Beecham, who sold his own brand of liver pills that customers' described as 'worth a guinea a box'. His pills and powders made Beecham's fortune although his son, Thomas, a musical genius, brought worldwide fame to the family.

PARBOLD

This is a charming village of pretty stone cottages as well as grand, late-Victorian houses built by wealthy Manchester cotton brokers. It is also home to Parbold Hill, one of the highest points for miles around and from which there are superb views of the West Lancashire plain. At the summit stands a rough hewn monument, erected to commemorate the Reform Act of 1832, that is locally known, due to its shape, as the Parbold Bottle. Ashurst Beacon, another local landmark, was re-erected on Ashurst Hill by Lord Skelmersdale in 1798 when the threat of a French invasion was thought to be imminent.

PRESTON

Lancaster may have the distinction of being the county town, but Preston is Lancashire's administrative centre and its location makes it an excellent place from which to explore the whole region. Despite first appearances, Preston is a town of ancient history and it is strategically positioned on the highest navigable point of the River Ribble. However, the port activity has declined, the dockland area, now called Riversway, has become an area of regeneration, and the marina caters now for pleasure craft, yachts, and windsurfers. Though the town has both a Roman and a medieval past nothing of this is visible today. However, the lasting legacy of those days is reflected in the famous Guilds Celebrations which have been taking place every 20 years since 1500. The Royal Charter establishing the rights to hold a Guild Merchant was granted by Henry II in 1179. Preston also featured in the Domesday Book, though, at that time it was known as Priest-town and, in the 1260s, the Greyfriars settled here.

The Catholic traditions of Preston continued, as they did elsewhere in the county, and this has, along with the associated loyalty to the crown, had a great part to play in the town's history. During the Civil War, it was the Battle of Preston, in 1648, which confirmed the eventual defeat of the supporters of Charles I and, later, at the time of the 1745 Jacobite rebellion, Preston played host to Prince Charles Edward. The many public buildings of Preston all reflect the prosperity of the town during the Victorian age. This wealth was built upon the textile industry and helped by the general location of the town: midway between London and Glasgow, on a major railway route, and with the docks.

Though the town's prosperity was built on cotton, textiles were not new to Preston as linen had been produced here from as far back as Tudor times. Preston was also the place where, in 1768, the single most important machine of the textile industry was invented: Richard Arkwright's water-frame cotton spinning machine. Almost overnight, the cottage industries of spinning and handloom weaving were moved from the workers' homes into factories and the entrepreneurs of Preston were quicker than most to catch on. One gentleman in particular, John Horrocks, saw the potential of combining the spinning and weaving operations under the same roof and so he was able to take

raw cotton in and produce the finished article on delivery. His firm became the largest of its kind in the

world, further adding to the town's prosperity, but it did not do Horrocks himself much good as, by the age of 36, he was dead. Although the great days of the textile industry are long gone in Preston, as elsewhere in Britain, the cotton workers of the town are remembered in a statue which stands outside the old **Corn Exchange**.

Looking at the town now it is hard to imagine those hectic days and may be even hard to believe that, when the docks were completed here in 1892, Preston was the second largest

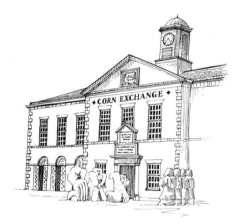

Cotton Martyrs, Corn Exchange

container handling port in Britain. In 1900, 1,285 vessels carrying nearly half a million tons of cargo entered and left the port. Unfortunately, the battle of keeping the channel open and free of silt became too expensive, particularly as trade was lost to other, nontidal ports, and the docks eventually closed.

One of the best places to start any exploration of the town is the **Harris Museum and Art Gallery**. Housed in a magnificent neoclassical building which dominates the Market Square, the museum and art gallery were opened in 1893. Funded by a successful local businessman and reminiscent of the British Museum, it has a fine collection of paintings and watercolours by major 19th century British artists as well as an excellent exhibition of the story of Preston. The two other museums in the town are

78

regimental. Housed in the former county court building, and with limited opening, the County and Regimental Museum, which is guarded by a giant Howitzer gun, has galleries dedicated to three regiments: the 14th/20th Kings Hussars, the Duke of Lancaster's Own Yeomanry, and the Queen's Lancashire Regiment. There is also an interesting and very informative display on the history of Lancashire. The Fulwood Barracks, which were built in 1848 of Longridge stone, are also home to the Loyal Regiment (North Lancashire) Museum. With a rich history that covers many campaigns, the exhibits here are numerous and include the famous silver mounted Maida Tortoise, items connected with General Wolfe, souvenirs from the Crimea War, and artefacts from the Defence of Kimberley, the diamond town in South Africa which the 1st Battalion the Loyals defended single-handedly.

Preston's Guild Hall, built in 1972 to celebrate that year's Guild, is known, or at least its interior, to many snooker and bowls fans as it is the venue for the UK World Snooker and the World Indoor Bowls Championships. Another building, less well-known but still a distinctive landmark, is Preston Prison. Built in 1789, it replaced the town's first House of Correction. In an interesting move in providing the inmates with work, during the 19th century, looms were installed in the prison and the prisoners were paid for their labour. Industrial unrest in the area soon followed and, in 1837, it was only the threat of a cannon which saved the prison from invasion by an angry mob intent on destroying the machines. Although the prison was closed in 1931, it re-opened in 1948 and remains in use.

As might be expected for a town on the banks of a river, there are many bridges, but two crossings are particularly worthy of note. PPPenwortham old bridge is perhaps the most attractive in Lancashire; slightly hump-backed and built of a mixture of stone. Constructed chiefly of buff gritstone and pink sandstone in 1756, it replaced a bridge that had collapsed and, by 1912, its use by motor cars and heavy carts was prohibited. For over 150 years, the bridge was the lowest crossing of the River Ribble. By contrast, the **Ribble Viaduct** is a completely different structure. One of the oldest works of railway engineering in the area and a construction of great elegance and dignity, it was built in 1838 and brought the railway from Wigan to the centre of Preston.

RIVINGTON

A delightful village surrounded by moorland of outstanding natural beauty that forms the western border of the Forest of Rossendale. Overlooking the village, and with splendid views over West Lancashire, Rivington Pike, at 1,191 feet, is one of the area's high spots. It was once a site of one of the country's chain of signal beacons. Just to the south of the village lies **Lever Park**, situated on the lower slopes of Rivington Moor, which was made over to the public in 1902 by William Hesketh Lever, who later became Lord Leverhulme. The park comprises an awe-inspiring pot pourri of ornamental, landscaped gardens, tree-lined avenues, cruck-framed barns, a Georgian hall, and a treasure trove of natural history within its 2,000 acres. The park's moorland setting, elevated position, and adjoining reservoirs provide scenery on a grand scale which leaves a lasting impression.

RUFFORD

Notable for its pretty houses, its church and its beautiful old hall. Built in 1869, the church is a splendid example of the Gothic revival period and its tall spire dominates the skyline. The ancestral home of the Hesketh family who were involved in reclaiming the mosslands on their estates, **Rufford Old Hall** is without a doubt one of the finest 15th century buildings in the county. Particularly noted for its magnificent Great Hall, this impressive black and white timbered house is well worth exploring. From the superb, intricately carved movable wooden screen to the solid oak chests and long refec-

Rufford Old Hall

tory table, the atmosphere here is definitely one of wealth and position. It is now in the hands of the National Trust, and within the outbuildings there are not only a shop and a popular restaurant but also the Philip Ashcroft Museum of Rural Life, with its unique collection of items that illustrate village life in pre-industrial Lancashire.

SCARISBRICK

The village, which is the largest parish in Lancashire, lies in the heart of rich agricultural land that is intesively cultivated for vegetables, including carrots, Brussels sprouts, cabbages and early potatoes. It follows that a feature of the area is the large number of roadside farm shops selling produce fresh from the fields. The first Scarisbrick Hall was built in the reign of King Stephen but, in the middle of the 19th century, the Hall, which is screened from the road by thick woodland, was extensively remodelled by the Victorian architect Augustus Welby Pugin for Charles Scarisbrick. In 1945, the hall and surrounding extensive grounds were sold by the last member of the family to live here, Sir Everard Scarisbrick, and today it is an independent boarding school.

SEFTON

This quiet old village lies on the edge of a rich and fertile plain of farmland that lies just behind the West Lancashire coast. Part of the estate of the Earls of Sefton (descendents of the Molyneux family) up until 1972, the 16th century village church has several monuments to the family as well as a 14th century spire. Though this is a small village, its name has also been given to the large metropolitan district of north Merseyside which stretches from Bootle to Southport.

SOUTHPORT

The rise of this popular and still elegant Victorian seaside resort lies in the tradition of sea bathing that began at nearby Churchtown centuries ago. As the number of people celebrating Bathing Sunday grew, the need for a more accessible beach also grew and a stretch of sand two miles south of Churchtown was deemed suitable. As the crowds flocked over the sand dunes more accommodation was needed and a local entrepreneur, known as Duke Sutton, built the first hotel of driftwood in 1792. It was Doctor Barton who, when christening Sutton's ho-

tel with a bottle of champagne, coined the name Southport (the South Port Hotel) and the town grew up around the ramshackle building. The driftwood hotel was replaced by a grander stone building, known as the Duke's Folly as its construction resulted in Sutton losing all his money and being imprisoned in Lancaster jail in 1803. Now an established town, the expansion of Southport came as a result, as with all of the region's famous resorts, of the extension of the railway services from the mill towns of Lancashire and from Manchester and Liverpool.

Of all these places, none has managed to retain is air of Victorian grandeur more than Southport. The town's central, main boulevard, **Lord Street**, is a mile long wide road that was built along the boundary bordering the lands of the two neighbouring lords of the manor. A superb shopping street today, the exceptionally wide pavements, with gardens along one side and an elegant glass-topped canopy along most of other side, make this one of the most pleasant places to shop in the country. Many of the town's classical style buildings are found along its length and is has been designated a conservation area. Off Lord Street is one of town's several covered arcades; built in 1898, Wayfarers Arcade is one of the best. The modest entrance opens out into a beautiful cast iron and glass conservatory, with its first floor gallery and splendid central dome. Originally named the

Lord Street, Southport

80

Leyland Arcade after the town's Member of Parliament, it took its present name in 1976 after the arcade's most successful leaseholder. In a central position along Lord Street lies Southport's rather modest Town Hall. Built in 1852 and of a classical design, above the balcony is a beautiful carving in bold relief of the figures of Justice, Mercy, and Truth picked out in white against a Wedgwood blue background. Further along, the Atkinson Central Library was built in 1879 as the premises of the Southport and West Lancashire Bank. The original ceiling of the banking hall can still be seen as can its fireplace. On the first floor is the Atkinson Art Gallery which contains collections of British art and Chinese porcelain.

However, not all the buildings in Southport are Victorian and the Top Rank Bingo Club, originally called the Garrick Theatre, was held to be the finest theatre when it was opened in 1932. With much of its exterior as it would have appeared when it first opened, it is a wonderful example of the Art Deco style. Finally, Lord Street is also home to the town's war memorial, The Monument. Opened on Remembrance Day, 1923 by the Earl of Derby, this is a large and grand memorial that remains the town's focal point. The central obelisk is flanked by twin colonnades in which the names of the town's World War I dead (over 1,000) are inscribed. As every Victorian resort had a Promenade, so does Southport and this is a typical example, flanked by grand hotels on the land side and a series of formal gardens on the other.

As the silting up of the Ribble estuary progressed unchecked, the Marine Lake was constructed at the northern end of the promenade. At over some 86 acres, this man-made lake is the largest in Britain and, as well as being an attractive site and a place for the pursuit of all manner of watersports, it is also host to an annual 24-hour yacht race.

From the centre of the promenade extends Southport's Pier which, at 1,460 yards long, was the longest pier in the country until 1897. Following a fire in 1933 it was shortened but it remains the second longest in the country. Looking at the pier today it is hard to imagine that at the end of the last century pleasure steamers were able to depart from here to Barrow in Cumbria, Bangor, Wales, and the Isle of Man. Along the shore line, and opened in the spring 1998, the new sea wall and Marine Drive is a wonderful modern construction, the length of Southport's sea front, that blends well with the town's Victorian heritage. The normal attractions of a seaside resort have not been forgotten and Pleasureland is the obvious choice for those seeking thrills and hair-raising rides. Keen gardeners will know of Southport for its splendid annual Flower Show, second only to Chelsea, and golfers will be familiar with the name of Royal Birkdale Golf Course, just south of the town centre. Southport has one more sporting association of which it is justly proud. From behind a car show room in the 1970s, Ginger McCain trained Red Rum on the sands of Southport to a record breaking three magnificent wins in the Grand National at Aintree. A statue of the great horse can be seen in Wayfarers Aracade.

STANDISH

This historic old market town has several reminders to its past and not least of these is the splendid **St Wilfrid's Church**. Built in a size and style that befitted the importance of the town in the late 16th century, the building stands on the site of a church that was certainly here at the beginning of the 13th century. A look around the interior of the church will provide a potted history of the area: there are tombs and memorials to all the local families, including the Wrightingtons, Shevingtons, and the Standish family themselves. The Standish family came from Normandy and crossed the channel with William the Conqueror. One of the family members became the Warden of Scarborough Castle and another, Ralph de Standish, was knighted after his part in quelling the Peasants' Revolt, there was even a Standish at Agincourt. However, the most famous member of the family is Miles Standish, who sailed to the New World on board the Mayflower with the Pilgrim Fathers in 1620. This may seem strange as the Standish family were staunch Catholics. Though there is little left in the way of monuments to the family in this country, their home (put up for sale in 1920 after the last family member died) was demolished and parts transported to America; Miles Standish is remembered in the town of Duxbury in America.

WIGAN

Although to many this town is a product of the industrial age, Wigan is one of the oldest places in Lancashire. As far back as the 1st century AD there was a Celtic Brigantes settlement here that was taken over by the Romans who built a small town called Coccium. Little remains of those far off days but, during the construction of a gasworks in the mid-19th century various burial urns were unearthed during the excavation work. The town's name comes from Wic-Ham, which is probably Anglo-Saxon or Breton in origin but, following the departure of the Romans, the settlement lay in that part of the country that was forever fluctuating between the kingdoms of Mercia and Northumbria so the derivation is uncertain

The medieval age brought more settled times and, by the end of the 13th century, the town had not only been granted a market charter but was also sending two members to Parliament. A staunchly Catholic town, Wigan fared badly during the Civil War. The Earl of Derby, whose home, Lathom House, lay on the outskirts of the town, was a favourite with the King and this was where Charles I made his base for his attacks on Roundhead Bolton. The bitter attacks on Wigan by the Cromwellian troops saw the fortifications destroyed and both the parish church and the moot hall were looted. The Battle of Wigan Lane, the last encounter between the warring forces in Lancashire, is commemorated by a monument which stands on the place where a key member of the Earl of Derby's forces was killed. Wigan's development as an industrial town centred around coal mining, which began as early as 1450. By the 19th century, there were over 1,000 pit shafts in operation in the surrounding area, supplying the fuel for Lancashire's expanding textile industry.

The Leeds and Liverpool Canal, which runs through the town, was a key means of transporting the coal to the cotton mills of Lancashire and **Wigan Pier**, the major loading bay, remains one of the most substantial and interesting features of the waterway. A well-known musical hall joke, first referred by George Formby senior as he told of the virtues of his home town over Blackpool, it was the 1930s novel by George Orwell, *The Road to Wigan Pier*, that really put the old wharf on the map. Today, the pier has been beautifully restored and it is now a key attraction in the area. There are canal boat rides and a superb exhibition, The Way We Were, based on local social history and with costumed actors playing the part of the townsfolk of the 19th century. The pier is also home to **Trencherfield Mill**, where not only is the largest working mill engine in the world on display but also a collection of old textile machines and other engines. However, Wigan is not a town living in the past but, as well as having a modern town centre with all the usual amenities, there is some fine countryside on the doorstep, including the Douglas Valley Trail, along the banks of the River Douglas. Even the town's coal mining past has interesting links with the natural world: Pennington Flash is a large lake formed by mining subsidence that is now a wildlife reserve and a country park. To the north of the town lies Haigh Country Park, one of the first to be designated in England, formed from the estate of the Earls of Crawford. Although Haigh Hall is not open to the public, the park includes areas of mixed woodland as well as a children's play area and a café.

Wigan Pier

82 The Blue Anchor

21 South Road,
Bretherton,
Lancashire
PR26 9AB
Tel: 01772 600270

Directions:
From Preston A59
southwest to
Becconsall then
B5247. From
Chorley A581 to
Croston then
B5247.

On a corner site in the scattered village of Bretherton, the **Blue Anchor** is an immaculate redbrick building dating from mid-Victorian times. Inside, the bars are similarly neat and pristine, with comfortably upholstered banquettes or roundback chairs set at little wooden tables, fresh flowers, a gleaming brass bar rail and a judicious assortment of prints and other objects.

Michele Fielding and Martin Wilcock, a brother and sister team, took over the lease in March 2001 after Michele has worked as bar manager for three years. Easily reached from all points of the compass, it's a really delightful spot to drop anchor for a drink - four real ales are always on tap - or a meal. The printed menu and the daily specials provide a particularly interesting and varied choice that is constantly changing, and the food is served every lunchtime and evening and all day on Saturday, Sunday and Bank Holiday Mondays. Every six weeks they hold a theme night, with appropriate music to accompany the style of the food. The pub has good off-road parking, a beer garden and a children's play area, and a gazebo is soon to be added.

The coast and the countryside provide plenty of opportunity for combining pleasant walks with splendid views, and among the attractions within an easy drive of the Blue Anchor are Camelot Theme Park, the historic farming village of Croston, the Commercial Museum at Leyland, the Wildfowl and Wetlands Trust at Martin Mere and the National Trust's Rofford Old Hall, one of the county's finest 16th century buildings, with a spectacular Great Hall.

Opening Hours: Lunchtime and evening; all day Fri, Sat & Sun.

Food: Bar meals.

Credit Cards: Diners, Mastercard, Visa.

Accommodation: None.

Facilities: Car Park, beer garden, children's play area.

Entertainment: None.

Local Places of Interest/Activities: Leyland 3 miles, Preston 6 miles, Martin Mere 4 miles.

Brook House

83

Barmskin Lane,
Heskin,
Lancashire
PR7 5PZ
Tel: 01257 451314

Directions:

From junction 27 of
the M6 take the
B5250; turn left in
Wrightington End
down Church Lane
and turn right at
the end. Brook
House is a little way
along on the right.

A real hidden gem in a rural setting not far from the M6. Formerly a farmhouse and later an alehouse, it was called The Windmill until the 1950s, since when it has been known locally as **The Brook**. The house was in a sad state when John and Christine took over as leaseholders in the autumn of millennium year, but they have quite literally transformed the place, refurbishing the interior and creating the most delightful garden at the rear, with trees, pathways and a little lake; at the front, picnic benches are set out under parasols.

Gleaming brass ornaments, old prints and pictures and a massive stone hearth take the eye in the public area, which includes a 28-cover non-smoking restaurant. Brook House has quickly established a name for itself under the new tenants, and John's cooking is a major contributor, attracting an ever-widening clientele (so it's always best to book). A blackboard announces the day's dishes, which put original touches on familiar themes using the best available ingredients: cod fillet poached in an orange and rosemary sauce; sirloin steak topped with black pudding covered with a brandy and wholegrain mustard sauce; chicken breast filled with apple sauce served with a mushroom, port, blue cheese and cream sauce. The food is served from noon to 9.30 daily, and there's always a good selection of beers and wines to accompany. Happy Hour for beer is between 5 o'clock and 7 Monday to Friday.

The quiet countryside around Brook House provides excellent walking and splendid views, and there are several delightful villages to explore, including Heskin itself, Wrightington and Mawdesley, past winner of the Best Kept Village of Lancashire award.

Opening Hours: All day, every day.

Food: A la carte menu.

Credit Cards: All the major cards.

Accommodation: None.

Facilities: Car Park, beer garden.

Entertainment: None.

Local Places of Interest/Activities: Chorley 4 miles, Standish 4 miles, Camelot Theme Park.

84 The Farmers Arms

36 New Lane,
Burscough,
Nr. Ormskirk,
Lancashire
L40 8JA
Tel: 01704 896021
*   or 01704 895623*

Directions:

From Ormskirk take the A59 north for about 1½ miles. Turn left after the A59/A5209 junction on to Higgins Lane, which leads to New Lane. The pub is situated by a swing bridge on the Leeds & Liverpool Canal.

In March 2001 Brian and Diane Hopkins took over the lease of the **Farmers Arms**, a most welcoming pub located by a swing bridge on the Leeds & Liverpool Canal. It is their first venture into this type of business, and they are already making their mark. The pub is a collection of linked redbrick buildings with a central conservatory, plenty of off-road parking, tables and chairs set outside and, at the back, a garden area being developed by the tenants.

Inside, the decor and furnishings are smart and stylish, and as well as spacious bar areas there's a cosy restaurant in traditional style. The pub provides plenty of variety among the popular pub classics, and the food is available every lunchtime and every evening. Booking is needed for larger groups or special occasions. Heading the liquid list are three real ales, two Tetleys and a rotating guest. Happy Hour on beer, lager and the house wines is from 5 till 8 on Friday, and the doubles bar is always in operation. Happy Hour turns into Disco Delight at 9 o'clock on Friday with music from the 1960s and 1970s.

Moorings on the canal can be arranged for boat-borne arrivals at this point, which is about halfway in its course between Wigan and Liverpool close to the Rufford branch. Rufford is most notable for Rufford Old Hall, a 16th century timber-framed house with gardens laid out by the National Trust in the style of the 1820s. Even closer, in Burscough itself, stands a parish church that was one of the Million, or Waterloo churches built as a thanks to God after the final defeat of Napoleon in 1815.

Opening Hours: All day, every day.

Food: Bar meals.

Credit Cards: None.

Accommodation: None.

Facilities: Car Park, moorings.

Entertainment: Disco Friday.

Local Places of Interest/Activities: Leeds & Liverpool Canal, Burscough, Ormskirk, Rufford.

Heatons Bridge Inn | **85**

2 Heatons Bridge Road,
Scarisbrick,
Ormskirk,
Lancashire
L40 8JG
Tel: 01704 840549

Directions:

The inn is located
on the B5242 two
miles north of
Ormskirk, next to
the Leeds &
Liverpool Canal.

Starting life as corn mill offices, this neat redbrick building has been a pub since 1837. Inside, one of the rooms is as inviting and homely as granny's parlour, with a collection of well-chosen objects and memorabilia adding to the cosy appeal; a particular attractive feature is the use of stained glass in some of the windows both here and in the bar.

A warm welcome and great hospitality are provided by Christine and Martin Donley, local people who took over the lease in April 2001. Traditional ales (Tetleys Cask, Tetleys Mild and a rotating guest) and a rotating guest cider are among the drinks dispensed at the well-stocked bar, and hot and cold food is served lunchtime and evening and all day on Sunday. The leg of lamb and the mixed grill are well able to deal with even the most ravenous, but there's something to suit lighter appetites, too, and children are welcome in the dining area (though not in the bar). Darts, dominoes and a fruit machine provide everyday entertainment in the bar, where Happy Hour is from 5 till 8 on Friday. Occasional theme nights are organised, and for really big occasions a marquee is set up in the beer garden.

Moorings on the canal can be organised with a little notice, and the pub has facilities for caravan rallies; there's also plenty of off-road parking and canalside seating. The village of Scarisbrick is part of the largest parish in Lancashire, and lies in an area of rich agricultural land producing abundant crops of vegetables.

Opening Hours: All day, every day.

Food: Bar meals / Restaurant

Credit Cards: None.

Accommodation: None.

Facilities: Car Park.

Entertainment: Occasional theme nights.

Local Places of Interest/Activities:
Ormskirk, Rufford Old Hall, Southport, Formby.

86   Kirkless Hall

Canal Bank, Top Lock, New Springs,
Lancashire WN2 1JW
Tel: 01942 242821

Directions:

From Wigan take the Horwich road. Just inside Aspull town boundary, at traffic lights, take a right turn marked Kirkless Industrial Estate. Follow road and turn third left into Albion Drive. On a few yards to T junction then turn right; follow the road round the corner to the pub on the right.

A real hidden gem of a place situated at the top of a series of locks on the Leeds & Liverpool Canal. Two private houses in mock Tudor style were turned into one to create a public house more than 100 years ago, and the outstanding location is just one of the attractions.

It's run by Jill and Bob Jolly, here since 1998 after 25 years as hoteliers, and Bob takes the leading role in the kitchen. Among his specialities are lamb Henry (with mint and redcurrants), chicken Italiano and steak au poivre, while Jill's home made pies (steak, steak & kidney, chicken & mushroom) are equally scrumptious. Sandwiches, made to order with a great variety of fillings, provide lighter snacks. Food is served from 12 to 2 (though lunch-time opening is limited in winter) and in the evenings till 9 o'clock (till 8 on Sunday); in high summer the food is served all day. The range of ales is appealing, too, with Burtonwood Bitter and Mild, Top Hat and Smooth among the options. The upstairs function room is to be converted into a top of the range fish restaurant, which it is planned to open by the autumn of 2001.

The comings and goings on the Leeds & Liverpool Canal provide plenty of entertainment and interest, especially in the summer, when the canalside picnic benches are a real boon; on Saturday evenings the call of the canal has a serious rival in the shape of the inn's weekly karaoke session. One of the main visitor attractions in the vicinity of this outstanding inn is Haigh Country Park, one of the first in England to be so designated. There's also excellent walking in the area, and golfers and anglers are also well catered for. And if you want to arrive by boat, there are moorings available at the inn.

Opening Hours: Lunchtime (limited opening in winter) and evening; all day Sat & Sun.

Food: Bar meals; fish restaurant planned.

Credit Cards: None.

Accommodation: None.

Facilities: Car Park, canalside tables.

Entertainment: Karaoke Saturday.

Local Places of Interest/Activities: Leeds & Liverpool Canal, Wigan, Haigh Country Park.

The Original Ship 87

95 Towngate, Leyland,
Lancashire PR25 2LQ
Tel: 01772 456674

Directions:
The pub is located in the heart of Leyland,
a short drive from junction 28 of the M6.

First The Ship, then The Seven Stars, now **The Original Ship**, this very sociable pub is located in the centre of Leyland, very close to junction 28 of the M6 and a short drive from Preston (to the north) and Chorley (to the southeast).

Samantha and Mick Hill took their first steps in the licensed trade when they took over as tenants at the end of 1999, and they have recently enhanced the traditional appeal of the place with a complete refurbishment inside and out. Food is served Tuesday to Sunday lunchtimes, and in addition to the main menu there's a daily specials board with dishes ranging from bacon or sausage barms to chicken or Aberdeen Angus burgers, T-bone steaks, minted lamb Henry and home-made chicken Madras. The bar always has a real ale on tap (the brew changes weekly) and other excellent thirst-quenchers include a locally brewed traditional scrumpy cider. Children are welcome at The Original Ship until 7.30 in the evening, after which there's something going on here most nights of the week: a free-for-all jamming session on the first Monday of the month, a quiz on Tuesday, a disco on Friday, a live soloist or duo on Saturday; karaoke on Sunday. Picnic benches are arranged on the patio at the front, and at the back is a capacious car park.

Preston and Chorley are both easily reached by car, and among other places to visit are the Camelot Theme Park at Charnock Richard and the fortified manor house of Hoghton Tower, where tradition has it that Shakespeare once lived. Leyland itself is best known for its association with the motor industry, and the British Commercial Museum, the largest of its kind in Europe, is well worth a visit.

Opening Hours: All day, every day.

Food: Bar meals lunchtime.

Credit Cards: None.

Accommodation: None.

Facilities: Car Park, beer garden.

Entertainment: see above.

Local Places of Interest/Activities: Preston, Chorley.

88   The Pear Tree Inn

155 Leyland Road,
Penwortham,
Lancashire
PR1 9QB
Tel: 01772 742536

Directions:

On Leyland Road, five minutes drive south of Preston; A59 then turn left on to the B5254.

Old weavers' cottages built in the late 18th century were converted into a grand little pub that's full of character, a cosy, welcoming spot to pause for refreshment on the road that runs south from Preston to Leyland by way of Tardy Gate.

The pub is run by Terry Sloper, who came here early in 2001 with 36 years experience in the business, with the assistance of bar manager Andy Croft and an excellent team. Victorian fireplaces with tiled surrounds are among the attractive features in the bar, where the brews on offer include John Smiths Cask and Smooth, Chestnut Mild and a good range of lagers. Food is served every lunchtime in the bar and in the non-smoking dining area, and there's no shortage of choice on the printed menu and the daily specials board; favourite dishes include mixed grills and the excellent home-made steak & kidney pie. Terry has plans to introduce meals in the evening and to add to the choice of real ales. Happy Hour for draught ales is 11-2 and 6-7 Monday to Friday. Quiz night is Sunday, starting at 9 o'clock. The Pear Tree has a large beer garden, and there's off-road parking on either side.

Nearby Preston, the administrative capital of Lancashire, has much to interest the visitor, including the Harris Museum, two regimental museums, a fine Guild Hall (well known to followers of snooker and bowls on TV), and the splendid Ribble Viaduct, built in 1838 to bring the railway from Wigan to Preston. The unique British Commercial Vehicle Museum is a short distance south of the Pear Tree at Leyland, and the coastal resorts of Southport, Lytham and Blackpool are all an easy drive away.

Opening Hours: All day, every day.

Food: Bar meals at lunchtime (evening meals in future).

Credit Cards: None.

Accommodation: None.

Facilities: Car Park, beer garden.

Entertainment: Quiz Sunday.

Local Places of Interest/Activities: Preston 2 miles, Leyland 2 miles, Southport, Lytham, Blackpool.

The Plough

46 Church Street,
Ormskirk,
Lancashire
L39 3AW
Tel: 01695 572290

Directions:

Situated centrally in
Ormskirk opposite
the parish church
and previously
called the Hatters
Arms.

Paul and Christine, in the licensed trade for over 20 years, took over at the Plough in 1995, and have an equally warm welcome for regular patrons and new faces. Three real ales (two Tetleys and a guest), two draught lagers and McEwans Scotch Bitter are among the liquid refreshments always on offer, and food is served at lunchtime Thursday to Sunday. The printed menu is supplemented by a daily specials board, and for many the all-day breakfast is the thing to go for - a tasty and satisfying prelude to an amble round the town or a great way to recharge the batteries after the walk. Other options might be light snacks (sandwiches, jacket potatoes), sausage with mashed potatoes and gravy, and the cool-weather favourite of traditional Lancashire hot pot served with beetroot salad and cabbage; this is a dish which disappears as quickly as they make it! Children are welcome and they have their own section of the menu.

There's no lack of entertainment in the bar, with darts, dominoes, pool, chess, two fruit machines and a juke box that's reputed to be the best in the whole of Lancashire. There's a Pay & Display car park behind the pub, which stands opposite the parish church of St Peter & St Paul in the centre of town. This church is unusual in having both a steeple and a tower. The latter was added in the 16th century to house the bells of Burscough Priory after the religious community had been disbanded by Henry VIII. Ormskirk's most famous son was a market trader called Beecham, who sold his own brand of liver pills and earned himself fame and fortune. Even greater fame awaited his son, the illustrious conductor Sir Thomas Beecham.

Opening Hours: All day, every day.

Food: Bar meals lunch Thursday to Sunday.

Credit Cards: None.

Accommodation: None.

Entertainment: The best juke box in Lancashire!

Local Places of Interest: Ormskirk Church of St Peter & St Paul (opposite the pub), Southport.

90 The Railway Hotel

69 Watkin Lane,
Lostock Hall,
Preston,
Lancashire
PR5 5HA
Tel: 01772 697233

Directions:

2 miles south of Preston, the village of Lostock Hall is more or less joined with the village of Tardy Gate, reached off the A582.

The pub sign is an A4 Pacific of the Mallard class in its blue LNER livery, and the pub itself stands by the main line railway. Built in the early part of the 19th century, it once had its own stables and brewery attached. Hanging baskets and window boxes adorn the white-painted exterior, and inside all is cosy and inviting, a very relaxed, popular place to meet for a quiet drink and a chat.

The tenants are Barbara and Graham Catterall, who, ably assisted by their daughter Sharon, have turned the **Railway Hotel** once more into a thriving local since their arrival in November 2000. The rollcall of cask-conditioned ales is particularly strong, with six usually on offer, including Ruddles, Magnet, John Smiths, Black Sheep and Bombardier. They serve food here lunchtime and evening every day except Monday; Barbara and Sharon share the cooking, and their main dishes include hearty classics such as steak & ale pie and a tasty, satisfying mixed grill; roghan josh is also zooming up the popularity charts. Happy Hours for draught beers and lagers are 11-2 and 5-7 Monday to Friday. Monday night is quiz night. The pub has good off-road parking, a beer garden with a safe children's play area, and a bowling green.

The Railway Hotel is located within an easy drive of Preston, which now has a thriving yacht marina in addition to its other amenities and attractions; also close by are the Commercial Vehicle Museum at Leyland and the baronial residence of Hoghton Hall, visited by James I and William Shakespeare and devastated by Cromwell's troops.

Opening Hours: All day, every day.
Food: Bar meals.
Credit Cards: None.
Accommodation: None.

Facilities: Car Park, beer garden with play area, bowling green.
Entertainment: Quiz Monday.
Local Places of Interest/Activities: Preston, Leyland, Hoghton Hall.

The Red Lion   91

138 Liverpool Road,
Longton,
Preston,
Lancashire
PR4 5AU
Tel: 01772 612168

Directions:

From Preston take
the A59 for about 3
miles; turn right on
to a minor road
signposted Longton.

The Red Lion is the social hub of a village standing in isolation on the south side of the River Ribble. A sturdy mid-Victorian building in redbrick and stone, with flourishing creeper and window boxes, it has the most atmospheric of bars, where the talking points include a collection of clocks showing the time in various parts of the world, gleaming copper and brass ornaments, old pots and bottles, pictures and prints - and pride of place must go to the full-size red telephone box!

The leaseholders since the beginning of 2001 are Ray and Debbie Heaney, whose first venture with their own pub this is. Ray's earlier career was as a sportsman, playing professional football for Liverpool and professional rugby league for Wigan and Salford. He now gets his kicks running this terrific pub, where among the plans for the near future are a complete refurbishment and the serving of food at lunchtime and in the evening. Ray keeps an excellent range of real ales, including Timothy Taylor Landlord, McEwans 80/-, Theakstons Cool and Directors. There are two regular entertainment slots each week in the form of a quiz on Thursday and live performers on Saturday, both events starting at 9.30. The pub has a very pleasant beer garden with an extensive children's play area.

This region of Lancashire offers the whole range of the county's heritage to explore, from the elegant resort of Southport and the unbroken miles of coastal walks to the rich, fertile countryside and the bustling centres of commerce.

Opening Hours: All day, every day.

Food: Planned.

Credit Cards: Planned.

Accommodation: None.

Facilities: Car Park, beer garden, children's play area.

Entertainment: Quiz Thursday, live show Saturday.

Local Places of Interest/Activities: Ribble Estuary, Ribble Way footpath, Preston 5 miles, Southport 10 miles.

92 Town Green Inn

17 Town Green Lane,
Aughton,
Nr. Ormskirk,
Lancashire
L39 6SE
Tel: 01695 422165

Directions:

Aughton lies 3 miles southwest of Ormskirk off the A59.

In the centre of a picturesque village off the main Ormskirk-Liverpool road (A59), **Town Green Inn** is a very striking late 18th century building constructed of the locally quarried Aughton stone. Originally a tied farmhouse, it started brewing early in its life, and under the aegis of business partners Vera Critchlow and Dave Corrin the tradition of hospitality continues in fine form.

The interior has a real old-world quality with half-panelling, nicotine-coloured walls, some splendid old furniture and lots of prints and pictures. One room has on display a fully documented history of local celebrity William Harvey Hartley, who was the bandmaster on the *Titanic* when it sank on its maiden voyage in 1912. The inn is a member of CAMRA, and three real ales - the choice is constantly changing - are always available. Food is also taken seriously here, and the specialities include curried chicken, a really tasty steak & Guinness pie and wicked home-made chips. Children are welcome, and the bars have some designated no-smoking areas. Food is served on Sunday from 12 to 3 and other days from 12 to 7 (except Monday lunch).

This is the most sociable of inns and a major focal point of the local community; it sponsors two football teams - Town Green and the Lancashire Police Veterans - and there's in-house entertainment three evenings a week. The quiz starts at 9 o'clock on Thursday, live entertainment on Friday, and on Monday local musicians gather for a jam session (visitors from further afield are always welcome to join in). Tables and chairs are set out under parasols at the front of the pub, and there's a car park to the rear. The village of Aughton is dominated by the spire of St Michael's Church, much of whose medieval framework survives.

Opening Hours: Monday from 5, all day other days.

Food: Bar meals.

Credit Cards: All the major cards.

Accommodation: None.

Facilities: Car Park.

Entertainment: Jam session Monday, quiz Thursday, live show Friday.

Local Places of Interest/Activities:
Ormskirk 3 miles, Liverpool, Formby.

The Travellers Rest 93

Dawbers Lane, Euxton,
Lancashire PR7 6EG
Tel: 01257 451184 Fax: 01257 450620

Directions:

From Preston take the A49 to Euxton; turn right on to the A581; the pub is about a mile along this road.

Three 18th century cottages, each with its own pretty little porch, were combined and expanded to make this very pleasant and welcoming inn, which has throughout its life been a popular place to pause between the industrial areas of Lancashire and the seaside resorts. Tony and Diane Hogan, here as tenants since 1997, continue to offer excellent hospitality, and the carefully modernised bars make eye-catching use of wood for ceiling beams, panelling, fireplace surrounds and bookshelves.

Patrons with a sporting interest can admire the photographs and prints on the themes of motor racing and association football; not surprisingly, the soccer teams featured are the heroes of Lancashire - Blackburn, Bolton, Burnley and Preston. Three real ales change on a regular basis, and there's also a constant reworking of the menu, with a specials board announcing daily supplements to the printed list. Everything is prepared on the premises, and the chef has a particularly good way with soups and sauces, pies and curries. But it's all excellent, and the lunchtime and early evening special deals offer outstanding value for money. Food is served every lunchtime and evening and all day on Sunday, and booking is recommended for Friday and Saturday evening and Sunday lunch. Children are welcome, and there are some non-smoking tables in the dining area. A fruit machine, juke box and pool table (free on Mondays) provide entertainment in the bar, and the quiz gets under way at 9 o'clock every Thursday evening. Outside, the pub has plenty of off-road parking space and a beer garden with a children's play area.

Two of the biggest visitor attractions in the vicinity are the Camelot Theme Park at Charnock Richard and the superb Elizabethan Astley Hall at Chorley.

Opening Hours: Lunchtime and evening; all day Sunday (also Saturday in the summer holiday).

Food: Bar meals.

Credit Cards: Mastercard, Visa.

Accommodation: None.

Facilities: Car Park, beer garden, children's play area.

Entertainment: Quiz Thursday.

Local Places of Interest/Activities: Chorley 1 mile, Camelot Theme Park 2 miles, Leyland 2 miles, Preston 4 miles.

94   The Tudor Inn

117 Mossey Lea Road,
Wrightington,
Lancashire
WN6 9RE
Tel: 01257 425977

Directions:

Wrightington lies
8 miles northeast
of Ormskirk on
the B5250 (take
the A59, A5209
then B5250); from
Wigan A5209
then B5250.

This really charming inn enjoys a convenient location in a quiet village easily reached from Wigan, Ormskirk or the M6 (leave at J27). The premises were originally two cottages, with a smithy at the back, and in its earlier days as an inn was called the White Lion, known locally as Old Bobs. The neat, compact, brick-and-stone exterior hides a wealth of old-world character and atmosphere: small-paned windows, black-and-white Tudor features, open brickwork, old beams, well-chosen pictures on yellow-painted walls, burnished copper and brass ornaments, a snug corner with comfortable sofas to sink into, a dining area with neatly laid tables and an elaborate chandelier.

The inn is closed Monday and Tuesday lunchtime in winter, but food is served every other lunchtime and every evening, and all day on Saturday and Sunday. The non-smoking restaurant, with waitress service, has seats for 54, and booking is essential on Sunday, when the three-course carvery pulls in the crowds. Home-made pies and sizzling platters are popular fixtures on the main menu, which is supplemented by daily specials typified by Chinese spring rolls, cheese and chilli melts, garlic chicken and mushroom & nut fettuccine, with tempting desserts such as spotted dick or chocolate pudding. Children are welcome and they even have their own special section of the menu. Beers include Greenalls Cask and Dark Mild and Worthington Creamflow.

The tenant, who took over at Easter 2000, is Louise Leyland, who has very able assistance from fiancé Carl, who is the head chef, Mum, Jean and David. The Tudor Inn has a beer garden at the back, along with a large car park. Wednesday is quiz night, starting at 9.30, and a live music event takes place once a month.

Opening Hours: Lunchtime and evening; all day Sat & Sun. Closed lunchtime Mon & Tues in winter.

Food: Bar meals, a la carte.

Credit Cards: Mastercard, Visa.

Accommodation: None.

Facilities: Car Park, beer garden, disabled entrance and toilets.

Entertainment: Quiz Wednesday.

Local Places of Interest/Activities: Wigan, Ormskirk, Camelot Theme Park.

The Wheatsheaf Hotel | 95

Ormskirk Road, Rainford,
St Helens, Lancashire WA11 7TA
Tel: 01744 884346

Directions:
From St Helens take the A570 Southport road. Ignore the turn-off signs to Rainford; follow the dual carriageway, pass under the railway bridge and find the inn on the right at the next road junction.

A mellow stone building dating back to the early part of the 18th century, standing on a prominent corner site on the A570. Once a staging post on the St Helens-Ormskirk route, with stables, a blacksmith and a wheelwright, it is now a village ale and eating house par excellence, with en suite accommodation for overnight guests. Window boxes brighten the exterior, while inside, wood panelling, Victorian fireplaces and displays of ornaments and memorabilia add to the charming, homely feel.

Brendan and Cathy Houlihan, members of the British Institute of Innkeepers, have been in the trade in the Northwest since 1978 and took over the lease of the Wheatsheaf in 1999. Visitors can look forward to warm hospitality, traditional cask beers and home-cooked food served all sessions and all day on Sunday, when booking is recommended and roast meats are added to the main menu. The options run from baguettes, toasties, burgers and jacket potatoes for snacks to starters such as oriental spring rolls or deep-fried mushrooms and main courses that include all the pub classics (cod, scampi, gammon, steaks, steak pie) and always a choice for vegetarians. Children are welcome, and there are designated no-smoking areas in the bars. The Houlihans are happy to cater for business lunches, buffets, parties and all sorts of special occasions.

The overnight guest accommodation comprises two en suite rooms - a twin and a family room - available all year round. They are let on a Bed & Breakfast basis, with discounts for extended stays. There's open countryside on either side of the main A570, while Ormskirk lies to the north and St Helens (Rugby League, Pilkington glass, home of Sir Thomas Beecham) is a short drive south.

Opening Hours: Lunchtime and evening; all day Sat, Sun & summer Fridays.

Food: Bar meals.

Credit Cards: Amex, Mastercard, Visa.

Accommodation: 2 en suite rooms.

Facilities: Car Park.

Entertainment: None.

Local Places of Interest/Activities:
Ormskirk 5 miles, St Helens 3 miles.

96 The White Horse

32-36 Chorley Road,
Heath Charnock,
Chorley,
Lancashire
PR6 9LJ
Tel: 01257 481766

Directions:

From Chorley take the A6 south then, where it forks to the right, take the left fork, which is the A683 (called Chorley Road) heading for Bolton. The pub stands by a mini-roundabout 3 miles south of Chorley.

Excellent hospitality is guaranteed at the White Horse, which is located in a tiny village (not on many maps) by a mini-roundabout on the A683. Elaine Lawson, here since September 1999, runs a really delightful old inn with abundant character and a good deal of history. It is said that a tunnel once connected the inn to a nearby monastery - was it for locals to seek sanctuary in an emergency or for monks to wet their whistles without letting the whole world know? Local scenes of bygone times adorn the walls of the inn, and the Victorian tiles surrounding the fireplace are one of several attractive features in the bar, where today's whistles are wetted by an excellent range of beers and lagers.

This is splendid walking country, and a morning ramble will generate the kind of appetite the **White Horse** is more than capable of satisfying. Food is served from noon to 2 o'clock Wednesday to Sunday, and favourites on the menu include gammon steaks, the house curry, chilli con carne and the really tasty home-cooked pies, notably chicken & ham and steak & ale. The two-course Sunday lunch with a choice of roasts is a weekly must for many of the regular patrons, and on Wednesday pensioners can enjoy a special two-course meal at a bargain price. The evenings may be without food but they're certainly not without entertainment, with a quiz on Tuesday, a pool competition on Wednesday, darts and dominoes on Thursday and the occasional DJ-hosted music evening on a Saturday. The pub has plenty of off-road parking at the rear.

The morning may be for walking, but after a splendid lunch visitors to the area will find plenty to see and do within a short drive: major attractions the Camelot Theme Park and the magnificent Astley Hall at Chorley, an Elizabethan mansion with a notable collection of furniture spanning four centuries.

Opening Hours: Lunchtime and evening; all day Saturday and Sunday.

Food: Bar meals Wed-Sun lunch.

Credit Cards: None.

Accommodation: None.

Facilities: Car Park.

Entertainment: See above.

Local Places of Interest/Activities: Chorley 3 miles, Rivington (walks).

4 West Cheshire and the Wirral

PLACES OF INTEREST:

PUBS AND INNS:

The Hidden Inns of Lancashire and Cheshire

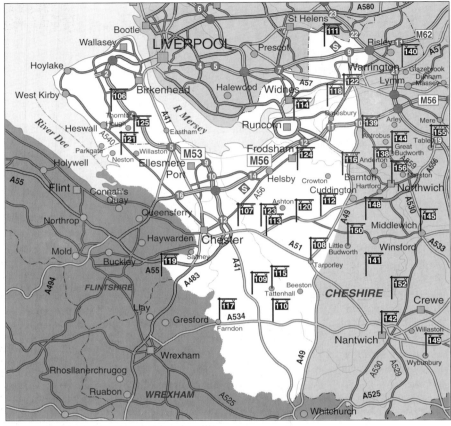

© MAPS IN MINUTES ™ 2001 © Crown Copyright, Ordnance Survey 2001

106	The Basset Hound, Wirral	116	The Maypole Inn, Weaverham
107	The Bird in Hand, Guilden Sutton	117	The Nags Head, Farndon
108	The Bulls Head Inn, Clotton	118	The Red Lion, Moore
109	The Calveley Arms, Handley	119	The Royal Oak, Higher Kinnerton
110	The Copper Mine, Broxton	120	Royal Oak Hotel, Kelsall, nr Tarporley
111	The Fiddle i'the Bag Inn, Burtonwood	121	The Royal Oak, Little Neston,
112	The Fishpool Inn, Delamere	122	The Stag Inn, Walton Warrington
113	The George and Dragon, Tarvin	123	The Stamford Bridge, Tarvin,
114	The Halfway House, Runcorn	124	The Travellers Rest, Frodsham
115	The Letters Inn, Tattenhall	125	The Wheatsheaf Inn, Raby

Please note all references refer to page numbers

West Cheshire and the Wirral

Around the 1890s, guide-book writers took a fancy to describing the topography of various counties by comparing their outlines to some appropriate emblem or object (The Times has recently done something similar with American States). In Cheshire's county boundaries they were unable to discern anything more imaginative than the shape of a teapot. Its base is the Staffordshire border, its handle the strip of land running from Stockport up to the Yorkshire border, with the Wirral providing the spout. And, tucked away at the base of the spout, is the capital of the county, the City of Chester. The city's position, a strategic site on

King Charles Tower

the River Dee close to the Welsh border, was important even before the Romans arrived in AD70 to establish the head-quarters of the famous 20th Legion, the *Valeria Victrix*. They based a large camp, or 'caster', here and called it Deva after the Celtic name for the river. It was during this period that the splendid city walls were originally built - two miles round, and still the most complete in the country. In Saxon times 'Ceastre' became the administrative centre of a shire, and was the last major town in England to fall to William the Conqueror during his dreadful Harrowing of the North. William pulled down half Chester's houses and reinforced the message of Norman domination by building a castle over-looking the Dee. Subsequent Earls of Chester (the present Prince of Wales is the current Earl) were given a free, and very firm hand, in dealing with the local Saxons and with the still-rebellious Welsh who continued to make a nuisance of themselves right through the Middle Ages. In return for its no-nonsense dealing with these problems Chester received a number of royal privileges: borough status, a licence for a market and, around 1120, the first commission in England for a Sheriff - long before his more famous colleague in Not-tingham received his. The Mayor of Chester can still claim the medieval title of 'Admiral of the Dee'. The problem with the Welsh was finally resolved in 1485 when a Welsh-based family, the Tudors, defeated Richard III at Bosworth Field and Owen Tudor claimed the throne as Henry VII. For more than 150 years Chester enjoyed an unprecedented period of peace and prosperity. Then came the Civil War. Chester supported the King but Charles I had the galling experience of watching from the city walls as his troops were defeated at nearby Rowton Moor. For two long years after that rout, the city was under siege until starvation finally forced its capitulation. The King Charles Tower on the wall is now a small museum with displays telling the story of that siege. Seventy years later, in the course of his *Tour through the Whole Island of Great Britain*, Daniel Defoe came to Chester by the ferry over the River Dee. He liked the city streets, "very broad and fair"; admired the "very pleasant walk round the city, upon the walls", disliked its cathedral, "built of red, sandy, ill looking stone", but had nothing but praise for its "excellent cheese".

Cheshire cheese had been famous for generations. John Speed, the famous Elizabethan map-maker and a Cheshire man himself, noted: "The soil is fat fruitful and rich....the Pas-tures make the Kine's udders to strout to the pail, from whom the best Cheese of all Europe is made". Later, some enthusiasts even promoted the idea that the name Cheshire was

100

actually short for cheese-shire. The county's other major industry was salt, mined here even before the Romans arrived. By the time of the Domesday Book, the salt towns, or "wiches" - Nantwich, Northwich, Middlewich, were firmly established. The process then involved pumping the salt brine to the surface and boiling it to produce granular salt. In 1670, huge deposits of rock salt were discovered and these are still being mined, mostly for use in keeping the country's roads free from ice. Both these historic industries have been overtaken in the 20th century by tourism. Chester, with its long history, varied and fascinating "magpie" architecture, and huge range of shops, restaurants and inns, is now the fourth most visited location in England after the "golden triangle" of London, Stratford and Oxford. One small disappointment, though. Visitors don't get to see the county's best known character, the grinning Cheshire Cat. The phrase "To grin like a Cheshire cat" was in use long before Lewis Carroll adopted it in

Ness Gardens, Neston

Alice in Wonderland. Carroll spent his childhood in the Cheshire village of Daresbury and would have regularly seen the local cheeses moulded into various animal shapes, one of which was a grinning cat.

Two Old English words meaning heathland covered with bog myrtle gave The Wirral its name and well into modern times it was a byword for a desolate place. The 14th century author of *Sir Gawayne and the Green Knight* writes of:

"The wilderness of Wirral: few lived there
Who loved with a good heart either God or man"

The Wirral's inhabitants were infamous for preying on the shipwrecks tossed on to its marshy coastline by gales sweeping off the Irish Sea. The 19th century development of shipbuilding at Birkenhead brought industry on a large scale to the Mersey shore but also an influx of prosperous Liverpool commuters who colonised the villages of the Caldy and Grange Hills and transformed the former wilderness into leafy suburbia. The 1974 Local Government changes handed two thirds of The Wirral to Merseyside leaving Cheshire with by far the most attractive third, the southern and western parts alongside the River Dee. Tourism officials now refer to The Wirral as the 'Leisure Peninsula', a fair description of this appealing and comparatively little-known area. One of its major attractions is Ness Botanic Gardens, a 64-acre tract of superbly landscaped gardens on the banks of the River Dee. The gardens are run by the University of Liverpool as an Environmental and Horticultural Research Station and are planned to provide magnificent displays all year round. The planting of Lombardy poplars, oaks and pines has provided shelter for the wide range of exotic and specialist plants for which the Gardens are known. There are children's play and picnic areas, and well-marked interest trails, and licensed refreshment rooms.

PLACES OF INTEREST

ASHTON

A couple of miles to the northeast of the village of Ashton stretch the 4,000 acres of **Delamere Forest**, a rambler's delight with a wealth of lovely walks and many picnic sites, ideal for a peaceful family day out. In Norman times, a 'forest' was a part-wooded, part-open area, reserved as a hunting ground exclusively for royalty or the nobility. There were savage penalties for anyone harming the deer, even if the deer were destroying crops, and household dogs within the forest had to be deliberately lamed to ensure that they could not harass the beasts. James I was the last king to hunt deer here, in August 1617, and so enjoyed the day's sport that he made his Chief Forester a knight on the spot. Even at that date, many of the great oaks in the forest had already been felled to provide timber for ship-building, as well as for Cheshire's familiar black and white half-timbered houses. Since the early 1900s, Delamere Forest has been maintained by the Forestry Commission which has undertaken an intensive programme of tree planting and woodland management. Delamere is now both an attractive recreational area and a working forest with 90% of the trees eventually destined for the saw mills.

BEESTON

A craggy cliff suddenly rising 500ft from the Cheshire Plain, its summit crowned by the ruins of **Beeston Castle** (English Heritage), Beeston Hill is one of the most dramatic sights in the county. Built around 1220, the castle didn't see any military action until the Civil War. On one rather ignominious occasion during that conflict, a Royalist captain and just

eight musketeers managed to capture the mighty fortress and its garrison of 60 soldiers without firing a

101

shot. A few years later, Cromwell ordered that the castle be 'slighted', or partially destroyed, but this 'Castle in the Air' is still very imposing with walls 30ft high and a well 366ft deep. An old legend asserts that Richard II tipped a hoard of coins, gold and jewels down the well, but no treasure has yet been discovered. The castle hill is a popular place for picnics, and it's worth climbing it just to enjoy the spectacular views which extend across seven counties and over to a 'twin' castle. **Peckforton Castle** looks just as medieval as Beeston but was, in fact, built in 1844 for the first Lord Tollemache who spared no expense in re-creating features such as a vast Great Hall and a keep with towers 60ft tall. The architect Gilbert Scott later praised Peckforton as "the very height of masquerading". Its authentic medieval appearance has made the castle a favourite location for film and television companies, and on Sundays and Bank Holidays during the season the Middle Ages are brought to life here with mock battles and tournaments. The castle also offers guided tours, refreshments and a speciality shop.

If you continue south from Beeston on the A49, after about six miles you will reach **Cholmondeley Castle** and its famous gardens. They were first laid out in the early years of the 19th century shortly after the Castle was built. The Castle itself, a marvellous mock-medieval construction, is not open to the public, but visitors are welcome to explore the 30 acre garden which includes a water garden and woodland walks. There are plants for sale, a lakeside picnic area, a gift shop and tea room.

CHESTER

James Boswell, Dr Johnson's biographer, visited Chester in the 1770s and wrote "I was quite enchanted at Chester, so that I could with difficulty quit it". He was to return again, declaring that "Chester pleases my fancy more than any town I ever saw". Modern visitors will almost certainly share his enthusiasm.

Probably the best introduction to this compact little city is to join one of the frequent sightseeing tours conducted by a Blue Badge guide. These take place every day, even Christmas Day, and leave from the Chester Visitor Centre. The Centre can also provide you with a

Beeston Castle

102

wealth of information about the city, including a full calendar of events that range from the Chester Regatta, the oldest rowing races in the world and Chester Races, the oldest in Britain, to the Lord Mayor's Show in May and the Festival of Transport, featuring an amazing parade of vintage cars, in August.

Towering above the city centre is **Chester Cathedral**, a majestic building of weathered pink stone which in 1992 celebrated its 900th birthday. It was originally an Abbey and is one of very few to survive Henry VIII's closure of the monasteries in the 1540s. The cloisters are regarded as the finest in England and the monks' refectory is still serving food although nowadays it is refreshments and lunches for visitors. It was at Chester Cathedral, in 1742,

Chester Cathedral

that George Frederick Handel personally conducted rehearsals of his oratorio *The Messiah* before its first performance in Dublin: a copy of the score with annotations in his own hand remains on display.

Chester is famous for its outstanding range of museums, from the Deva Roman Experience where you can re-live the sights, sounds and even the smells of daily Roman life, through the Grosvenor Museum with its furnished period rooms, to the Chester Heritage Centre which tells the city's story from the Civil War siege to the present day. On The Air broadcasting museum chronicles the world of radio and

television from the pioneering days of BBC radio to satellite TV, while the Chester Toy & Doll Museum is a nostalgic treasure-house of antique playthings

Quite apart from its historical attractions, Chester is also one of the major shopping centres for the north west and north Wales. All the familiar High Street names are here, often housed in much more appealing buildings than they usually inhabit, along with a great number of specialist and antique shops. For a unique shopping experience, you must visit the world-famous, two-tiered galleries of shops under covered walkways known as **The Rows** which line Eastgate Street and part of Bridge Street. The Rows are an architectural one-off: no other medieval town has anything like them. Many of the black and white, half-timbered frontages of The Rows, so typical of Chester and Cheshire, are actually Victorian restorations, but crafted so beautifully and faithfully that even experts can have difficulty distinguishing them from their 13th century originals.

Close by in Eastgate is the famous **Jubilee Clock**, a beautifully ornate contsruction that must be among the most photographed clocks in the world. It was made by Joyce of Whitchurch and erected in 1897 to celebrate Queen Victoria's Diamond Jubilee. If your timing is right and you arrive hereabouts at 12 noon in the summer, you should see, and certainly hear, the Town Crier delivering some stentorian civic message.

A few steps bring you to Chester's famous **City Walls** which were originally built by the Romans to protect the fortress of Deva from attacks by pesky Celtic tribes. Nowadays, the two-mile long circuit, - an easy, level promenade, provides thousands of visitors with some splendid views of the River Dee, of the city's many glorious buildings and of the distant Welsh mountains. Here, during the summer months, you may come across Caius Julius Quartus, a Roman Legionary Officer in shining armour conducting a patrol around the fortress walls and helping to re-create the life and times of a front-line defender of the Empire. At one point, the wall runs alongside St John Street, which has a curious history. In Roman times it was the main thoroughfare between the fortress and the Amphitheatre, the largest ever uncovered in Britain, capable of seating 7,000 spectators. During the Middle Ages however this highway was excavated and turned into a defensive ditch. Over the years, the ditch gradually filled

ers show a Mock Turtle, a March Hare and a Mad Hatter. This is of course the Lewis Carroll Memorial Window, commemorating the author of *Alice in Wonderland*. Carroll himself is shown at one side, dressed in clerical garb and kneeling. His father was Vicar of Daresbury and he was born here in 1832 and baptised as Charles Lutwidge Dodgson. The boy enjoyed an apparently idyllic childhood at Daresbury until his father moved to another parish when Charles/Lewis was eleven years old.

EASTHAM

Eastham Woods Country Park is a 76-acre oasis of countryside amidst industrial Merseyside and enjoys considerable status amongst birdwatchers as one of few northern woodlands with all three species of native woodpecker in residence. Just a mile or so from the Park is Eastham village, another little oasis with a church and old houses grouped around the village green. The venerable yew tree in the churchyard is reputed to be the oldest in England.

FARNDON

Built on a hillside overlooking the River Dee, Farndon is literally a stone's throw from Wales. Most travellers agree that the best approach to the principality is by way of this little town and its ancient bridge. Records show that building of the bridge began in 1345 and it is one of only two surviving medieval bridges in the county, the other being in Chester. From Farndon's bridge, riverside walks by the Dee extend almost up to its partner in Chester. During the Civil War, Farndon's strategic position between Royalist North Wales and parliamentarian Cheshire led to many skirmishes here. Those stirring events are colourfully depicted in a stained glass window in the church, although only the Royalist heroes are included. One Farndon man who deserves a memorial of some kind but doesn't have one is John Speed, the famous cartographer, who was born here in 1542. He followed his father's trade as a tailor, married and had 18 children, and was nearly 50 before he was able to devote himself full time to researching and producing his beautifully drawn maps. Fortunately, he lived to the age of 87 and his fifty-four Maps of England and Wales were the first really accurate ones to be published.

The Rows

up and by Elizabethan times St John Street was a proper street once again. The heart of the old city is now reserved for pedestrians only and Foregate Street is part of this walker-friendly area. Rivers always add a special attraction to a city and Chester certainly makes good use of the River Dee. Rowing boats, motor boats, canoes, are all available for hire, and comfortable cruisers offer sightseeing tours along the river as far as the Crook of Dee, opposite the Duke of Westminster's stately residence of Eaton Hall.

No visit to Chester would be complete without a trip to **Chester Zoo** on the northern edge of the city. Set in 110 acres of landscaped gardens, it's the largest zoo in Britain, caring for more than 5000 animals from some 500 different species. The Zoo also provides a refuge for many rare and endangered animals which breed freely in near-natural enclosures. What's more, it has the UK's largest elephant facility and is the only successful breeder of Asiatic elephants in this country. Offering more than enough interest for a full day out, the Zoo is open every day of the year except Christmas Day.

CROWTON

Crowton has many times been voted the Best Kept Village in Cheshire and its 18th century hostelry, The Hare & Hounds, enjoys a particularly scenic position in this appealing village.

DARESBURY

All Saints' Church in Daresbury has a unique stained glass window: there are panels depicting a Gryphon and a Cheshire Cat, while oth-

104

FRODSHAM

This is an attractive town with a broad High Street lined with thatched cottages and spacious Georgian and Victorian houses. During the 18th and early 19th centuries, Frodsham was an important coaching town and there are several fine coaching inns. Built in 1632, The Bear's Paw with its three stone gables recalls the bear-baiting that once took place nearby. Of the Earl of Chester's Norman castle only fragments remain, but the Church of St Laurence overlooking the town from below the steep face of Overton Hill is noted for the fine 17th century panelling in its exquisite north chapel. The Vicar here from 1740 to 1756 was Francis Gastrell, a name that is anathema to all lovers of Shakespeare. Gastrell bought the poet's house, New Place, at Stratford and first incensed the towns-people by cutting down the famous mulberry tree. Then, in order to avoid paying the Corporation poor rate, he pulled the house itself down. The outraged citizens of Stratford hounded him from the town and he returned to the parish at Frodsham that he had neglected for years.

HELSBY

There are seven Iron Age forts scattered across Cheshire, but only the one at Helsby, maintained by the National Trust, is open to the public. The climb out of the village along pretty woodland paths to the red sandstone summit is quite steep but the views across the marshes to the Mersey Estuary and the mountains of North Wales repay the effort.

NESTON

Right up until the early 19th century, Neston was the most significant town in The Wirral, one of the string of small ports along the River Dee. In Tudor times, Neston had been one of the main embarkation points for travellers to Ireland but the silting up of the river was so swift and inexorable that by the time the New Quay, begun in 1545, was completed, it had become useless. Visiting Neston in the late 1700s, Anna Seward described the little town set on a hill overlooking the Dee Estuary as "a nest from the storm of the ocean".

PARKGATE

After Neston port became unusable, maritime traffic moved along the Dee Estuary to Parkgate which, as the new gateway to Ireland, saw some notable visitors. John Wesley, who made regular trips to Ireland, preached here while waiting for a favourable wind, and George Frederick Handel returned via Parkgate after conducting the first performance of *The Messiah* in Dublin. JMW Turner came to sketch the lovely view across to the Flintshire hills. A little later, Parkgate enjoyed a brief spell as a fashionable spa. Lord Nelson's mistress, Lady Hamilton (who was born at nearby Neston) took the waters here in an effort to cure an unfortunate skin disease, another visitor was Mrs Fitzherbert, already secretly married to the Prince Regent, later George IV. When Holyhead developed into the main gateway to Ireland, Parkgate's days as a port and watering-place were numbered. But with fine Georgian houses lining the promenade, this attractive little place still retains the atmosphere of a gracious spa town.

SALTNEY

For centuries, the ferry boat from Saltney on the south side of the River Dee provided a vital link for travellers from north Wales making their way to the great city of Chester. Modern roads put the ferrymen out of business a long time ago but their memory is honoured at The Saltney Ferry public house.

TARPORLEY

In the days when most of this area was part of Delamere Forest, Tarporley was the headquarters of the verderers or forest wardens. It was from Tarporley in the early 17th century that John Done, Chief Forester and Hereditary Bowbearer of Delamere entertained King James to a hunt. The chase was, he reported, a great success: "deer, both red and fallow, fish and fowl, abounded in the meres". A gratified King rewarded his host with a knighthood. At that time, the verderers had their own courts in which they meted out rough justice to offenders against the forest laws. One such court was at Utkinton, just north of the town, and in an old farmhouse there stands a column formed by an ancient forest tree, its roots still in the ground. When the court was in session, the wardens would place on this tree the symbol of their authority, the Hunting Horn of Delamere. The farmhouse is not open to the public but the horn, dating from around 1120, has survived and can be seen at the Grosvenor Museum in Chester. Another impressive survivor is the Tarporley Hunt Club which is primarily a dining club for hunting people and still has an annual banquet in the town. Founded in 1762, it is now the oldest Hunt Club in the country.

TATTENHALL

Tattenhall is a fine old village within sight of the twin castles of Beeston and Peckforton perched atop the Peckforton Hills. There are some attractive old houses and a Victorian church with a graveyard which gained notoriety during the 19th century because of the activities of a gang of grave-robbers. They lived in caves in the hills nearby and, once they had disposed of the bodies to medical gentlemen, used the empty coffins to store their booty from more conventional thieving. At that time Tattenhall was a busy little place. The Shropshire Union Canal passed close by and the village was served by two railway stations on different lines. Today, only one railway line survives (and no stations), the canal is used solely by pleasure craft, but the village is enjoying a new lease of life as a desirable community for people commuting to Chester, a short drive away.

Small though it is, Tattenhall has entertained some distinguished visitors. No less a personage than King James I once stayed at The Bear & Ragged Staff.

THORNTON HOUGH

The huge village green at Thornton Hough, covering some 14 acres and surrounded by half-timbered black and white houses, is one of the most picturesque spots in Cheshire.

WILLASTON-IN-WIRRAL

Hadlow Road Station, a short distance from the centre of Willaston, hasn't seen a train since 1962. But everything here is spick and span, the signal box and ticket office apparently ready for action, a trolley laden with milk churns waiting on the platform. Restored to appear as it would have done on a typical day in 1952, the station is an intriguing feature on the Wirral Way. This 12 mile long linear nature reserve follows the track of the old railway between Hooton and West Kirkby and was, in 1973, one of the first Country Parks to be opened.

106   The Basset Hound

Barnston Road, Thingwall, Heswall,
Wirral, Cheshire CH61 1AS
Tel: 0151 648 2223 Fax: 0151 929 5909

Directions:

The inn is located in the hamlet of
Thingwall, on the A551 Gayton-
Birkenhead road just north of Barnston.

The picturesque building built in 1965, with its small paned windows and tiled roofs at first
and second floor levels makes for a pretty sight on the A551 Gayton - Birkenhead road. It's
equally appealing inside, with hale panelling, beams, rustic furniture and prints giving it a
look and feel much older than its actual years.

Welcoming customers for the past five years, Steve and Tricia Snee, have built the inns'
good reputation for both fine food and ale. Four real ales including Boddingtons and local
Liverpool ale Cains with two regularly changing "guest ales" are on tap to quench thirsts.
A wide and varied selection of wines are on hand to complement the fine cooking. Food is
served from 12 o'clock right through to 9.30 pm from both the pubs' varied table menu and
the exciting chefs' specials boards. The dining areas, which can seat up to 130, include a
section designated non-smoking and dedicated staff are on hand to cater for larger parties
and groups with a variety of different needs.

This part of the Wirral Peninsula is full of interesting places to see and pleasant scenery
to enjoy. Thornton Hough, a little way south of the Basset Hound, is notable for its huge
village green, covering some 14 acres and known as one of the most picturesque spots in
Cheshire. Another major attraction is Ness Botanic Gardens at Neston, 64 acres of superbly
landscaped gardens on the banks of the Dee, with marvellous displays, play areas and
waymarked trails. The walking is excellent hereabouts and includes the Wirral Way, a long,
linear nature reserve running from Hooton and West Kirby. And when the walking's done,
the Basset Hound beckons!

Opening Hours: All day, every day.

Food: A blend of traditional meals and
modern cuisine

Credit Cards: Mastercard, Visa, Switch, Delta

Accommodation: None.

Facilities: Large beer garden, car park.

Entertainment: Quiz Thursday.

Local Places of Interest/Activities:
Birkenhead 3 miles, Thornton Hough 2 miles,
Ness Gardens, Wirral Way.

Internet/Website:
bassethound.heswall@whitbread.com

The Bird in Hand   107

Church Lane,
Guilden Sutton,
Nr. Chester,
Cheshire
CH3 7EW
Tel: 01244 300341

Directions:

Guilden Sutton lies 2
miles east of Chester
on a minor road
north of the A51 or
south of the A56.

An old coaching inn dating back well over 200 years, **The Bird in Hand** is the social hub of the tiny community of Guilden Sutton, a couple of miles east of Chester (take the A51 or A56). Set peacefully on a no through road near the church, it has a very inviting look that is more than confirmed inside, where all is old-world cosy, with an ornately panelled bar counter and a dining area with roundback chairs and comfortably upholstered banquettes at neatly clothed tables.

Food is taken very seriously by the delightful leaseholder Susan Parry and is available every lunchtime and evening. The choice is wide and very tempting, and everything on the standard menu, specials blackboard and curry board being wholesome and full of flavour. Specialities include mussels, curries and the Joanna Lumley steaks (absolutely fabulous!), while among the daily specials could be roasted cod with couscous, whole boned trout and pork fillet with a sweet apricot gravy. Booking is necessary at the weekend, and children are welcome in the pub until 8 o'clock - later if eating. Four real ales are among the brews dispensed at the bar - Boddingtons, Flowers, Timothy Taylor Landlord and a guest.

Outside, there's a well-tended beer garden and an off-road parking area. It's no distance at all from this hidden gem of a pub to the walled city of Chester on the River Dee, with 2,000 years of history, innumerable fascinating buildings, a superb zoo and the country's most unusual and atmospheric racecourse.

Opening Hours: Lunchtime and evening daily.

Food: Bar meals.

Credit Cards: Mastercard, Visa.

Accommodation: None.

Facilities: Car Park, beer garden.

Entertainment: None.

Local Places of Interest/Activities: Chester 2 miles.

108 The Bulls Head Inn

Clotton, Tarporley,
Cheshire CW6 0EG
Tel: 01829 781354

Directions:
From Chester, take the A51 east for about
6 miles.

Situated on the A51 a mile or so west of its junction with the A49, this one-time coaching inn retains many delightful period features, including oak beams and a splendid inglenook fireplace.

Richard and Joan came here as tenants in the spring of 2001, bringing with them a wealth of experience in the business. Richard is the chef, and visitors can settle down to enjoy his food anywhere in the pub. Wholesome bar snacks include sandwiches (the steak sandwich is a great favourite), ploughman's lunch and 'les trois oeufs au bacon' - pan-fried bacon topped with three eggs and baked French-style. The main menu runs from soup, prawn cocktail ad deep-fried brie to cod with mushy peas, steaks, lasagne and chicken breast served with a mushroom or peppercorn sauce. There are also children's meals and an ever-changing choice of desserts. In the summer, barbecues are popular events in the beer garden, where there is a children's play area. At least two real ales are always available, plus a full range of keg beers, lagers, cider and stout.

Pool, darts, dominoes and cards are played in the bar, where there's also a tv and fruit machine, and have regulars make a weekly date with the quiz night (Wednesday) and the music night (Friday). The area around **The Bulls Head** is full of interesting places to visit, including the nearby town of Tarporley, Oulton Park motor-racing circuit, Delamere Forest with a number of lovely walks, historic Beeston Castle and the Shropshire Union Canal.

Opening Hours: Lunch and evening; all day Sat & Sun.

Food: Bar meals.

Credit Cards: Mastercard, Visa.

Accommodation: None.

Facilities: Car Park, beer garden.

Entertainment: Quiz Wednesday, live music Friday.

Local Places of Interest/Activities:
Tarporley 2 miles, Delamere Forest, Oulton Park.

The Calveley Arms 109

Whitchurch Road,
Handley,
Nr. Tattenhall,
Cheshire
CH3 9DT
Tel/Fax:
 01829 770619

Directions:

From Chester 6 miles south on the A41; from Whitchurch 8 miles north on the A41.

First licensed in 1638, **The Calveley Arms** stands in the pleasant village of Handley, just off the A41 road that links Chester and Whitchurch. The smart black and white facade promises much, and in the bars the scene is as traditional as could be, with a mass of wall and ceiling timbers and a collection of jugs and pots, pictures, pints and ornaments. This is the atmospheric setting for enjoying first-class cooking under the supervision of experienced leaseholders Grant Wilson and Chrissy Manley.

The food is a major attraction here, served every lunchtime and every evening, and the 45 covers soon fill up, so booking is always a good idea. The daily changing specials board supplements a printed menu of unusual range and interest, and the fresh fish dishes are something of a speciality. Typical items on the main menu include hot avocado and stilton (one of the best-selling dishes), Creole-style crab cakes, tarte flambée like they make it in Alsace, Madras-style curry, a classic moules à la crème and Breton chicken - grilled chicken breast with a sauce of bacon and mushrooms topped with cheddar cheese and finished with cream. Sandwiches, baguettes and special salads are among the lighter options. Four real ales - Boddingtons and three guests - are popular orders at the bar, and in fine weather they can be enjoyed watching or playing a game of boules in the beer garden. Happy hour is 6 till 7 Monday to Friday, and on Sunday night a fun quiz starts at 9 o'clock.

Among the attractions in the vicinity are two famous castles: Beeston, built in the 13th century and partially destroyed by Cromwell; and 19th century Cholmondeley, a mock-medieval construction in a 30-acre garden.

Opening Hours: Lunchtime and evening every day.

Food: Bar meals.

Credit Cards: Diners, Mastercard, Visa.

Accommodation: None.

Facilities: Car Park, beer garden.

Entertainment: Quiz Sunday.

Local Places of Interest/Activities: Chester, Whitchurch, Castles at Beeston, Cholmondeley.

Website/Internet: www.calveleyarms.co.uk

110 The Copper Mine

Nantwich Road,
Broxton,
Cheshire
CH3 9JH
Tel: 01829 782293

Directions:

Take the A41 south
from Chester/north
from Whitchurch and
turn left (from
Chester) or right
(from Whitchurch)
on to the A534 for
about 2 miles beyond
Broxton village.

Standing all alone alongside the A534 a couple of miles east of its junction with the A41, **The Copper Mine** is a very appealing cream-painted building with plant boxes and ornamental hedges in a stone trough. Inside, the bar is invitingly and comfortably furnished, with carpeted floors, half-panelling and a display cabinet full of little pots.

Beyond the bar is one of the pub's most attractive features, a delightful conservatory that overlooks the beer garden. There are seats for over 50 in the bar and conservatory (the latter non-smoking), and it's best to book to be sure of a table at the weekend. The menu provides abundant choice to suit all tastes and appetites, and one of the very best dishes, a firm Copper Mine favourite, is the really excellent home-made steak pie. Children can choose from their own special menu, and when the weather allows, the beer garden is a very pleasant spot where families can enjoy an alfresco drink: grown-up brews include Bass and Boddingtons real ales, John Smiths Smooth and several lagers. The pub also has a large off-road car park.

The leaseholders Kathryn and Noel Morris were previously in charge of the Golden Grove Inn in Rossett, Denbighshire, moving to Broxton in January 1999. The Copper Mine is particularly well located for access to the major towns of the region - Chester, Whitchurch, Wrexham, Nantwich - as well as to many local sites of interest, including Beeston and Cholmondeley Castles and the Iron Age hill fort of Maiden Castle. And at Malpas, a little way south, the Church of St Oswald is one of the most splendid in the region.

Opening Hours: Lunchtime and evening every day.

Food: Bar meals.

Credit Cards: Amex, Mastercard, Visa.

Accommodation: None.

Facilities: Car Park, beer garden.

Entertainment: none

Local Places of Interest/Activities: Chester, Whitchurch, Beeston and Cholmondeley Castles, Malpas.

The Fiddle i'the Bag Inn   111

Alder Root Lane,
Burtonwood,
Cheshire
WA5 4BJ
Tel: 01925 225442
Directions:

Take the A49 northwards off junction 9 of the M62 (north of Warrington). Turn left after ½ at traffic lights. The pub is on the right after 1 mile. Also accessible off the B5204.

New tenants Sharon Hutchinson and Mike Sayers took over the running of this grand old inn in March 2001 and began a major programme of refurbishment. Real fires, stained glass windows and homely furnishings are among the features that make the bar a very pleasant place to relax with a drink, and the soon-to-be-built conservatory will provide an equally agreeable alternative.

Food is big business here, and Carol, the talented cook, prepares everything to order on a menu that is available lunchtime and evening Monday to Friday and all day Saturday and Sunday. The choice is wide, with something to please everyone, from generously filled and garnished sandwiches and wholesome salads to classics such as chilli, steak pie, jumbo scampi, a variety of steaks and a hearty North Country hot pot. Two real ales are always on tap, along with John Smiths Smooth, Theakstons Bitter, Greenalls Mild and a good selection of wines.

There are great views from the pub, which is situated in a village on a minor road that runs between Warrington and Newton-le-Willows. Warrington is North Cheshire's largest town, with plenty to see, including an exceptionally interesting museum and art gallery. It was in the neighbouring village of Winwick that an invading force of Scots under the Duke of Hamilton made its last stand in a battle that began at Preston. The M62, reached in a few minutes from the inn, provides ready access to Liverpool and Manchester.

Opening Hours: Lunchtime and evening; all day Sat, Sun & Bank Holidays.

Food: Bar meals.

Credit Cards: Planned.

Accommodation: None.

Facilities: Car Park.

Entertainment: None.

Local Places of Interest/Activities: Warrington, Newton-le-Willows.

112   The Fishpool Inn

Fishpool Road, Delamere,
Cheshire CW8 2HP
Tel: 01606 883277 Fax: 01606 889576

Directions:
From Chester take the A54 eastward, from Congleton/Winsford take the A54 westward. The inn stands in Delamere where the A54 meets the B5152.

Gerry and Gloria O'Dwyer came out of retirement following many years in the hotel trade to take over the lease at this lovely old inn. Named after a nearby pool where monks would come to fish, the inn dates from the late 18th century, and behind the white-painted frontage the various rooms are full of character, with old prints and memorabilia adding to the appeal.

Hospitality is second to none, and the inn is a hugely popular spot for a meal. Gloria cooks with the best, and among the favourites in her repertoire are the Fishpool battered cod, steak & kidney pie and baked ham in a peach sauce. The 'international collection' section of the menu includes British stalwarts like Cumberland sausage or roast chicken, and dishes from further afield such as lasagne verdi, chicken tikka masala or Thai green chicken curry. Vegetarians have a choice of main courses and a lite bite menu caters for smaller appetites or those in a hurry. The Sunday roasts are guaranteed to bring in the crowds, so booking is essential, also for Friday and Saturday evenings.

The Fishpool has not one but two beer gardens, one at the front and one at the side, and there's plenty of off-road parking. Budding masterminds assemble in the bat at 9.15 for the Wednesday quiz. Historic Chester, an easy drive away, provides a wealth of sightseeing, and closer attractions include ancient Delamere Forest, once a royal hunting ground, Little Budworth Common Country Park and the motor-racing circuit at Oulton Park.

Opening Hours: Lunchtime and evening; all day Bank Holidays.

Food: Bar snacks and meals.

Credit Cards: Diners, Mastercard, Visa.

Accommodation: None.

Facilities: Car Park, beer gardens.

Entertainment: Quiz night Wednesday.

Local Places of Interest/Activities: Chester (historic sights, flat racing) 10 miles, Little Budworth Common Country Park 4 miles, Oulton Park 4 miles.

The George and Dragon | 113

67 High Street,
Tarvin,
Cheshire
CH3 8EE
Tel/Fax:
  01829 741446

Directions:

In the centre of
Tarvin, 5 miles east
of Chester on the
A54/A51.

Tarvin suffered the fate of many towns in the 18th century when it was ravaged by fire in 1752. The result of the rebuilding is a large number of handsome Georgian buildings one of the most notable being **The George and Dragon**.

Behind the black and white bay-windowed facade the interior is full of character, with a unique feature in a huge, brightly painted mural depicting the village (the pub takes centre stage) as it was in the 19th century. By that time, the George and Dragon has been dispensing good cheer for more than a century, an unbroken tradition that passed four years ago into the care of Mel and Karen Corrall.

Regulars, of whom there are many, sing the praises of Karen's cooking, which offers a truly comprehensive choice of dishes, from light snacks to three-course meals; all-time favourites include chilli, curries and the splendid steak pies, with ale, with mushrooms or with kidney. Food is served from 11.30 till 4 on Monday, till 6 on Wednesday, till 7 on Thursday, Friday and Saturday, and from noon to 7.30 on Sunday. On Wednesday and Thursday there are special deals on meals ordered by 5 o'clock. To accompany the hearty food there are three real ales (one a guest) and plenty of other thirst-quenchers.

Apart from being a great place for food, the George and Dragon is a very sociable pub, with a quiz on Thursday, karaoke on the first and third Saturdays of the month, a pool competition on Sunday night and occasional horse-racing nights. There's adjacent off-road parking and a secluded suntrap beer garden.

Opening Hours: All day, every day.

Food: Bar meals (no food Tuesday).

Credit Cards: Mastercard, Visa.

Accommodation: None.

Facilities: Car Park, beer garden.

Entertainment: see above.

Local Places of Interest/Activities: Chester 5 miles, Shropshire Union Canal, Tarporley 4 miles, Delamere Forest.

114 The Halfway House

Halton Road,
Runcorn,
Cheshire
WA7 5NR
Tel: 01928 563756

Directions:

The pub is located about 1 mile to the east from the centre of Runcorn Old Town towards Norton village.

Midway between Runcorn Old Town and Norton village - hence the name - **The Halfway House** dates from the middle of the 19th century. A handsome redbrick building, it is partly painted white, with a jaunty row of window boxes outside the first-floor windows.

A lovely local couple, Bob and Kath Conway, took over as tenants in millennium year for their first venture into the business, and the friendly greeting they always have for visitors is a major plus point. In the comfortably furnished open-plan bar thirsts are quenched by real ales and a good selection of other beers, and special prices are always on offer at the Double Spirits Bar. Appetites are satisfied by a wide-ranging selection of home-cooked dishes on the printed menu and the specials board. Minted lamb and steak pies are two of the specialities, and there's also a monthly changing list of Chinese dishes to ring the changes. Food can be ordered to take away. This is a very sociable pub, with bingo on Wednesday, a disco on Friday, karaoke on Saturday and both bingo and Open the Box on Sunday. The beer garden is a pleasant spot when the sun has got his hat on, and the pub has plenty of secure off-road parking.

The remains of Norton Priory, set in 38 acres of woodland, are a major local attraction in the care of the National Trust, and other places of interest within a short drive include the agreeable town of Frodsham, with its thatched cottage and spacious Georgian and Victorian houses; the National Trust's Iron Age fort site at Helsby Hill, with great views across the marshes to the Mersey and Liverpool; and Daresbury, where All Saints Church has a unique stained glass window commemorating local man Lewis Carroll.

Opening Hours: All day, every day.

Food: Bar meals.

Credit Cards: None.

Accommodation: None.

Facilities: Car Park, beer garden.

Entertainment: see above.

Local Places of Interest/Activities: Runcorn, Norton Priory, Frodsham, Helsby Hill.

The Letters Inn

High Street,
Tattenhall,
Cheshire
CH3 9PX
Tel: 01829 770221

Directions:

From Chester, take the A41 south; minor roads signposted Tattenhall lead off on the left. About 8 miles from Chester.

A superbly appointed old-world pub on the main street of Tattenhall, a village easily accessible from all directions. The A41 runs just to the left (Chester-Whitchurch), the A49 to the right (Whitchurch -Warrington), and the A534 links those two roads. The building, smartly done out in black and white, dates from the 18th century and part of it was once a postal sorting office - a fact remembered in the pub's name and in its sign of a traditional red letter box.

Inside, it's a real gem of old-world charm, complete with beams and brasses, ancient artefacts and grand old barrels labelled brandy, rum and whisky. An area called the Post Room is neatly laid with tables and Windsor chairs ready for visitors taking lunch or dinner. Food is served every session except Sunday and Monday evenings, and the standard menu is augmented by a splendidly varied board of chef's specials and some very tempting fish specials on Friday. To accompany the food or to enjoy on their own are four real ales and an excellent selection of wines including many Old World bottles. The pub has a beer garden and there's plenty of on-road and nearby off-road parking.

Tattenhall is a fine old village with some attractive period houses and a Victorian church. The Shropshire Canal passes close by, once busy with commercial barges but now the domain of pleasure craft. Mr & Mrs Cooke, in the licensed trade since 1969, have held the lease at this outstanding pub since August 1999.

Opening Hours: Lunchtime and evening; all day Sat & Sun.

Food: Bar meals (not Sun or Mon eves).

Credit Cards: All major cards except Amex and Diners

Accommodation: None.

Facilities: Beer garden.

Entertainment: None.

Local Places of Interest/Activities: Chester 8 miles, Shropshire Union Canal, Beeston and Peckforton Castles.

116   The Maypole Inn

Hilltop Road,
Acton Bridge,
Weaverham,
Nr. Northwich,
Cheshire
CW8 3RA
Tel: 01606 853114

Directions:

From Northwich
B5153 west for about
5 miles; or take the
A533 and turn left
on to A49.

For many years a popular place of refreshment for the local community, **The Maypole** has excellent leaseholders in Brenda and Keith Morris. They've been in the trade for 30 years, and here for ten, and there's no doubting the warmth of the welcome that awaits visitors. Outside, floral displays provide a lovely blaze of colour, while inside, the low-beamed ceilings, open log fires and an assortment of ornaments and memorabilia add to the cosy, intimate atmosphere.

Excellent ales and traditional home-cooked food keep the inner man happy, and booking in advance is recommended to be sure of a table, particularly at the weekend. Blackboard and vegetarian specials supplement the main menu, which is available lunchtime and evening every day. Long-time favourites include steak pie, braised steak in onion and mushroom gravy, and chicken breast in a creamy leek and stilton sauce; traditional roasts offer pork, beef, ham and lamb with lemon and mint seasoning; there's a choice of ten salads; and a fish menu with the likes of salmon with prawn sauce or sea bass with a Mediterranean sauce. They also offer a lighter menu of closed, open and toasted sandwiches, filled jacket potatoes and hot snacks. Sweets from the trolley, speciality coffees, good selection of wines, ales and liqueurs.

The River Weaver and the Trent & Mersey Canal are both close to the inn, and other attractions in the vicinity include Delamere Forest (great for ramblers) and historic Northwich.

Opening Hours: Every lunchtime and evening.

Food: Snack and full bar menus.

Credit Cards: Diners, Mastercard, Visa.

Accommodation: None.

Facilities: Car Park.

Entertainment: None.

Local Places of Interest/Activities: Northwich (Salt Museum) 5 miles, Delamere Forest 4 miles.

The Nags Head ·117·

High Street,
Farndon,
Cheshire
CH3 6PU
Tel: 01829 270261

Directions:

From Chester take the
B5130. Farndon lies
just off this road
immediately before it
joins the A534
Nantwich-Wrexham
road.

Close to the River Dee and the border with Wales, **The Nags Head** started life as a coaching inn during the 18th century. It remains a very popular refreshment stop in a village which is one of the favourite entry routes for motorists driving to Wales; its ancient bridge, which dates from the 14th century, is one of only two surviving medieval bridges in the county.

New tenants Christine and Geoffrey Nevitt took over the lease of the Nags Head in the spring of 2001, and their plans include enhancing the already attractively decorated and furnished interior, and providing live entertainment on Friday evenings (the Wednesday night quiz remains a popular fixture). Food is served lunchtime and evening every day except Monday, and children are welcome if eating; the non-smoking dining area has seats for 30, and it's essential to book in advance for a table on Saturday evening or Sunday. The menu includes sandwiches and light snacks, fish dishes, grills, pies and curries, vegetarian dishes and the house speciality rack of lamb served with a minted gravy and a selection of vegetables. All the meat, poultry and game comes from Griffiths Butchers in the village. The pub serves a full range of real ales, keg bitters, draught lagers, cider and stout. Amenities include a games room, outside tables, a good off-road car park and a field at the back with room for six to eight caravans.

A walk from the old bridge along the Dee is a very pleasant way to work up a thirst and an appetite, and it's also worth taking time to visit Farndon's church, whose stained glass windows depict Civil War skirmishes in and around the village.

Opening Hours: Every lunchtime and evening.

Food: Bar meals.

Credit Cards: Planned.

Accommodation: None.

Facilities: Car Park, caravan park, games room.

Entertainment: See above.

Local Places of Interest/Activities: Chester 7 miles, walks by the Dee.

118   The Red Lion

Runcorn Road,
Moore,
Cheshire
WA4 6UD
Tel: 01925 740205
Fax: 01925 740676

Directions:

Moore is located 5 miles south of Warrington, 3 miles east of Runcorn, on a minor road off the A56.

Starting life in the 17th century as one of the dozen or so farmhouses that then made up the village of Moore, **The Red Lion** adopted its present role a century later, when the nearby Bridgewater Canal was being constructed.

Hospitality has been dispensed here ever since, a tradition carried on in fine style by the current tenants Nicholas and Vikki Broome, who, along with Dad Gerald, took over the reins in August 2000. They brought with them many years experience in the catering/licensed trade, and visitors to the Red Lion are guaranteed the warmest of welcomes as well as an excellent choice of food and drink to enjoy in the civilised surroundings of the bars with their low beamed ceilings, wood panelling and old prints and pictures of local scenes. Nicholas is the chef, and his printed menu and blackboard specials offer a good, varied selection - his curries are particularly popular. Food is served every lunchtime and evening and all day Sunday and Bank Holidays. Children are very welcome. There are four real ales on offer - Greenalls, Theakstons and rotating guests - and when the weather's fine a drink and a snack can be enjoyed at picnic benches on the front patio. The pub is closed in winter from 3 to 6 midweek, and in the summer the price of drinks is reduced by 10% between those times. Quiz night is Tuesday, and there's live music on the last Saturday of the month.

It's an easy drive from the Red Lion to Warrington, the largest town in North Cheshire, where Chris Evans was born and George Formby is buried. Other local places of interest include Walton Gardens and the nearby town of Daresbury, whose All Saints Church contains a stained glass window commemorating Lewis Carroll, who was born in the town as Charles Lutwidge Dodgson - his father was the vicar.

Opening Hours: All day, every day

Food: Bar meals.

Credit Cards: All the major cards.

Accommodation: None.

Facilities: Off-road parking.

Entertainment: Quiz Tuesday, live entertainment last Saturday of the month.

Local Places of Interest/Activities: Walton Gardens, Daresbury 2 miles, Warrington 5 miles.

Internet/Website:
www.the-red-lion-moore.co.uk

The Royal Oak

Higher Kinnerton,
Flintshire
CH4 9BE
Tel: 01244 660871
Fax: 01244 661395

Directions:

Six miles
southwest of
Chester off the
A55/A5104.

Exceptional food and quality ales put this outstanding pub firmly at the top of the tree. Lying just over the border in Wales, it is one of the oldest and most attractive coaching inns in the region, a real hidden gem standing at a leafy crossroads off the A55 six miles southwest of Chester.

Derek and Lee Thompson, ably assisted by manageress Jackie, provide a cheery welcome for visitors to 'the first tavern in Wales', and in the bars log fires crackle and a collection of old pots and water jugs adds to the charm and character. The most unusual feature is Derek's depiction of the tale of the Kinnerton Oak, which once stood on this spot. It is renowned as the tree where King Charles I hid in September 1644, fleeing Cromwell's troops after his defeat at Chester.

The Royal Oak has established an enviable reputation for the quality of its food, which is served every lunchtime and evening and all day Sunday in the modern annexe of Thompson's Restaurant (booking advised, especially at the weekend). A team of highly talented chefs prepare superb dishes using raw materials from top local sources and introducing ideas from near and far into the mouthwatering menu. The choice is very varied, a few examples being mushrooms filled with mozzarella and basil with a creamed herb dressing; Thai fish cakes; pan-fried tuna with roasted vegetables, chilli and sesame dressing; T-bone, fillet and sirloin steaks; sausage and black pudding on a bed of mash with onion gravy and apple sauce; mushroom and courgette stroganoff; iced lemon charlotte with raspberry compote. Lighter snacks are available at lunchtime, with an excellent choice of sandwiches, ploughman's platters and jacket potatoes. Four real ales are always on offer, and the pub has one of the best selections of Irish malts in the country.

Opening Hours: Every lunchtime and evening; all day Sat & Sun.

Food: Bar snacks and à la carte menu.

Credit Cards: Mastercard, Visa.

Accommodation: None.

Facilities: Car Park.

Entertainment: None.

Local Places of Interest/Activities: Chester 6 miles.

120   Royal Oak Hotel

Chester Road,
Kelsall,
Nr. Tarporley,
Cheshire
CW6 0RR
Tel: 01829 751208

Directions:
A54 east from Chester, about 6 miles, or west from Winsford 10 miles.

A ramble in Delamere Forest, just north of the village of Kelsall, will generate an appetite which the **Royal Oak** is well able to satisfy at almost any time of day. The hotel, which marked its centenary in 2000, has the friendliest of leaseholders in Eleanor and Ken Rothwell, who came here in the autumn of 1999.

Eleanor is a superb cook, and in addition to the main lunchtime and evening menus breakfast is served on Sunday from 9 o'clock. Bar snacks include toasties and burgers, while for 'a bite more' there's fish & chips, cottage pie, an all-day breakfast, mixed grill and Yorkshire pudding filled with Cumberland sausage and onion gravy. No food on Monday.

The Royal Oak is also an excellent place for a pint, with four real ales including two rotating guests heading the list, and for an overnight stay. Bed & Breakfast accommodation is provided in five letting rooms - a double and four family rooms - available all year round, with washbasins and a number of thoughtful little extras to make a stay even more homely and comfortable. Other facilities of the hotel include a children's room, toilets equipped for disabled guests, an excellent beer garden with a grassed play area, a large car park and a 50-seat function room for parties or special occasions. The weekly quiz starts at 9 o'clock on Sunday evening, and there's live entertainment every other Saturday.

Delamere Forest really is a rambler's delight, with a number of lovely walks. Once a royal hunting ground (James I was the last monarch to use it as such), it is now both an attractive recreational area and a working forest.

Opening Hours: All day, every day.

Food: Bar meals.

Credit Cards: Diners, Mastercard, Visa.

Accommodation: Five rooms.

Facilities: Car Park, beer garden, play area.

Entertainment: Quiz night Sunday, live

performance every other Saturday.

Local Places of Interest/Activities: Chester (historic sights, flat racing) 6 miles, Delamere Forest.

Internet/Website:
www.royaloakcheshire.co.uk

The Royal Oak | 121

23 Town Lane,
Little Neston,
South Wirral,
Cheshire
CH64 4DE
Tel: 0151 336 2364
Fax: 0151 336 5974

Directions:

Take the A540 northwest from Chester for about 10 miles. Little Neston lies just off this road.

Built in 1904 to replace its thatched predecessor, which burnt down, the **Royal Oak** is a splendidly homely and inviting place, very popular with local patrons and a winner with motorists who come across it in their travels. It's well worth the short detour from the main road, and Barry and Donna, leaseholders since 1991, offer warm and genuine hospitality.

The bars have a very traditional look, with lots of highly polished wood, brass counter and foot rails at the bar, some fine prints and plenty of comfortable seating. In the raised dining area food is served lunchtime and evening Monday to Friday, from 12 till 8 on Saturday and from 12 till 5 on Sunday (best to book). The 56 covers are split about 50/50 between smoking and non-smoking. There's always plenty to choose from, including an excellent snack menu of sandwiches, toasties, baguettes, burgers and jacket potatoes. The main menu offers all the familiar favourites, from fish and chips with mushy peas to steak & kidney pie, steaks, lots of ways with chicken (filled with ham and pineapple in a barbecue sauce, rotisserie-style, Kiev, Cajun, with vegetables in a pie) and always plenty of options for vegetarians.

Children are very well catered for at the Royal Oak with their own Little Oaks menu and a play area with a bouncy castle in summer. The play area is part of the splendid beer garden, and the pub has plenty of off-road car parking space. There's a pool table in a separate part of the bar, and regular weekly entertainment includes live performers on Friday and a quiz on Sunday. Chester is an easy drive from the pub, while more or less on the premises are the Dee Estuary and Ness Botanic Gardens, 64 acres of superbly landscaped gardens on the banks of the Dee.

Opening Hours: All day, every day.

Food: Bar meals.

Credit Cards: None.

Accommodation: None.

Facilities: Car Park, beer garden with children's play area.

Entertainment: Live show Friday, quiz Sunday.

Local Places of Interest/Activities: Chester 10 miles, Ness Botanic Gardens.

122

The Stag Inn

Chester Road,
Walton,
Warrington,
Cheshire
WA4 6EG
Tel: 01925 261680
Fax: 01925
210338

Directions:

From Warrington 1 mile south on the A56.

Built in the 1920s on the site of a centuries-old inn, **The Stag** is a distinctive redbrick building with a steeply raked roof and tall chimneys. Inside, it's smart and well furnished, very cosy and comfortable, with a good atmosphere generated by leaseholders Alf and Ilona, a lovely couple who have been in the licensed trade in Cheshire pubs for 30 years. They've been at the Stag for the past four, and their patrons know that they can be sure of a friendly welcome and true hospitality.

Three real ales - Greenalls and two rotating guests - are on hand to quench thirsts, and satisfying home-cooked food is served lunchtime and evening Monday to Saturday and from noon to 5 o'clock on Sunday. No bookings are taken at present, and visitors can eat anywhere they like; children are welcome if they are dining. The menu is nicely varied, and among the dishes that are always high up in the popularity list are braised steak and lamb Henry, although there is always a vegetarian option . The tasty Sunday roasts are extremely popular and it is advisable to arrive early to eat. Darts and TV provide diversions in the TV lounge, and the inn plays host to two quizzes each week, general knowledge on Sunday and with an entertainment theme on Wednesday. A bowling green, with seating for spectators, can be hired with notice.

The Stag is situated close to the swing bridge over the Manchester Ship Canal, on the A56 a mile south of Warrington. There's easy access to the M6, M56 and M62. Among the local attractions are Walton Hall Gardens, a series of formal gardens in the grounds of a grand Victorian mansion with a prominent clock tower.

Opening Hours: Lunchtime and evening; all day Fri, Sat & Sun.

Food: Quality pub food

Credit Cards: Amex, Mastercard, Visa.

Accommodation: None.

Facilities: Car Park, Bowling Green

Entertainment: Quiz Sun & Wed.

Local Places of Interest/Activities: Walton Gardens, Warrington, Daresbury.

The Stamford Bridge | 123

Tarvin Road, Tarvin,
Nr. Chester,
Cheshire CH3 7HN
Tel: 01829 740229

Directions:
Tarvin is located 3 miles east of Chester on the A51/A54. The pub is a mile from the centre of Tarvin, just off the A51 and very close to Great Barrow.

Ann and Stan Higginson and their son Paul are the tenants of **The Stamford Bridge**, which stands outside Tarvin close to the neighbouring village of Great Barrow. They're local people, and they know exactly what their customers want, which is quality food and ale served in relaxed, convivial surroundings.

A coaching inn in days gone by, it retains a good deal of period appeal behind its long, flower-decorated frontage. The ceilings are timbered, and the decor includes plants, prints, pictures and displays of china. Sitting on attractively upholstered stools and chairs set at neat little tables, visitors can relax with a glass of real ale or settle down to a snack or something more substantial. Booking are not taken, so it's first come, first served for the very reasonably priced menu, which is available from noon onwards every day. There are seats for up to 120, and the main dining areas are non-smoking. Outside, there's a beer garden, a patio area with picnic benches, and lots of off-road parking space.

It's worth taking time for a stroll round Tarvin, which boasts a number of handsome Georgian buildings - the result of the reconstruction of the village after a fire in 1752 destroyed many of the old houses. The Stamford Bridge, deservedly one of the most popular pubs in the region, is well placed for the motorway network (M53, M56), for the Dee and Mersey estuaries, and for historic Chester with its ancient buildings, its museums, its zoo and its marvellous racecourse.

Opening Hours: All day, every day.

Food: Extensive menu and specials board

Credit Cards: Amex, Mastercard, Visa.

Accommodation: None.

Facilities: Car Park, beer garden.

Entertainment: None.

Local Places of Interest/Activities: Chester 3 miles, Ellesmere Port, Runcorn, Chester Zoo 4 miles, Blue Planet Aquarium 4 miles

124 The Travellers Rest

Kingsley Road,
Frodsham,
Cheshire WA6 6SL
Tel: 01928 735125

Directions:

Frodsham is 10 miles northeast of Chester on the A56. The pub is located about a mile outside Frodsham on the B5152 towards Delamere.

A distinctive redbrick building standing alongside the road that runs south from Frodsham through Delamere Forest. Family-run since July 1999 by Ann and David Lamb with their daughter Nicola, it's one of the most popular places in the area to pause for refreshment and a warm and friendly welcome.

Inside, the scene is pleasingly traditional, with tiled floor, soberly patterned wallpaper, handsome wooden panelling and photographs of the locality in days gone by. All in all, a very pleasant setting for the enjoyment of a glass of real ale or keg bitter, and also much recommended for its food, which ranges from traditionally home cooked pies to something from the specials boards. And its always worth leaving some space for one of the calorie busting desserts! The pub, whose name is particularly apt, is open all day seven days a week; children are always welcome and there's plenty of off-road parking.

The town of Frodsham is well worth taking time to visit, with its fine Georgian and Victorian houses and the exceptional Church of St Lawrence. Ramblers will head south to explore the 4,000 acres of Delamere Forest, once a royal hunting ground, now both an attractive recreational area and a working forest maintained by the Forestry Commission.

Opening Hours: All day, every day.

Food: Bar meals.

Credit Cards: All the major cards, except American Express.

Accommodation: None.

Facilities: Off-road parking.

Entertainment: None.

Local Places of Interest/Activities:
Frodsham 1 mile, Delamere Forest 2 miles, Chester 10 miles, Runcorn, Ellesmere Port.

The Wheatsheaf Inn 125

The Green,
Raby Mere Road,
Raby,
Wirral,
Cheshire
CH63 4JH
Tel: 0151 336 3416
Fax: 0151 353 1976

Directions:

From Chester, take
the A540 north-
wards; turn right at
Red Farm on to
Upper Raby Road.

Good ale and good food are the stock in trade of the **Wheatsheaf Inn**, combined with as much old-world charm and character as any pub in the county can offer. Beer was brewed here as long ago as 1290, and behind the wonderful thatched frontage the bars boast open stonework, rafters and old gnarled beams, a copper-hooded fire in a huge stone hearth, gleaming horse brasses, copper pots and plates and an assortment of mugs hanging from the ceiling.

There could be no more atmospheric setting for taking time out to relax with a glass of real ale, and the choice here is very impressive, with a number of guests supplementing Tetleys, Thwaites, Theakstons Best, XB and Old Peculier and Old Speckled Hen. The chefs are just as generous in the choice they offer, with both à la carte and table d'hote options. The menus, French and English inspired, change with the seasons, making excellent use of what is freshest and best in the markets. The daily fish specials are always in demand, but everything is worth trying, and it's all available every session except Sunday and Monday evenings. There are seats for more than 70 in total, including 30 in the non-smoking conservatory, and booking is advisable on Friday and Saturday. Park-style wooden benches are set out at the front, and at the back is a lovely beer garden. Other amenities include ramps to allow wheelchair access into the pub and toilet facilities for disabled visitors.

This truly outstanding pub has been owned and run since 1995 by Wes and Sue Charlesworth. Wes was previously a farmer, and the pub stands right in the middle of the land he once farmed. Ness Botanic Gardens, ten minutes down the road, is a major local attraction in this lovely part of the world.

Opening Hours: Mon-Sat 11.30-23.00; Sun 12.00-22.30

Food: Mon-Sat 12.00-14.00; Tue-Sat 18.00-21.30; Sun 12.00-14.30

Credit Cards: All major cards except Amex and Diners

Accommodation: None

Facilities: Disabled ramps and toilets. Beer garden and patio

Entertainment: None

Local Places of Interest/Activities:

The Hidden Inns of Lancashire and Cheshire

5 Central Cheshire

PLACES OF INTEREST:

PUBS AND INNS:

The Hidden Inns of Lancashire and Cheshire

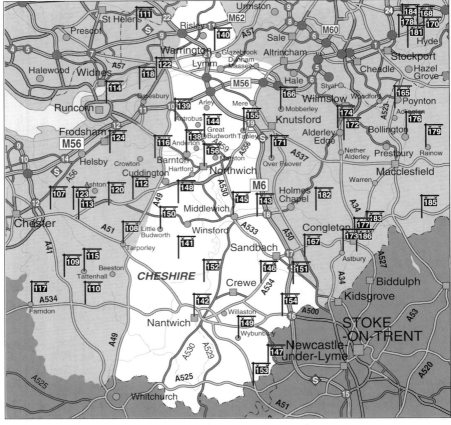

© MAPS IN MINUTES ™ 2001 © Crown Copyright, Ordnance Survey 2001

138 The Beech Tree, Barnton

139 The Birch and Bottle, Higher Whitley

140 The Black Swan, Rixton

141 The Boot & Slipper, Wettenhall

142 The Cheshire Cheese, Nantwich

143 The Fox & Hounds Inn,
       Sproston Green

144 The George & Dragon,
       Great Budworth

145 The Golden Lion, Middlewich

146 The Hawk Inn, Haslington

147 The Old Swan Inn, Madeley Heath

148 The Plough Inn, Whitegate

149 Red Lion Inn, Wybunbury

150 The Red Lion, Tarporley

151 The Romping Donkey, Sandbach

152 The Royal Oak, Worleston

153 The Swan, Woore, nr Crewe

154 The White Lion Inn, Barthomley

155 The Windmill Inn, Tabley

156 The Witton Chimes, Northwich

Please note all references refer to page numbers

Central Cheshire

The central section of Cheshire contains several major towns and cities, with Nantwich and Crewe in the southern part; Nantwich, with a history stretching back beyond Roman times, and Crewe, with no history at all until 1837. That was when the Grand Junction Railway arrived and five years later moved all its construction and repair workshops to this green field site. A workforce of nine hundred had to be housed so the company rapidly built cottages, each one shared by four of the lowest paid workers, and detached 'mansions' which accommodated four families of the more highly skilled. Later, in 1887, the railway company also provided the town with one of the most splendid parks in the north of England, Queens Park, some 40 acres of lawns and flowerbeds together with an ornamental lake. Rolls Royce's engineering works brought further prosperity to the town, but it is as a railway centre that Crewe is best known. The Railway Age museum offers a fascinating insight into Crewe's place in railway history with hands-on exhibits, steam locomotive rides, model railway displays and a children's playground.

In the centre is the famous old salt town of Nantwich, with Knutsford, the original of Mrs Gaskell's Cranford, a little further west, and in the north, towards Merseyside, lies Warrington, an important industrial centre since Georgian and Victorian times. There are plenty of wide open spaces, too, in this part of the world, notably the gently undulating pastures and woods that drop down to the Cheshire Plain. This is an area of sudden and striking contrasts. Within half a mile you can find yourself travelling out of lowland Cheshire into some of the highest and wildest countryside; acres of lonely uplands with rugged gritstone crags, steep valleys watered by moorland streams. Here too is the old salt town of Middlewich, and Sandbach with its famous Saxon crosses, along with a host of quiet, attractive villages.

The Vale Royal is an attractive name for a very attractive part of the county. It was Prince Edward, later Edward I, who named it so and it was he who founded the great Abbey of Vale Royal in fulfilment of a solemn vow made in dramatic circumstances. He was returning from the Crusades when his ship was struck by a violent storm. The Prince made a pledge to the Virgin that if his life were spared he would found an Abbey for one hundred monks. Lo!, the ship was tossed ashore, the Prince and his companions waded through the surf to safety. In 1277, Edward, now King and with his young wife Eleanor of Castile by his side, honoured his vow by placing the first stone of Vale Royal Abbey. "No monastery" he decreed "shall be more royal than this one in liberties, wealth and honour, throughout the whole world". Vale Royal Abbey indeed became the largest and most powerful Cistercian Abbey in England, a building reputedly even more glorious than Tintern or Fountains. Unlike those Abbeys, however, barely a stone of Vale Royal now remains in place. The abuse by the medieval Abbots of their vast wealth, and of their unfettered power of life and death over the inhabitants of the Vale, may partly explain why their magnificent building was so quickly and completely destroyed after Henry VIII's closure of the monasteries. Over the centuries, the county has lost many fine buildings unnecessarily but the deliberate destruction of Vale Royal Abbey must take prime place in the litany of crimes against sublime architecture.

PLACES OF INTEREST

ANDERTON

One of the most stupendous engineering feats of the canal age was the **Anderton Boat Lift**, built in 1875 and recently restored. This extraordinary construction was designed to transfer boats from the Trent & Mersey Canal to the Weaver Navigation 50ft below. Two barges would enter the upper tank, two the lower, and by pumping water out of the lower tank, the boats would exchange places. Thousands of visitors come every year to marvel at this impressive structure conceived and designed by Edward Leader Williams, who later went on to engineer the Manchester Ship Canal.

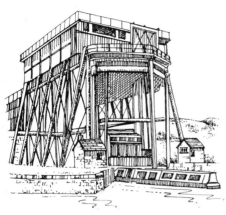

Anderton Boat Lift

About a mile north of Anderton, **Marbury Country Park** was formerly part of a large country estate, but the area is now managed by Cheshire County Council whose wardens have created a variety of habitats for plants, trees and animals. The Park lies at the edge of Budworth Mere and there are attractive walks and bridleways around the site where you'll also find an arboretum, picnic area and garden centre.

ANTROBUS

Just a couple of miles from the magnificent Arley Hall and its world-famous gardens, is the pleasing little village of Antrobus, the only place in Britain to bear this name. Even the Oxford Dictionary of English Place Names is baffled by Antrobus: "Unexplained" it says curtly, adding as its excuse, "Hardly English".

ARLEY

There are many grand houses in Cheshire, and many fine gardens, but at **Arley Hall and Gardens** you will find one of the grandest houses and one of the finest gardens in perfect har-

mony. The present Hall was completed in 1845, a few years after Rowland Egerton-Warburton arrived at Arley with his new bride, Mary Brooke. The couple took possession of a dilapidated old mansion, infested with rats and with antiquated drains from which an unbearable stench drifted through the house. Understandably, Rowland and Mary soon demolished the old hall and in its place rose a sumptuous early-Victorian stately home complete with (bearing in mind those drains) such state-of-the-art innovations as Howden's Patent Atmospheric Air Dispensers. Rowland and Mary were both ardent gardeners and it was they who masterminded the magnificent panoramas of today's Arley Gardens. Rowland is credited with creating what is believed to be the first herbaceous border in England; his descendant, the present Viscount Ashbrook, has continued this tradition by cultivating The Grove, an informal woodland garden planted with spring bulbs, flowering shrubs and exotic trees, a pleasing contrast to the more formal design of the main gardens.

CUDDINGTON

Cuddington is at the western end of the Whitegate Way, a pleasant rural walk of about 5 miles which follows the trackbed of the old railway that used to carry salt from the Winsford mines. There is a picnic site and car park at the former Whitegate Station.

DUNHAM MASSEY

Dunham Massey Hall and Park are in the care of the National Trust. On the 3,000-acre estate, fallow deer roam freely, there's a restored water-mill which is usually in operation every Wednesday, and splendid walks in every direc-

Dunham Massey Hall

tion. The Hall, once the home of the Earls of Stamford and Warrington, is a grand Georgian mansion of 1732 which boasts an outstanding collection of furniture, paintings and Huguenot silver in its sumptuous Edwardian interior. The Hall is open Saturday-Wednesday from late March to late September; the Park is open every day between those dates.

GLAZEBROOK

A grand old farmhouse, built in 1851, stands at the heart of the **Mount Pleasant Farm Craft Centre** at Glazebrook. The converted old barns surrounding it house a huge variety of attractions with something to appeal to all the family. The popular Coffee Shop, with its quarry-tiled floor and welcoming log fire, offers an excellent choice of light meals, home made treats and daily specials and is attractively decorated with samples of the many quality crafts on sale in other parts of the complex. Toys, linen, jewellery, walking-sticks - the centre is brimming with gift ideas. The Craft Shop itself offers an extensive range of gifts, crafts, knitwear and furnishings while the 3,000 sq. ft. conservatory furniture showroom displays the very latest in cane suites, occasional furniture and accessories. The Needlework Stable stocks every item a needlewoman could ever need and also arranges Embroidery Workshops about five times a month. In the Nursery Room, grandparents will find the perfect keepsake for a grandchild's christening day, birthday - or indeed any day. And yet another showroom is devoted to painted furniture along with dried and silk flowers, sold either in bunches or in ready-made basket arrangements.

GREAT BUDWORTH

A charming small village nowadays, Budworth was accorded the designation 'Great' at a time when it was the largest ecclesiastical parish in all Cheshire, the administrative centre for some 35 individual communities. The imposing church on the hill, built in the 14th and 15th centuries, reflects its importance during those years. **St Mary & All Saints** attracts many visitors to its host of quaint carvings and odd faces that peer out at unexpected corners: some with staring eyes, others with their tongues poking out. There's a man near the pulpit who appears to be drowsing through some interminable sermon. Under the roof of the nave you'll find a man with a serpent, another in mid-somersault,

and a minstrel playing bagpipes. The distinguished 17th century historian, Sir Peter Leycester, is buried in the Lady Chapel, and in the Warburton Chapel there is a finely carved Tudor ceiling and 13th century oak stalls - the oldest in Cheshire. During the 19th century, Great Budworth was part of the Arley Hall estate and it is largely due to the energetic Squire Egerton-Warburton, a conservationist well ahead of his time, that so many of the attractive old cottages in the village are still in place.

HARTFORD

No self-respecting 16th century house should be without its resident ghost and **Hartford Hall** has quite a sociable one, a nun who goes by the name of Ida. She is believed to have some connection with Vale Royal Abbey and has manifested herself on many occasions, perhaps seeking out the sister nuns who lived here when Hartford Hall was a nunnery.

KNUTSFORD

Knutsford and its people were the heroes of one of the most durable of Victorian novels, Elizabeth Gaskell's *Cranford*. This gently humorous, sympathetic but sharply-observed portrait of the little Cheshire town, and the foibles and preoccupations of its citizens, was first published in 1853 and it is still delighting readers today. Elizabeth was scarcely a month old when she came to Knutsford. Her mother had died shortly after her birth; her father sent her here to be brought up by an aunt who lived in a road which has now been re-named Gaskell Avenue. The motherless child grew up to be both strikingly beautiful and exceptionally intelligent. Early on she evinced a lively interest in the town's characters and its history. (She was intrigued, for example, to find that in the house next door to her aunt's had once lived a notorious highwayman, Edward Higgins, hanged for his crimes in 1767. She wrote a story about him). Marriage to William Gaskell, a Unitarian pastor in Manchester, took her away from Knutsford, although she returned often and for long periods, and after her death in 1865 was buried in the grounds of the Unitarian Chapel here.

The Knutsford that Elizabeth Gaskell knew so well and wrote about so vividly has expanded a great deal since those days of course, but in

132

its compact centre, now designated an outstanding area of conservation, the narrow streets and cobbled alleys still evoke the intimacy of a small Victorian town. Two parallel roads, Toft Street and King Street, form a rectangle surrounding the old town. But Mrs Gaskell would surely be astonished by the building erected in King Street to her memory by Mr Richard Harding Watt in 1907. A gifted entrepreneur, Mr Watt had made a huge fortune in Manchester as a glove manufacturer, but what really aroused his enthusiasm was the flamboyant architecture he had seen during his travels through Spain, southern Italy and the Near East. On his return, he spent lavishly on trying to transform Knutsford in Cheshire into Knutsford-on-the-Mediterranean. At the north end of the town, he built a laundry complete with Byzantine domes and a minaret. A vaguely Ottoman style of architecture welcomed serious-minded artisans to his Ruskin Reading Rooms. In Legh Road, he erected a series of villas whose south-facing frontages are clearly in need of a really hot sun. And in King Street, as homage to the town's most famous resident, Richard Watt spent thousands of Victorian pounds on the **Gaskell Memorial Tower**. This tall, blank-walled building seems a rather incongruous tribute to the author who was herself so open and so down-to-earth. But it is eccentrics like Richard Watt who make English architecture as interesting as it is. He was so proud of his contribution to the town's new buildings that, travelling on his coach to the railway station, he would rise to his feet and raise his hat to salute them. As he did so, one day in 1913, his horse suddenly shied, the carriage overturned, and Richard Watt was thrown out and killed. What other changes he might have made to this grand old town, had he lived, we can only imagine.

An unusual exhibition and well worth visiting is the **Penny Farthing Museum**, located in a courtyard off King Street. These bizarre machines were in fashion for barely twenty years before the last model was manufactured in 1892. The collection includes a replica of the famous Starley Giant with a front wheel 7ft in diameter. Close by, in Tatton Street, is the Knutsford Heritage Centre. Knutsford is a town with a long history: Edward I granted the town a Charter in 1262; at the same time, the local landowner, William de Tabley, was given a money-making licence to control the market. The Heritage Centre is housed in a restored 17th century timber-framed building which in Victorian times was a smithy and during the restoration, the old forge and bellows were found in a remarkable state of preservation. The wrought iron gate in front of the centre was specially created for the Centre and depicts dancing girls taking part in Knutsford's famous Royal May Day celebrations - Royal because in 1887 the Prince and Princess of Wales honoured the festivities with their presence.

Every May Day the town centre streets are closed to all traffic except for the May Queen's procession in which colourful characters such as Jack in Green, Highwayman Higgins and Lord Chamberlain, Morris and Maypole dancers, and many others take part. One curious tradition whose origins are unknown is the practice of covering the streets and pavements with ordinary sand and then, using white sand, creating elaborate patterns on top. Sweeping up to the very edge of Knutsford are the grounds of **Tatton Park**, 2,000 acres of exquisite parkland landscaped in the 18th century by the celebrated Humphrey Repton. This lovely park, where herds of red and fallow deer roam at will, provides a worthy setting for the noble Geor-

Gaskell Memorial Tower

gian mansion designed by the equally celebrated architect Samuel Wyatt. The combination of the two men's talents created a house and park that have become one of the National Trust's most visited attractions. Tatton's opulent staterooms, containing paintings by artists such as Canaletto and Van Dyck along with superb collections of porcelain and furniture, provided the television series Brideshead Revisited with a sumptuous setting for Marchmain House. More than 200 elegant pieces of furniture were commissioned from the celebrated cabinet-makers, Gillow of Lancaster. Particularly fine are the superb bookcases in the Library, constructed to house the Egerton family's collection of more than 8,000 books. By contrast, the stark servants' rooms and cellars give a vivid idea of what life below stairs was really like. The Egerton family built Tatton Park to replace the much earlier Old Hall which nestles in a wood in the deer park and dates back to around 1520. Here, visitors are given a guided tour through time from the late Middle Ages up to the 1950s. Flickering light from candles reveals the ancient timber roof of the Great Hall, supported by ornate quatrefoils, while underfoot, the floor is strewn with rushes, providing a warm place for the medieval Lord of the Manor and his servants to sleep. There's much more: Home Farm is a working farm, but working as it did in the 1930s, complete with vintage machinery. Traditional crafts, (including pottery), stables and many farm animals provide a complete picture of rural life some sixty years ago. Tatton's famous gardens include a Victorian maze, an orangery and fernery, a serene Japanese garden, American redwoods, and a splendid Italian terraced garden. There's also a busy programme of educational activities for children, an adventure playground, shops, and a restaurant. You can even get married in the sumptuous mansion and hold your reception either in the house itself, in the recently refurbished Tenants Hall which can cater for parties of up to 430, or in a marquee in the magnificent grounds. With so much on offer no wonder Tatton Park has been described as the most complete historic estate in the country.

LITTLE BUDWORTH

A few miles east of the village of Willington is Little Budworth Common Country Park, a pleasant area of heathland and woods ideal for picnics and walking. The nearby village enjoys splendid views over Budworth Pool but will be better known to motor racing enthusiasts for the Oulton Park racing circuit a mile or so to the south.

LOWER PEOVER

The village of Lower Peover (pronounced Peever) is effectively made up of two hamlets. One is grouped around the village green on the B5081, the other is at the end of a cobbled lane. It's a picturesque little group: a charming old coaching inn, The Bells of Peover, a handsome village school founded in 1710, and a lovely black and white timbered church, more than 700 years old. **St Oswald's** is notable as one of the few timber-framed churches in the country still standing. Inside, there is a wealth of carved wood - pews and screens, pulpit and lectern, and a massive medieval chest made from a single log of bog oak. At one time local girls who wished to marry a farmer were required to raise its lid with one hand to demonstrate they had the strength to cope with farm life. Former guests at **The Bells of Peover** have included Generals Patton and Eisenhower during World War II, and the American flag still flies here alongside the Union Jack. About three miles east of Lower Peover is **Peover Hall**, very much hidden away at the end of a winding country road but well worth tracking down. During World War II, General George Patton lived for a while at the Hall which was conveniently close to his then headquarters at Knutsford. There's a memorial to him in the church nearby, but many many more to the Mainwaring family whose fine monuments crowd beside each other in both the north and south chapels. The Hall is only open to the public on Monday afternoons between May and September, the gardens on Monday and Thursday.

LYMM

During the stage coach era, Eagle Brow was notorious, a dangerously steep road that dropped precipitously down the hillside into the village of Lymm. To bypass this hazard, a turnpike was built (now the A56), so preserving the heart of this ancient village with its half-timbered houses and well-preserved village stocks. The Bridgewater Canal flows past nearby and the church is reflected in the waters of Lymm Dam. Popular with anglers and bird-watchers, the dam is a large man-made lake, part of a lovely woodland centre which is linked

134

to the surrounding countryside and the canal towpath by a network of footpaths and bridleways. The village became an important centre for the fustian cloth (corduroy) trade in the 19th century but is now best known simply as a delightful place to visit. Lymm stands on the sides of a ravine and its streets have actually been carved out of the sandstone rock. The same rock was used to construct Lymm's best-known landmark, the ancient cross crowned with a huge cupola that stands at the top of the High Street.

MARSTON

In Victorian times, the Old Salt Mine at Marston was a huge tourist attraction. About 360 ft deep and covering 35 acres, it even brought the Tsar of Russia here in 1844. Ten thousand lamps illuminated the huge cavern as the Emperor sat down to dinner here with eminent members of the Royal Society. By the end of the century, however, subsidence caused by the mine had made some 40 houses in the village uninhabitable, and one day in 1933 a hole 50ft wide and 300ft deep suddenly appeared close to the Trent & Mersey Canal. Happily, the village has now stabilised itself, and at the **Lion Salt Works Museum** on most afternoons you will find volunteer workers keeping alive the only surviving open pan saltworks in Britain.

MERE

One of the more notorious guests at Mere's Kilton Inn, back in the 18th century, was Dick Turpin. The intrepid highwayman made this historic old inn the base from which he plundered travellers along the Knutsford to Warrington road (now the comparatively safe A50). After one such robbery (and murder) Turpin, on his famous horse Black Bess, "galloped to the Kilton and, altering the clock, strolled on to the bowling green and proved an alibi by the short time he took to cover the four miles".

MIDDLEWICH

The Romans called their settlement here Salinae, meaning saltworks. Excavations have revealed outlines of their long, narrow, timber workshops, brine pits and even a jar with the word AMYRCA scratched on it. (Amurca was the Latin name for brine waste and was used throughout the Empire as a cleansing agent).

In modern times, it was the need for Cheshire's salt manufacturers to get their cumbersome product to markets in the Midlands and the south which gave a great impetus to the building of canals in the county. Middlewich was particularly well-provided for with its own Middlewich Branch Canal linking the town to both the Shropshire Union and the Trent & Mersey canals. During the Civil War, Middlewich witnessed two of the bloodiest battles fought in the county. In March 1644, Royalists trapped Cromwell's men in the narrow lanes and alleys of the town and slaughtered 200 of them. A few managed to find refuge in **St Michael's Church**, which has changed greatly since those days but has some notable old carvings and a curiosity in the form of a carved coat of arms of the Kinderton family of nearby Kinderton Hall. Their crest shows a dragon eating a child, a reference to the occasion on which Baron Kinderton killed a local dragon as it was devouring a child. The incident apparently took place at Moston, near Sandbach, and a lane there is still called Dragon Lane.

NANTWICH

The most disastrous event in the long history of Nantwich was the Great Fire of 1583 which consumed some 600 of its thatched and timber-framed buildings. The blaze raged for 20 days and the terror of the townspeople was compounded when some bears kept behind the Crown Hotel escaped. (Four bears from Nantwich are mentioned in Shakespeare's comedy "The Merry Wives of Windsor"). Queen Elizabeth contributed the huge sum of £2000 and also donated quantities of timber from Delamere Forest to assist in the town's rebuilding. The most striking of the buildings to survive the conflagration, perhaps because it was surrounded by a moat, is the lovely black and white house in Hospital Street, known as **Churche's Mansion** after the merchant Richard Churche who built it in 1577. Astonishingly, when the house was up for sale in 1930, no buyer showed any interest and the building was on the point of being transported brick by brick to America when a public-spirited local doctor stepped in and rescued it. The ground floor is now a restaurant, but the upper floor has been furnished in Elizabethan style and is open to the public during the summer.

The Great Fire also spared the stone-built 14th century church. This fine building, with an

Churche's Mansion

unusual octagonal tower, is sometimes called the **Cathedral of South Cheshire** and dates from the period of the town's greatest prosperity as a salt town and trading centre. Of exceptional interest is the magnificent chancel and the wonderful carvings in the choir. On the misericords (tip-up seats) are mermaids, foxes (some dressed as monks in a sharp dig at priests), pigs, and the legendary wyvern, half-dragon, half-bird, whose name is linked with the River Weaver, 'wyvern' being an old pronunciation of Weaver. An old tale about the building of the church tells of an old woman who brought ale and food each day from a local inn to the masons working on the site. The masons discovered that the woman was cheating them by keeping back some of the money they put 'in the pot' for their refreshment. They dismissed her and took revenge by making a stone carving showing the old woman being carried away by Old Nick himself, her hand still stuck in a pot. During the Civil War, Nantwich was the only town in Cheshire to support Cromwell's Parliamentary army. After several weeks of fighting, the Royalist forces were finally defeated on 25th January, 1644 and the people of Nantwich celebrated by wearing sprigs of holly in their hair. As a result, the day became known as 'Holly Holy Day' and every year, on the Saturday closest to January 25th, the town welcomes Cromwellian pikemen and battle scenes are re-enacted by members of the Sealed Knot.

There are records of the Civil War in the **Nantwich Museum** in Pillory Street which also has exhibitions about the town and its dairy and cheese-making industries. But it was salt that had once made Nantwich second only in importance to Chester in the county. The Romans had mined salt here for their garrisons at Chester and Stoke where the soldiers received part of their wages in 'sal', or salt. The payment was called a "salarium", hence the modern word salary. Nantwich remained a salt producing

town right up to the 18th century but then it was overtaken by towns like Northwich which enjoyed better communications on the canal system. But a brine spring still supplies Nantwich's outdoor swimming pool!

NORTHWICH

The Vale Royal is now a district borough centred on the old salt town of Northwich. Even before the Romans arrived, Cheshire salt was well known and highly valued. But production

Nantwich

on a major scale at Northwich began in 1670 when rock salt was discovered in nearby Marston. Salt may seem an inoffensive sort of product, but its extraction from the Keuper marl of the Cheshire Plain has had some quite spectacular side-effects. In Elizabethan times, John Leland, recorded that a hill at Combermere suddenly disappeared into underground workings, and Northwich later became notorious for the number of its buildings leaning at crazy angles because of subsidence. Even today, the White Lion Inn in Witton Street lies a complete storey lower than its original height. The arrival in the 19th century of new processes of extraction brought different problems. In 1873, John Brunner and Ludwig Mond set up their salt works at Winnington on the northern edge of the town to manufacture alkali products based on brine. The ammonia process involved cast an appalling stench over the town and devastated vegetation for miles around. On the other hand, Brunner and Mond were model employers. They paid their work-force well, built houses for them and were amongst the first firms in

136

the country to give their employees annual holidays with pay. The long involvement of Northwich and Cheshire with salt production is vividly recorded at the **Salt Museum**, the only one of its kind in Britain. It stands in London Road and occupies what used to be the Northwich Workhouse which, like so many of those dreaded institutions, is an exceptionally handsome late-Georgian building, designed by George Latham, the architect of Arley Hall. With its unique col-

Salt Museum, Northwich

lection of traditional working tools, and lively displays which include working models and videos, the Salt Museum recounts the fascinating story of the county's oldest industry. Not only can ancient remains such as Roman evaporating pans and medieval salt rakes be seen, but there is also much to remind visitors of the vital part that salt plays in the modern chemical industry.

SANDBACH

Sandbach's former importance as a stopping place for coaches (both stage and motor) is evident in the attractive old half-timbered inns and houses, some of them thatched, which line the main street. Sandbach's handsome market square is dominated by its two famous stone crosses, 16 and 11 feet tall. These superbly carved crosses (actually only the shafts have survived) were created some time in the 9th century, and the striking scenes are believed to represent the conversion of Mercia to Christianity during the reign of King Penda. A plaque at their base notes that they were restored in 1816 "after destruction by iconoclasts" - namely the Puritans. The restorers had to recover fragments from here and there: some had been used as street paving, cottage steps or in the walls of a well. Somehow they fitted the broken stones together, like pieces of a jigsaw, and the result is immensely impressive.

Saxon Crosses, Sandbach

TABLEY

Just to the west of Knutsford, on the A5033, is **Tabley House**, home of the Leicester family from 1272 to 1975. Mrs Gaskell often came to picnic in the grounds of the last of their houses, a stately Georgian mansion designed by John Carr for the first Lord de Tabley in 1761. This Lord de Tabley loved paintings and it was his son's passion for art, and his hunger for others to share it, which led to the creation of London's National Gallery. His personal collection of English pictures, on display in Tabley House, includes work by Turner (who painted the house several times), Reynolds, Opie and Martin Danby, along with furniture by Chippendale, and fascinating family memorabilia spanning three centuries. The 17th century chapel next to the house looks perfectly in place but it was originally built on an island in Tabley Mere and only moved to its present site in 1927. Another attraction in Tabley, at the Old School, is the **Tabley Cuckoo Clock Collection**. Brothers Roman and Maz Piekarski are well-known horologists and clock restorers and over the last 25 years they have sought out and renovated some of the rarest and most notable examples of this 300-year-old craft. Also on display are some mid-19th century cuckoo clocks which included complex musical movements to reproduce popular tunes of the day.

WARRINGTON

Warrington is North Cheshire's largest town, an important industrial centre since Georgian and Victorian times and with substantial buildings of those days to prove it. Its imposing Town Hall was formerly Lord Winmarleigh's country residence, built in 1750 with all the appropriate grandeur: windows framed in painfully expensive copper, and elaborately-designed entrance gates 25ft high and 54ft wide. Along with

Tabley House

its park, it provides a dignified focus for the town centre. A major Victorian contribution to the town is its excellent **Museum and Art Gallery** in Bold Street, one of the earliest municipal museums dating from 1857. The exhibits are remarkably varied: amongst them are shrunken heads, a unique china teapot collection, a scold's bridle, Egyptian mummies, a Roman actor's mask and other Roman artefacts discovered in nearby Wilderspool. There are some fine paintings as well, most of which are Victorian watercolours and oils, and a rare Vanous still life. An interesting curiosity at Bridge Foot nearby is a combined telephone kiosk and letter box. These were quite common in the early 1900's, but Warrington's is one of the few survivors. Also associated with the town are two prominent entertainers: the television presenter Chris Evans was born here, and the durable comedian and ukelele player George Formby is buried in the town's cemetery.

WILLASTON

It was in the village of Willaston that one of the most unusual world records was established in 1994. Some 200 competitors had gathered at the Primary School here for the annual **World Worm Charming Championships**. The prize goes to whoever induces the greatest number of worms to poke their heads above a square metre of soil. Each contestant is allowed fifteen minutes and the current world champion charmed his worms out at the rate of more than ten a minute. His wonderful way with worms remains a secret.

WINSFORD

137

Winsford is another of the Cheshire salt towns which expanded greatly during the 19th century, swallowing up the old villages of Over and Wharton on opposite banks of the River Weaver. Two legacies of those boom years should be mentioned. One is Christ Church which was specifically designed so that it could be jacked up in the event of subsidence. The other is Botton Flash, a sizeable lake caused by subsidence but now a popular water recreation area for the town.

WYBUNBURY

South Cheshire's answer to the Leaning Tower of Pisa is the 100ft high tower of **St Chad's Church** in Wybunbury. It was built in 1470 above an unsuspected ancient salt bed. Subsidence has been the reason for the tower's long history of leaning sideways by as much as four feet and then being straightened up, most recently in 1989. It now rests on a reinforced concrete bed and is unlikely to deviate from the vertical again. The tower stands alone: the body of the church, once capable of holding a congregation of 1600, collapsed on no fewer than five occasions. In 1972, the villagers finally decided to abandon it and build a new church on firmer ground.

138 The Beech Tree

Runcorn Road,
Barnton,
Northwich,
Cheshire
CW8 4HS
Tel: 01606 77292

Directions:

On the main A533 at
Barnton, 1 mile west of
Northwich.

The Beech Tree is a handsome redbrick building set back from the main A533 Nantwich-Runcorn road. Built in 1940 to replace the original, which stood opposite, it wins top marks not only for the quality of the decor and furnishings but also for the warmth of the welcome provided by leaseholders Stuart and Mary Piper and their son William. Their hard work and friendly personalities have turned the Beech Tree into a real success, a popular place for motorists to pause for refreshment and a firm favourite with the locals.

A minimum of three real ales are always available, and good bar snacks and meals - choose from the printed menu or the specials board - are served lunchtime and evening Monday to Saturday and from 12 to 6 on Sunday and Bank Holiday Mondays. Themed food evenings are held on Wednesdays, and from Tuesday to Thursday there are special lunch-time deals for senior citizens.

Wednesday is also the day of the weekly quiz; there's a music quiz on the last Friday of the month and live entertainment every Thursday evening. A bowling green behind the back of the pub is available for hire. The Beech Tree is open lunchtime and evening and all day Friday, Saturday and Sunday.

The location, on the main Northwich-Runcorn road, provides easy access to those two important towns, and the minor roads in the vicinity lead to numerous places to visit, including the Anderton Boat Lift, Marbury Country Park and Arley Hall & Gardens. The Beech Tree is an excellent base for exploring these attractions, and the two comfortable, well appointed letting bedrooms willsoon become three, all with en suite facilities.

Opening Hours: Lunchtime and evening Mon-Thurs, all day Fri-Sun.

Food: Bar meals.

Credit Cards: None.

Accommodation: 3 rooms.

Facilities: Car Park, bowling green.

Entertainment: Quiz Wednesday, live music Thursday.

Local Places of Interest/Activities:
Nantwich 1 mile, Runcorn 8 miles, Anderton, Arley.

The Birch and Bottle | 139

Northwich Road,
Higher Whitley,
Warrington,
Cheshire
WA4 4PH
Tel: 01925 730225

Directions:

Higher Whitley is located on the A559 about 1 mile south of junction 10 of the M56.

A fine old inn, built around 1720, situated on the A559 a short drive south of the M56 (junction 10). The split-level bar areas have a particularly warm inviting feel, aided by wall and ceiling beams and plenty of comfortable chairs for relaxing with a drink; a conservatory looks out over the gardens to the rear.

Dorothy and Stephen Rothwell have made a great success of this, their first steps in the licensed trade, considerably enhancing the popularity of the inn since their arrival as tenants three years ago. A major part of the appeal is in the quality of the food, all freshly prepared to order by Stephen. His soups and sauces are a particular strength, and the standard menu, augmented by dishes of the day, runs from sandwiches and salad platters to pasta, pizza, pork ribs with a barbecue sauce, roast chicken, salmon au poivre and a variety of ways with steaks - plain, peppered, chasseur, Diane. A senior citizens special (3 courses and coffee for £5.25) is served every session except Saturday evening, Sunday lunch and Bank Holidays. Two real ales, keg bitters, lagers, ciders and a well-priced wine list provide the complement to the fine food, which is served lunchtime and evening and all day on Sunday. It's best to book on Saturday evenings and at all times for groups. Children are very welcome, and they have their own special section on the menu. There's a fruit machine and bagatelle board in the bar, and outside, the amenities include generous off-road parking and a beer garden, complete with fish pond, that is reached through the conservatory.

Among the attractions close to the **Birch and Bottle** are Arley Hall and Gardens, Marbury County Park and the Anderton Boat Lift, one of the most remarkable engineering feats of the canal age.

Opening Hours: Lunchtime and evening; all day Sunday.

Food: Bar meals.

Credit Cards: Diners, Mastercard, Visa.

Accommodation: None.

Facilities: Car Park, beer garden.

Entertainment: None.

Local Places of Interest/Activities: Arley Hall, Marbury Park, Anderton, Northwich, Warrington.

Internet/Website:
e-mail: birchv857@aol.com

140 The Black Swan

550 Manchester Road,
Hollins Green,
Rixton,
Warrington,
Cheshire
WA3 6LA
Tel: 0161 777 9673
Fax: 0161 776 9897

Directions:

On the A57 about four
miles east of
Warrington.

Once an important refreshment stop on the Liverpool-Manchester coaching run, this handsome hostelry has been dispensing hospitality for more than 300 years. It was originally called the Old Swan and acquired its present name when black swans, native to Australia, first appeared on the nearby Mersey and Glaze rivers. The tradition of serving good ale and good food is being carried on in fine style by Liz and Mike Morrison, who took over the lease in October 1999.

The three regularly changing real ales are popular thirst-quenchers, and the food, freshly prepared for a wide-ranging menu, is served lunchtime and evening Monday to Friday and all day Saturday and Sunday. Snacks include sandwiches, jacket potatoes, burger on a barm cake and hot roast beef baguette with onions and gravy, while main dishes run from jumbo battered cod to lasagne and an excellent steak & ale pie. Steaks and chicken fillets are accompanied by the diner's choice from a mouthwatering list of sauces: pepper, Diane, creamy stilton, honey & cider, redcurrant & red wine, and bosceolla - capers, peppers, onions, olives, mushrooms, cream, wine. Special deals are available for senior citizens during the week. It's advisable to book at the weekend to be sure of a table in the 50-cover non-smoking restaurant.

On the social side, there's something going on every night of the week at the Black Swan: quiz on Monday and Wednesday, fun bingo on Tuesday, Karaoke on Thursday and Saturday, Tote night on Friday, 50s night and Play Your Cards Right on Sunday. The Morrisons have many plans to broaden still further the scope of their very attractive pub, including the creation of a beer garden and the bringing on stream of six guest bedrooms, all upstairs, all with en suite facilities.

Opening Hours: Lunchtime and evening; all day Fri, Sat & Sun.

Food: Bar meals.

Credit Cards: Diners, Mastercard, Visa.

Accommodation: 6 en suite rooms planned.

Facilities: Car Park.

Entertainment: See above.

Local Places of Interest/Activities: Warrington (Museum & Art Gallery) 4 miles, Lymm 4 miles.

The Boot & Slipper | 141

Long Lane, Wettenhall,
Cheshire CW7 4DN
Tel: 01270 528238 Fax: 01270 528284

Directions:
Wettenhall is 7 miles north of Nantwich on a minor road off the B5074.

In a pretty village surrounded by open countryside, **The Boot & Slipper** is one of Cheshire's most popular inns. Part of the premises date back nearly 400 years, and until the 1930s the pub was called the Royal Oak.

Run for the past five years by Joan and David Jones, son Nick and daughter-in-law Joanne, this free house has abundant old-world charm, a place to be sought out whether for a drink, a snack, a full meal or an overnight stay. Food is served lunchtime and evening every day of the week, and at the weekend it's essential to book for a table in the restaurant. Snacks and full meals cover an excellent choice on the printed menu and specials board, and everything is fresh and tasty - steaks and steak pies are among the specialities. Drinks include two real ales and a good range of draught and bottled beers. The Boot & Slipper is a great base for exploring the region, and the letting accommodation comprises four upstairs bedrooms - two doubles and two singles - all with showers. The tariff is on a Bed & Breakfast basis, with discounts for extended stays.

And there's certainly plenty to see and do in the locality: Crewe and Nantwich, the two major towns of South Cheshire, are a short drive to the south, Middlewich to the northeast, and Oulton Park, which stages numerous motor racing events throughout the year, is just a few minutes away to the north.

Opening Hours: Lunchtime and evening; all day Sat & Sun.

Food: Bar snacks and à la carte menu.

Credit Cards: Amex, Mastercard, Visa.

Accommodation: Four rooms with showers.

Facilities: Car Park.

Entertainment: None.

Local Places of Interest/Activities: Crewe (Railway Museum), Nantwich, Shropshire Union Canal, Oulton Park.

142 The Cheshire Cheese

56 Crewe Road,
Nantwich,
Cheshire
CW5 6JD
Tel: 01270 628654

Directions:

Crewe Road is a
two-minute walk
from the town
centre.

The Cheshire Cheese is a good-looking redbrick gabled building on a corner site a short stroll from the centre of Nantwich. Lisa and Mike, with ten years experience in the trade behind them, took over as leaseholders in the spring of 2000, since when they have added to the pub's reputation as a spot where regulars and first-timers can be sure of an equally warm welcome.

There's a good atmosphere in the bars, where among the favourite thirst-quenchers are the two real ales - Greenalls and Boddingtons - that are always on tap. The whole place is cosy and inviting, and the happy hour (5 till 7.30 Monday to Friday) is a particularly good time for a visit. Pool, darts, dominoes and various card games keep many of the regulars busy, while outside in the beer garden children can play in their own secure space - there's even a bouncy castle when the weather is going through a kind patch.

There is a bar menu specialising in sea food and steak, and indeed, food is an item high on the agenda for expansion in the near future. Whilst there is a designated dining area, meals can be eaten throughout. The pub is closed lunchtime Monday to Friday except Bank Holidays, and open all day Saturday, Sunday and Bank Holidays.

Nantwich, once a centre of the salt industry, has plenty to attract the visitor, including the 14th century stone church, sometimes called the Cathedral of South Cheshire, and the Museum, where displays tell of Civil War days and the dairy and cheese-making industries.

Opening Hours: Mon to Fri evenings, all day Sat, Sun & Bank Holidays.

Food: Bar menu served when pub is open

Credit Cards: None.

Accommodation: None.

Facilities: Car Park.

Entertainment: Occasional karaoke Fridays.

Local Places of Interest/Activities: Nantwich, Crewe (Railway Museum) Stapeley Water Gardens 1 mile south on the A51, Willaston (World Worm Charming Championships).

The Fox & Hounds Inn   143

Holmes Chapel Road, Sproston Green,
Middlewich, Cheshire CW4 7LW
Tel: 01606 832303

Directions:

From junction 18 of the M6 take the A54 towards Middlewich. The inn is less than a mile along on the left.

Motorists driving along the M6 need only the briefest of diversions to find this excellent place of refreshment. **The Fox & Hounds Inn**, a handsome old black and white building, stands less than a mile from junction 18, and its motto 'happiness is a drink and good food' is very well chosen.

Run for the past five years by the French family, it has a history going back almost 300 years, and the traditional bar and restaurant are cosy and inviting. Food is served every lunchtime and evening except for non-Bank Holiday Monday evenings. A specials board and à là carte are available for both sessions with the addition of a snack menu for lunchtimes only. Daily fish specials are always worth looking out for, but everything is good and fresh, and such is the popularity of the place that from Thursday through the weekend booking is advisable to be sure of a table. Also very well attended are the special occasion themed evenings which are held from time to time. Three real ales - Greenalls, Bass and a rotating guest - are always available, along with the usual range of popular brews.

The inn has a large off-road car park and a beer garden with an old bowling green that is now used as an area for children to play in (kids also have their own menu). Other amenities include a toilet with facilities for disabled visitors.

With the M6 so close, access north and south is very easy, and in the immediate vicinity there are plenty of places worth a visit, including the old salt town of Middlewich, the little village of Holmes Chapel, where John Wesley preached outside St Luke's Church, Goostrey, which holds an annual gooseberry fair, and Jodrell Bank Science Centre.

Opening Hours: All day, every day.

Food: Snack and à la carte menus.

Credit Cards: Amex, Mastercard, Visa.

Accommodation: None.

Facilities: Car Park, beer garden.

Entertainment: None.

Local Places of Interest/Activities:
Middlewich 1 mile, Holmes Chapel 3 miles, Jodrell Bank 5 miles.

144 The George & Dragon

Great Budworth,
Cheshire
CW9 6HF
Tel: 01606 891317
Fax: 01606 892135

Directions:

From Northwich take the A559 for about 3 miles. Great Budworth is signposted on a minor road to the right.

In the centre of one of the county's most picturesque villages, **The George & Dragon** has been in the same family for 37 years, and Malcolm Curtin has been at the helm since 1982, ably assisted by his partner Rose. The historic inn was built in 1722, and the promise of the characterful redbrick exterior is more than fulfilled in the beamed bars, where a marvellous collection of gleaming brass and copper and old pictures and prints fill most of the wall space. An inscription in the front porch, accredited to Rowland Egerton Warburton of nearby Arley, delivers this message against intemperance:

> *"As St George in armed array*
> *Doth the fiery dragon slay*
> *So mayst thou with might no less*
> *Slay that dragon drunkenness."*

Other examples of his verse can be seen in the pub, in the village pumphouse and on the rhyming signposts of Arley. In the two downstairs bar areas - the Lounge Bar and Stocks Bar - hot and cold snacks and meals are served every lunchtime and evening, with filled rolls for quick bites and main courses running from jumbo cod in batter with chips and mushy peas to cheeseburgers, steaks, chicken with barbecue sauce and the day's curry (always a great favourite here). There are special offers on meals in the early evening (not Sunday), and from Wednesday to Sunday tables can be booked in the first-floor dining room. The pub has featured more than 500 guest beers from all over Britain in the last five years, and there's always an excellent selection to enjoy.

Great Budworth has a very splendid 14th century church that's well worth a visit, as are nearby Arley Hall & Gardens and Marbury Country Park.

Opening Hours: Lunchtime and evening; all day Friday, Saturday and Sunday.

Food: Bar meals and restaurant

Credit Cards: All the major cards.

Accommodation: None.

Facilities: Car Park.

Entertainment: None.

Local Places of Interest/Activities: Northwich 3 miles, Arley Hall, Marbury Country Park.

The Golden Lion | 145

61 Chester Road,
Middlewich,
Cheshire
CW10 9ET
Tel: 01606 737163

Directions:

Close to the centre
of Middlewich,
where the A54,
A530 and A533
meet.

The Golden Lion is a compact three-storey building constructed 150 years ago on the site of a 13th century hostelry. It enjoys a prime location close to the centre of town, and can be approached on the A54, A530 or A533; it is also only a short drive from junction 18 of the M6.

Barbara Horton, here as leaseholder for the past five years, is a really smashing hostess, and her pub epitomises charm and character, with real fires to keep things cosy when the wind blows. This is a splendid setting in which to meet the regulars for a chat over a glass of real ale or perhaps to join in a game of darts. The pub is open late afternoon until evening Monday to Thursday and all day Friday, Saturday and Sunday. Barbara organises the occasional quiz evening or murder mystery night, and private parties, meetings and buffet functions can also be catered. The only food served on a regular basis is breakfast for residents, for whom the pub is particularly well placed for access to all parts of the region. Four twin bedrooms, one of them with en suite facilities, are available all year round. Middlewich is a town with much to attract the visitor.

It was once a major centre of the salt industry (the 'wich' means salt) and even had its own canal built for the transportation of that vital commodity - the Middlewich Branch Canal linked the town with both the Shropshire Union and the Trent & Mersey Canals. Once a year, Middlewich really bounces on the occasion of the Folk Festival. Another famous salt town, Nantwich, is a short drive north, and Crewe, Sandbach and Congleton are all within easy reach by car.

Opening Hours: Mon-Thur 15.30-23.30 and all day Fri-Sun

Food: Buffets on request

Credit Cards: None.

Accommodation: 4 rooms, 1 en suite.

Facilities: Car Park.

Entertainment: Music evenings, quiz, impromptu darts, dominoes, competitions

Local Places of Interest/Activities:
Middlewich (St Michael's Church), Nantwich 4 miles. Salt Museum Northwich, Local craft centres and canals

146

The Hawk Inn

137 Crewe Road,
Haslington,
Cheshire
CW1 5RG
Tel: 01270 582181

Directions:

A532 from Crewe,
then left on to A534

Old-world charm really means what it says at this wonderful inn, whose 500 years of history are evident throughout. In former times it has been a farmhouse, ale house and coaching inn, and it now welcomes visitors with generous measures of hospitality, good food and drink (an inscription on one of the outside timbers reads: 'a jug of ale, a whispered word, can be found within these old walls'). Also within these old walls is a wealth of ancient black beams, some fine panelling and a framed section of the original wattle and daub. Add to this the traditional furnishings and an amazing collection of brass ornaments, and the picture is complete.

In this most atmospheric of settings David Howell-Jones is the tenant and Sue Batchelor the talented cook who produces an excellent range of snacks and meals served Monday to Friday lunchtimes. The freshly baked baguettes are real favourites, and other popular choices run from prawn cocktail to breaded plaice, gammon with egg <u>and</u> pineapple, salads, ham & mushroom tagliatelle and sirloin steak. Booking is recommended on Friday. The thirsty also have a wide choice, including Robinson's Best, Hatters Mild and Old Stockport Smooth. A separate dining room can be booked for private business lunches, and a function room is available for business or social meetings or private parties.

The inn has a beer garden and patio and plenty of off-road parking. Darts, dominoes and big-screen Sky TV provide permanent entertainment and each month there's a quiz on Thursday and a group performing live on a Friday. The two major towns of South Cheshire, Crewe and Nantwich, are both an easy drive away.

Opening Hours: Mon-Sat, 12.00-23.00; Sun 12.00-22.30

Food: Bar food Mon-Fri lunchtime.

Credit Cards: Mastercard, Visa.

Accommodation: None.

Facilities: Function Room, Car Park.

Entertainment: Monthly quiz and live group.

Local Places of Interest/Activities: Crewe 3 miles, Nantwich 4 miles.

The Old Swan Inn　　147

Keele Road,
Madeley Heath,
Nr. Crewe,
Cheshire
CW3 9LR
Tel: 01782 751199

Directions:

From Stoke take the
A525 west for about
5 miles; from Crewe
A5020, A52, A531.

George Panagi, tenant of the **Old Swan Inn** since April 2001, brought with him a wealth of experience in the licensed and catering trades, and his parents have run a hotel in the locality for 35 years. The Old Swan, which lies just across the border in Staffordshire, is a handsome redbrick building with a spacious, attractive interior in traditional style; in addition to the bar and non-smoking restaurant, a conservatory leading to the garden is soon to be added to the public rooms.

George is a top-class chef and his across-the-board menu takes in dishes from Britain and around the world. The lunchtime menu, served from 12 to 2 Monday to Saturday, offers three courses for a bargain £4.95, with a choice of half a dozen main courses such as cod with chips and mushy peas, roast chicken or the home-made pie of the day. On Sunday a traditional meal, with roast beef and another roast, is served from noon right through to 8 o'clock in the evening. The main à la carte choice runs from chicken tikka with salad and a minty yoghurt dip to Cumberland sausage ring with onion gravy, 16oz gammon steak, breaded scampi and sirloin steak. Also available are sandwiches, hot snacks, kiddies meals and some naughty but delicious desserts. Themed food evenings are held once a month.

A mile or so along the A525 is the village of Madeley, situated on an ancient packhorse route from Newcastle-under-Lyme. The focal point of this conservation area is The Pool, a haven to a multitude of birdlife. The grandest building in Madeley is the timber-framed 15th century Old Hall.

Opening Hours: Mon-Sat, 12.00-15.00, 18.00-23.00; Sun 12.00-23.00

Food: Bar meals.

Credit Cards: None.

Accommodation: None.

Facilities: Car Park.

Entertainment: None.

Local Places of Interest/Activities: Stoke 4 miles, Crewe 10 miles, Madeley 1 mile.

148 The Plough Inn

Beauty Bank,
Foxwist Green,
Whitegate,
Northwich,
Cheshire
CW8 2BP
Tel: 01606 889455
Fax: 01606 301717

Directions:

Reached off
Whitegate Road, 5
miles southwest of
Northwich on a
minor road off the
A54 or A556.

David Hughes, the tenant of seven years, runs a real gem of a pub, a genuine 'hidden place' tucked away down a No Through Road on top of Beauty Bank in the tiny hamlet of Foxwist Green near Whitegate. The setting, among fields, is serene and attractive, and the inn's two old-world bars are full of character and charm.

There are many reasons for seeking out this delightful place, the main one being the superb food cooked by the four chefs/cooks(and occasionally byDavid himself) and served in generous helpings at very reasonable prices. The quality and choice are quite outstanding, whether it's a quick snack or a three-course meal. The regular menu of sandwiches, salads, jacket potatoes and a dozen classic main courses is supplemented by what could just be the longest daily specials list you'll ever see, with inspiration drawn from all round the world: peach halves stuffed with stilton and grilled, deep-fried crab claws, chargrilled sea bass, spaghetti bolognese, boeuf bourguignon, sweet & sour chicken, pork or prawns. The inspiration may be worldwide, but the beef is all British, and David is a great supporter of British farming.

Real ales and a long list of well-chosen wines accompany the splendid fare, and this winning combination makes **The Plough** one of the most popular pubs in the area - booking is very much recommended, especially in summer. The garden has plenty of tables and chairs for alfresco quaffing, and a secure play area with huts and slides that no small person could resist (although they are not allowed inside the pub). Quiz night Monday. Good off-road parking.

Opening Hours: All day, every day.

Food: Bar meals and à la carte.

Credit Cards: Diners, Mastercard, Visa.

Accommodation: None.

Facilities: Car Park, superior outdoor children's play area, beer garden.

Entertainment: Quiz Monday.

Local Places of Interest/Activities:
Northwich (Salt Museum) 5 miles, Whitegate Way (pleasant rural walk), Winsford (recreational lake).

Internet/Website:
e-mail: david@the-plough.demon.co.uk

Red Lion Inn

5 Main Road,
Wybunbury,
Cheshire
CW5 7NA
Tel: 01270 842391

Directions:
About 4 miles
southeast of
Nantwich; take the
A51 or A52 then
B5071.

Once a coaching inn, the **Red Lion** has recently been taken over by Craig Harrop, diving into the world of the licensed trade for the first time. The inn has a very inviting, traditional feel, with old beams, apricot-coloured walls and seating at either smart Windsor-style chairs or comfortable banquettes. Greenall, Bass and a rotating guest make up the choice of real ales, and there is a good selection of other beers and lagers available at the bar.

The new leaseholder is currently refurbishing the kitchen, and when the work is completed (due date December 2001) bar snacks will be produced lunchtime and evening. Pool, darts, dominoes, card games, tv and a fruit machine provide diversions in the bar, with the occasional live entertainment evening thrown in for good measure. The beer garden is safe for children, being accessible only through the pub, and there's plenty of off-road parking space. Open lunchtime and evening Monday to Thursday and all day Friday to Sunday, the Red Lion is situated in the pretty village of Wybunbury, on the B5071, which links the A51 and A52.

The village is best known for the Church of St Chad, which was built on an unsuspected ancient salt bed in the 15th century. Subsidence caused the old church to collapse (a new one was built in the 1970s) and the tower to lean, sometimes by as much as 4 feet from the vertical. The tower now stands alone, fixed in the upright position in a concrete bed. Other local places of interest include Bridgemere Garden World, one of the largest garden centres in Europe, and the Railway Museum at Crewe.

Opening Hours: Lunchtime and evening; all day Fri, Sat & Sun.

Food: Bar snacks after Dec 2001.

Credit Cards: None.

Accommodation: None.

Facilities: Car Park.

Entertainment: See above

Local Places of Interest/Activities:
Nantwich 4 miles, Crewe 4 miles, Bridgemere Garden World 3 miles.

150 | The Red Lion

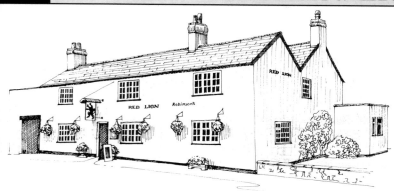

Vicarage Lane, Little Budworth,
Tarporley, Cheshire CW6 9BY
Tel: 01829 760275

Directions:
From Chester take the A54 for about 8 miles; turn right on to minor road signposted Little Budworth. From Tarporley take minor roads signposted off A49 or A54.

Built over 200 years ago as a coaching inn, the **Red Lion** retains a good deal of period detail, including the old mounting steps at the front of the building. Inside, the open fires, traditional furnishings and a collection of gleaming brass and copper lamps, kettles, pots and pans all add to the inviting, welcoming atmosphere generated by owners Alan and Pauline Burgess.

The inn is renowned for its food, and the reputation established by Pauline continues under a full-time professional chef. There are two separate restaurant areas, one of them non-smoking, with about 70 covers in all - but you'll still need to book for Saturday night and Sunday lunchtime. The menu offers an excellent choice of mainly classic pub dishes, from garlic mushrooms and breaded scampi to gammon and sirloin steaks, steak pie and battered cod with chips and mushy peas. Many of the dishes can be ordered in snack or main-course size, and at lunchtime an additional menu of sandwiches, ploughman's platters and jacket potatoes is available. Food is served lunchtime and evening Tuesday to Saturday and all day Sunday. To complement the food is a selection of wines from the Old and New Worlds, available in bottles or quarter-bottles.

Outdoor facilities at this splendid pub include a beer garden and a bowling green that can be hired for parties. The owners plan to bring on stream five en suite letting bedrooms, the front rooms overlooking St Peter's Church. Among the attractions in the vicinity are several golf courses, Little Budworth Common Country Park and the motor-racing circuit at Oulton Park.

Opening Hours: All sessions except Monday lunch (but open Bank Holiday Mondays).

Food: Snack and à la carte menus.

Credit Cards: Diners, Mastercard, Visa.

Accommodation: Five rooms planned.

Facilities: Car Park, beer garden.

Entertainment: None.

Local Places of Interest/Activities:
Tarporley 4 miles, Oulton Park 1 mile.

The Romping Donkey 151

Hassall Green, Sandbach,
Cheshire CW11 4YA
Tel: 01270 765202

Directions:

3 miles south of Sandbach on the A533

The village of Hassall Green, close to the Trent & Mersey Canal, is the attractive setting for **The Romping Donkey**, a real gem of an inn dating from the late 16th century. Part timber-framed, it has a traditional interior with low beams ('duck or grouse') and homely furniture including dressers with displays of china.

Two real ales are always among the drinks on offer, and food is served lunchtime and evening every day. The printed menu and specials board put the emphasis on British dishes, and booking is advisable, especially at the weekend. Children are welcome, and there are no-smoking areas within the bars. Outside is an extensive beer garden with parasols set at picnic tables, the scene of summer barbecues, and there's plenty of off-road parking.

The leaseholders and business partners are Bill Anderson and Bev and Mick Kozlowski, who all have many years' experience in the trade - Bill formerly ran the Stags Head at Great Warford. The Romping Donkey was originally called the Red Lion and at least two reasons are commonly given for the name change. One is that the locals were very unimpressed by the painting of a lion on the pub sign, thinking it looked more like a donkey than a lion; another is that a former licensee kept donkeys in the grounds and once rode one into the bar - photographs in the bar capture this memorable occasion!

Attractions within easy reach of this most delightful inn include the historic town of Sandbach with its famous Saxon stone crosses and the National Trust's Little Moreton Hall,

Opening Hours: 12.00-15.00, 18.60-23.00

Food: Bar meals.

Credit Cards: None.

Accommodation: None.

Facilities: Beer Garden, Car Park.

Entertainment: None.

Local Places of Interest/Activities:
Sandbach 3 miles, Astbury (Little Moreton Hall), Trent & Mersey Canal.

152   The Royal Oak

Main Road,
Worleston,
Nantwich,
Cheshire
CW5 6DN
Tel: 01270 624138
Fax: 01270 611663

Directions:

From Nantwich 1
mile on the A51
then right on to the
B5074 for about 1
mile.

The Royal Oak is the social hub of the village of Worleston, which lies on the B5074 a short distance from Nantwich. Built in the middle of the 19th century on the site of a much earlier hostelry, the pub is spacious and stylish, with plenty of comfortable seating, a restaurant area and a pool table.

Robert and Rachel Hollinshead have held the lease here for 12 years and Rachel, who was born in the village, knows everything there is to know about the village and the locality. She also does most of the cooking, and in addition to the extensive restaurant menu hot and cold bar snacks are available. The printed menu is supplemented by a specials board, and three-course set lunches widen the options still further. Food is served every session except Sunday evening, and booking is advisable for Tuesday and Saturday evenings and Sunday lunch. Meals are rounded off in fine style by a selection of mouth-watering home-made sweets. Boddingtons and Greenalls real ales are among the brews, which also include Worthington Creamflow. There are designated non-smoking areas in the newly decorated, smartly furnished bars, and children have their own play area in the beer garden. Good off-road parking. Country music is played from 8.45 on Tuesday evenings.

The River Weaver and the Shropshire Union Canal are both a short walk from the pib, while within easy reach for motorists are the important towns of Nantwich and Crewe, the former with a splendid 14th century church, the latter not to be missed by anyone interested in the history of the railways.

Opening Hours: Every lunchtime and evening.

Food: Bar meals and à la carte.

Credit Cards: Diners, Mastercard, Visa.

Accommodation: None.

Facilities: Car Park, Beer Garden

Entertainment: Country music Tuesday.

Local Places of Interest/Activities:
Nantwich 2 miles, Crewe 4 miles.

The Swan | 153

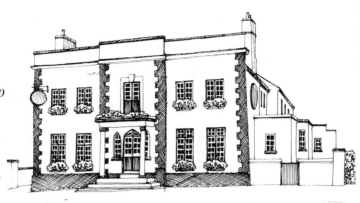

Nantwich Road,
Woore,
Nr. Crewe,
Cheshire
CW3 9SA
Tel: 01630 647220

Directions:

From Nantwich, south on the A51; from Stoke or Newcastle-under-Lyme, west on the A525. Woore is located at the junction of the A51 and A525.

The Swan is a renowned old inn with a history going back to 1539. Once a stop on the Liverpool-London coaching route, it is now a favourite choice both with the locals and with visitors to the area. The location, close to the junction of two major roads, the A51 and A525, makes it very accessible from all points of the compass, and the journey will certainly be worthwhile.

Food is a serious matter here, served during most of the pub's opening hours throughout the week. The choice is wide and varied, and the printed menu is supplemented by a specials board that changes every session. A light lunch menu, served from noon to 5 o'clock Monday to Saturday, offers soup and some really different sandwiches such as grilled aubergine and goat's cheese or roast beef with horseradish mayonnaise; 'stotties' and main courses like penne pasta with smoked salmon, bangers and mash with onion gravy or traditional Staffordshire oatcake filled with bacon, cheese and tomato. The main menu is also splendidly varied and inventive with the likes of vine tomato and crab cocktail with essence of sweet peppers; grilled breast of chicken with succotash in sweet and sour sauce; grilled pork cutlet on lentils with a tomato anise gravy; and, to finish in style, Old English sherry trifle or iced chocolate parfait with summer berries and coffee bean sauce. Booking is strongly recommended at the weekend to be sure of a table in the 90-cover non-smoking restaurant.

To drink: four real ales, keg bitters, lagers, fine wines. The bars are delightfully old-world, with quarry-tiled or wooden floors, panelled walls, prints, pictures and memorabilia.

Opening Hours: Lunchtime and evening; all day Sat & Sun.

Food: Bar meals and à la carte.

Credit Cards: Mastercard, Visa.

Accommodation: None.

Facilities: Games room.

Entertainment: None.

Local Places of Interest/Activities: Nantwich

154 The White Lion Inn

Barthomley,
Nr. Crewe,
Cheshire
CW2 5PG
Tel: 01270 882242

Directions:

From Crewe A5020 then A500; Barthomley is also very close to and signposted from the M6 (junction 16).

Built as an inn nearly 500 years ago, the **White Lion** took its name from the coat of arms of the local bigwigs, the Lords of Crewe. It stands in the pleasant village of Barthomley opposite the Church of St Bertoline, just off the A500 and very close to junction 16 of the M6. The black-and-white thatch-roofed exterior is picture-postcard pretty, and the appeal is maintained within, where quarry tiled floors, ancient beams hung with brasses, sturdy old furniture, leaded windows and real fires present a picture of immense old-world charm. A notable feature is a section of the original wattle and daub preserved in a quiet corner of the bar.

Terence Cartwright, the tenant here for the past 11 years, is ably assisted by his hardworking staff Barbara, Katie, Laura and Suzie. Terence does the cooking, and blackboards list an ever-changing selection of dishes, with freshly cooked joints a popular speciality. Other typical choices could include Ardennes paté, tuna mayonnaise, special ploughman's with Stilton and bacon or local roast ham, pork bangers and mash with onion gravy, pie with vegetables, lemon and pepper chicken breast and cheese and onion oatcakes with beans and tomatoes. This tasty fare can be washed down with a glass of excellent real ale. Children are welcome at the White Lion if they are eating.

Crewe, a mecca for railway enthusiasts, is an easy drive away, and Willaton, a couple of miles south of Crewe, is the venue of a typical British eccentricity, the Annual World Worm Charming Championships.

Opening Hours: Mon-Wed, Fri-Sat 11.30-23.00; Thurs 17.00-23.00; Sun 12.00-22.30

Food: Bar meals lunchtime.

Credit Cards: Mastercard, Visa.

Accommodation: None.

Facilities: Car Park.

Entertainment: None.

Local Places of Interest/Activities: Crewe (Railway Museum) 4 miles, Nantwich, Willaston.

The Windmill Inn 155

Chester Road,
Tabley,
Knutsford,
Cheshire
WA16 0HW
Tel: 01565 632670

Directions:

Tabley lies 2 miles west of Knutsford on the A5033. The inn is located beside the A556 near junction 19 of the M6.

Don't look for a windmill as a pointer to this grand old inn, as it was actually named after the horse Windmill. He came from the stable of the master of nearby Tabley Hall and was a winner of the Chester Gold Cup. Lord de Tabley sold one of his cottages for use as this public house, insisting that it be named after his great favourite.

Behind a very smart black and white frontage the inn has a number of delightful, cosy public rooms, all of which will have been totally refurbished by the end of 2001. A good glass of real ale and something to eat can be enjoyed in any of the various rooms, which include a dining room designated for non-smokers. Traditional English dishes are the mainstay of the menu and specials list, along with some vegetarian dishes; food is served lunchtime and evening every day of the week. Mark Barbe and his father Victor, who also own inns in Wales, have other plans in mind besides the refurbishment. Chief among these is additional letting accommodation, which will number five bedrooms by December 2001. All upstairs, these Bed & Breakfast rooms comprise doubles/twins and a family room, all with en suite facilities.

The nearby town of Knutsford, which Elizabeth Gaskell wrote about so evocatively, is well worth exploring, and within a short drive of the Windmill are two very grand Georgian mansions. On the outskirts of Knutsford, Tatton Park has marvellous paintings, porcelain and furniture along with renowned gardens, while in Tabley itself Tabley House, home of Windmill the horse's owner, has a fine collection of English paintings, including works by Turner and Reynolds, and furniture by Chippendale.

Opening Hours: Lunchtime and evening every day.

Food: Bar meals.

Credit Cards: Amex, Mastercard, Visa.

Accommodation: 5 en suite rooms.

Facilities: Car Park.

Entertainment: None.

Local Places of Interest/Activities:
Knutsford 2 miles, Tatton Park, Tabley (Tabley House, Tabley Cuckoo Clock Collection).

156 | The Witton Chimes

Witton Street,
Northwich,
Cheshire
CW9 5NW
Tel: 016506 47904

Directions:

In the centre of
Northwich at the
junction of Witton
Street and Venables
Road.

Originally an old coach house and for many years a Northwich landmark, the inn stands on a prominent corner site in the centre of town. The name was changed from the Watermans Arms to the **Witton Chimes** after the chiming of the local church. The handsome redbrick building, its upper part in black and white, is a popular local meeting place, and the beamed bars are full of character. Neil and Michele Partington, leaseholders since 1997, are a most pleasant and sociable couple, so it's not surprising that their pub has such a loyal following.

Open all day, every day, this free house is primarily a 'wet' pub, with a good selection of ales on tap, but straightforward bar snacks are available at lunchtime. The regular cask ale is Websters, and they occasionally have a guest ale, along with brews such as John Smiths Smooth and Tetleys Smooth. Pool and darts are among the popular games played here, but the entertainment is very varied, with something happening most nights of the week: karaoke on Thursday and Sunday, treasure runs for motorcyclists on Wednesday, a disco with DJ on Friday, live performances on Saturday. The Partingtons are expanding the scope of the pub by making Bed & Breakfast accommodation available from 1st October 2001. There's free parking at the back.

Northwich was, from the 17th to the 19th centuries, a major centre of the salt industry, and the long involvement of the town and the county in the production of salt is recorded in the Salt Museum, the only one of its kind in Britain. No visit to the area is complete without a look at the amazing Boat Lift at Anderton, a mile from Northwich. This extraordinary construction, built in 1875 and recently restored, was designed to transfer boats from the Trent & Mersey Canal to the Weaver Navigation 50 feet below.

Opening Hours: All day, every day.

Food: Lunchtime bar snacks.

Credit Cards: None.

Accommodation: 6 B&B rooms opening 1st Oct 2001.

Facilities: Car Park

Entertainment: Something most nights - see above.

Local Places of Interest/Activities: Northwich Salt Museum, Anderton boat lift 1 mile.

Internet/Website: www.thewittonchimes.co.uk

6 East Cheshire

PLACES OF INTEREST:

PUBS AND INNS:

The Hidden Inns of Lancashire and Cheshire

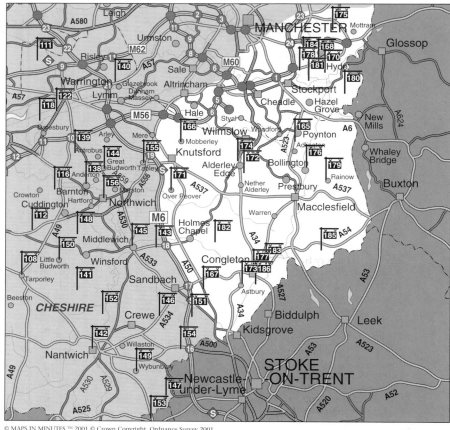

© MAPS IN MINUTES ™ 2001 © Crown Copyright, Ordnance Survey 2001

165	The Boars Head, Higher Poynton	**176**	The Poachers Inn, Bollington
166	The Bull's Head, Mobberley	**177**	Queens Head Hotel, Congleton
167	The Bull's Head, Smallwood	**178**	The Rising Sun, Bredbury, nr Stockport
168	The Buxton Inn, Gee Cross, nr Hyde	**179**	Robin Hood Inn, Rainow
169	The Church Inn, MillbrookStalybridge	**180**	The Royal Oak, Mellor, nr Stockport
170	The Clarence Hotel, Newton, nr Hyde	**181**	The Stock Dove, Romiley, nr Stockport
171	The Dog Inn, Over Peover	**182**	The Swettenham Arms, Swettenham
172	The Drum & Monkey, Alderley Edge	**183**	Throstles Nest Inn, Buglawton
173	Horseshoe Inn, Astbury, nr Congleton	**184**	The White Hart, Woodley
174	The Oakwood, Alderley Edge	**185**	The Wild Boar, Wincle
175	Old Hunters Tavern, Stalybridge	**186**	Ye Olde White Lion, Congleton

Please note all references refer to page numbers

The eastern part of Cheshire is bordered on the south by Staffordshire, on the east by Derbyshire and the Peak District National Park and on the north by Greater Manchester. This part of the county is particularly rich in history: Congleton, in the foothills of the Pennines, was an inhabited place as long ago as the Stone Age and the remains of a 5,000-year-old chambered tomb known as The Bridestones can be seen beside the hill road running eastwards from the town to the A523 road to Leek. The 'Panhandle' is a narrow finger of land pointing up to West Yorkshire; it was chopped off from Cheshire in the 1974 Local Government redrawing of boundaries, but a quarter of a century later most of its population still consider themselves Cheshire folk. At its northern end lie Longdendale and Featherbed Moss, Pennine scenery quite unlike anywhere else in the county. Visitors to Cheshire tend to overlook this orphaned quarter, but it is certainly worth a detour. Nestling below the hills of the High Peak, Macclesfield was once an important silk manufacturing town. Charles Roe built the first silk mill here, beside the River Bollin, in 1743 and for more than a century and a half, Macclesfield was known as the silk town. Congleton also developed as an important textile town during the 18th century with many of its mills involved in silk manufacture, cotton spinning and ribbon weaving. In Mill Green near the River Dane, you can still see part of the very first silk mill to operate here. Towards the Peak District National Park, the scenery and the views are among the most stunning in the whole of Britain

PLACES OF INTEREST

ADLINGTON

The village of Adlington boasts a very fine old house. **Adlington Hall** has been the home of the Legh family since 1315 and is now one of the county's most popular attractions. Quadrangular in shape, this magnificent manor house has two distinctive styles of architecture: black and white half-timbered buildings on two sides, later Georgian additions in warm red brick on the others. There is much to see as you tour the hall, with beautifully polished wooden floors and lovely antique furnishings enhancing the air of elegance and grandeur. The Great Hall is a breathtaking sight, a vast room of lofty proportions that set off perfectly the exquisitely painted walls. The beautifully-preserved 17th century organ here has responded to the touch

Adlington Hall

of many maestros, none more famous than George Frederick Handel, who visited the Hall in the 1740s. It wasn't long after Handel's visit to Cheshire that the county was gripped by a mania for building canals, a passion that has left Cheshire with a uniquely complex network of these environment-friendly waterways.

ALDERLEY EDGE

Alderley Edge takes its name from the long, wooded sandstone escarpment, nearly two miles long, that rises 600 ft above sea level and culminates in sandy crags overlooking the Cheshire Plain. In Victorian times, this spectacular area was the private preserve of the Stanley family and it was only under great pressure that they grudgingly allowed the 'Cottentots' of Manchester access on occasional summer weekends. It was the Stanley daughters who took great umbrage when the Wizard Inn hung up a new sign. They demanded its removal. The Merlin-like figure depicted could, they claimed, be taken as a representation of their father, Lord Stanley, at that time a virtual recluse and more than a little eccentric. Nowadays, however, walkers can roam freely along the many footpaths through the woods, one of

160

which will take them to **Hare Hill Gardens**, a little known National Trust property. These Victorian gardens comprise a walled garden and a fine woodland garden with over 50 varieties of holly, masses of rhododendrons, climbing roses and a pond crossed by wooden bridges. There is access by way of gravel paths for the less able.

The view from Alderley Edge over the Cheshire plain is one of the county's most memorable sights.

Little Moreton Hall

ALTRINCHAM

The writer Thomas de Quincey visited Altrincham in the early 1800s and thought its bustling market "the gayest scene he ever saw". The market is still very active although the old houses that de Quincey also noted have sadly gone. A modern bustling town, Altrincham nevertheless has a long history with a charter granted in 1290 and clear evidence that there was a settlement beside the River Bollin some 6,000 years ago. Even older than that is the prehistoric body preserved in peat discovered on Lindow Common nearby. From Victorian times, Altrincham has been a favoured retreat for Manchester businessmen and the town is well-supplied with inns and restaurants.

ASTBURY

The pretty little village of Astbury, set around a triangular village green, was once more important than neighbouring Congleton, which is why it has a much older church, built between 1350 and 1540. Arguably the finest parish church in the county, **St Mary's** is famous for its lofty recessed spire (which rises from a tower almost detached from the nave), and the superb timber work inside: a richly carved ceiling, intricate tracery on the rood screen, and a lovely Jacobean font cover. But just three miles down the A34 is an even more remarkable building. Black and white half-timbered houses have almost become a symbol for the county of Cheshire and the most stunning example is undoubtedly **Little Moreton Hall** (National Trust), a wibbly wobbly house which provided a memorable location for Granada TV's adaptation of *Moll Flanders*. The only bricks to be seen are in the chimneys, and The Hall's huge overhanging gables, slanting walls, and great stretches of leaded windows, create wonderfully complex patterns, all magically reflected in the

still flooded moat. Ralph Moreton began construction in 1480 and the fabric of this magnificent house has changed little since the 16th century. A richly panelled Great Hall, parlour and chapel show off superb Elizabethan plasterwork and woodwork. Free guided tours give visitors a fascinating insight into Tudor life, and features in the attractive grounds include a yew tunnel, a period herb garden and a lovely Elizabethan-style knot garden with clipped box hedges and a period herb garden. About a mile south of Cuttleford Farm is the Rode Hall Estate. It was an 18th century owner of the estate, Randle Wilbraham, who built the famous folly of **Mow Cop** (National Trust) to enhance the view from his mansion. This mock ruin stands atop a rocky hill 1100 ft above sea level, just yards from the Staffordshire border. On a clear day, the views are fantastic: Alderley Edge

Mow Cop

to the north, the Pennines to the north-east, south to Cannock Chase and Shropshire, and westwards across Cheshire.

BOLLINGTON

In its 19th century heyday, there were 13 cotton mills working away at Bollington, a little town perched on the foothills of the High Peak. Two of the largest mills, the Clarence and the Adelphi, still stand, although now adapted to other purposes. The Victorian shops and cottages around Water Street and the High Street recall those busy days. A striking feature of the town is the splendid 20-arched viaduct which once carried the railway over the River Dean. It is now part of the **Middlewood Way**, a ten mile, traffic-free country trail which follows a scenic route from Macclesfield to Marple. The Way is open to walkers, cyclists and horse riders and during the season cycles are available for hire, complete with child seats if required. Just as remarkable as the viaduct, although in a different way, is **White Nancy**, a round stone tower which stands on Kerridge Hill, more than 900ft above sea level. It was built to commemorate the Battle of Waterloo and offers sweeping views in all directions.

CONGLETON

In Elizabethan times, the townspeople of Congleton seem to have had a passion for bear-baiting. On one occasion, when the town bear died they handed 16 shillings to the Bear Warden to acquire another beast. The money had originally been collected to buy a town bible: this disgraceful misappropriation of funds gave rise to the ditty: "Congleton rare, Congleton rare, sold the bible to buy a bear". Known locally as the Bear Town, Congleton was the very last town in England to outlaw the cruel practice of bear-baiting. A more attractive distinction is the fact that it is also one the few towns in Cheshire where the medieval street pattern has remained intact and where the curfew bell is still rung each night at 8pm. Congleton's impressive Venetian Gothic style Town Hall, built in 1866, contains some interesting exhibits recalling its long history. Amongst them are displays recording the work of such ancient civic officials as the swine-catcher, the chimney-looker and the ale-taster, and aids to domestic harmony like the bridle for nagging wives which used to be fastened to a wall in the market place.

HOLMES CHAPEL

In the mid-18th century, the little village of Holmes Chapel was stirred by two important events. In 1738, John Wesley came and preached outside St Luke's Church. Fifteen years later, on July 10th, 1753, a disastrous fire swept through the village. When the flames were finally quenched, only two buildings had survived the blaze: St Luke's Church and The Old Red Lion alongside. On the A535 berween Holmes Chapel and Chelford is the **Jodrell Bank Science and Arboretum**. Visible from miles around, the huge white dish of the world famous Jodrell Bank radio telescope has a good claim to being the most distinctive building in the county. The Observatory came into service in 1957 and was used by both Americans and the Soviets in their exploration of space. Its Science Centre offers visitors a wonderful array of hands-on exhibits, including a 25ft telescope, while its Planetarium transports through the heavens, explaining the secrets of Rocky Dwarfs and Gassy Giants along the way. Outside, there's a superb 35-acre Arboretum planted with 2,500 species of trees and shrubs, each one helpfully labelled. The arboretum, which was begun in 1972, was the idea of Professor Sir Bernard Lovell, who also originated the Quinta Tree Garden at nearby Swettenham.

MACCLESFIELD

Macclesfield can boast the country's only **Silk Museum**, where visitors are given a lively introduction to all aspects of the silk industry, from cocoon to loom. The museum has an award-winning audio-visual presentation, there are fascinating exhibitions on the Silk Road across Asia, on silk cultivation, fashion and other uses of silk. The silk theme continues at nearby Paradise Mill. Built in the 1820s, it is now a working museum demonstrating silk weaving on 26 jacquard hand looms. Exhibitions and restored workshops and living rooms capture the working conditions and lives of mill workers in the 1930s. It is also possible to buy locally-made silk products here. The Silk Museum is housed in what used to be the Macclesfield Sunday School; the school finally closed in 1970 and the Silk Museum now shares this rather grand building with the town's Heritage Centre which has some interesting displays on Macclesfield's rich and exciting past (the town was occupied for five days by Scottish troops during the Jacobite Rebellion of 1745, for example), and on the Sunday School itself. In pre-Saxon times, Macclesfield was known as Hameston, the homestead on the rock, and on that rock is set the church founded

162

by King Edward I and Queen Eleanor. From the modern town, a walk to the church involves climbing a gruelling flight of 108 steps. St Michael and All Angels was extended in the 1890s but its 14th century core remains, notably the Legh Chapel built in 1422 to receive the body of Piers Legh who had fought at Agincourt and died at the Siege of Meaux. Another chapel contains the famous Legh Pardon brass, which recalls the medieval practice of selling pardons for sins past, and even for those not yet committed. The inscription on the brass records that, in return for saying five Paternosters and five Aves, the Legh family received a pardon for 26,000 years and 26 days. One of the Macclesfield area's most famous sons is Charles Frederick Tunnicliffe, the celebrated bird and wild-life artist, who was born at the nearby village of Langley in 1901. He studied at the Macclesfield School of Art and first came to public attention with his illustrations for Henry Williamson's *Tarka the Otter* in 1927. A collection of Tunnicliffe's striking paintings can be seen at the **West Park Museum** on the northwest edge of the town. This purpose-built museum, founded in 1898 by the Brocklehurst family, also includes exhibits of Egyptian artefacts, fine and decorative arts.

West Park Museum is on Prestbury Road and further along this road is Upton House, a grand Victorian detached house set in almost an acre of gardens. It was built around 1885 by a prosperous Macclesfield merchant who decided to build a house on the outskirts of the town that would reflect his wealth and his substantial position in society. To the east of the town centre runs the **Macclesfield Canal**, one of the highest waterways in England, running for much of its length at more than 500 ft above sea level. Thomas Telford was the surveyor of the 26-mile long route, opened in 1831, which links the Trent & Mersey and the Peak Forest canals. Between Macclesfield and Congleton, the canal descends over a hundred feet in a spectacular series of 12 locks at Bosley, before crossing the River Dane via Telford's handsome iron viaduct. Other unusual features of this superbly-engineered canal are the two roving bridges' south of Congleton. These swing from one bank to the other where the towpath changes sides and so enabled horses to cross over without having to unhitch the tow-rope.

MOBBERLEY

Mobberley village is scattered along the B5085, with its notable church set slightly apart. The main glory here is the spectacular woodwork inside: massive roof beams with striking winged figures and one of the finest rood screens in the country, dated 1500. The screen is covered with a rich tracery of leaves and fruit, coats-of-arms, and religious symbols. Two generations of the Mallory family held the rectorship here, one of them for 53 years. He is commemorated in the east window. Another window honours his grandson, George Mallory, the mountaineer who perished while making his third attempt to climb Mt Everest in 1924.

MOTTRAM

Mottram village is set on a breezy hillside on the edge of the Pennines. According to the 1930's guide-book writer Arthur Mee, the off-Atlantic gusts that scour the village are known locally as Captain Whitle's Wind. In the 16th century, the story goes, coffin-bearers carrying the late Captain were struggling up the steep hill to the church when gale-force winds swept the coffin from their shoulders.

NETHER ALDERLEY

The village of Nether Alderley lies on the A34 and here you will find **Nether Alderley Mill**, a delightful 15th century watermill that has been restored by the National Trust. The red sandstone walls are almost hidden under the huge sweep of its stone tiled roof. Inside is the original Elizabethan woodwork and Victorian mill machinery which is still in working order, with two tandem overshot wheels powering the mill. Nether Alderley Mill is open to the public on Wednesday and Sunday afternoons in April, May & October, and every afternoon except Monday from June to September. If you have time, visit the 14th century church of St Mary with its unusual richly carved pew, set up on the wall like an opera box and reached by a flight of steps outside.

PRESTBURY

A regular winner of the Best Kept Village title, Prestbury is a charming village where a tree-lined High Street runs down to a bridge over the River Bollin, ancient stocks stand against the church wall, old coaching inns and black and white buildings mingle with the mellow red brick work of later Georgian houses. The **Church of St Peter**, dating from the 13th century, still maintains a tradition which began in 1577. Every autumn and winter evening at 8pm a curfew bell is rung, with the number of chimes corresponding to the date of the month. Close by is a building known as the Norman Chapel with a striking frontage carved with the characteristic Norman zig-zags and beaked heads. Even older are the carved fragments of an 8th century Saxon cross preserved under glass in the graveyard. Opposite the church is a remarkable magpie timber-framed house which is now a bank but used to be the Vicarage. During the Commonwealth, the rightful incumbent was debarred from preaching in the church by the Puritans. Undaunted, the priest addressed his parishioners from the tiny balcony of his Vicarage.

RAINOW

A village situated on the edge of the Peak District National Park very close to Nab Head, the hill-top vantage point offering spectacular views across east Cheshire. And not far away is White Nancy, a round stone tower from whose summit, more than 900 feet above sea level, there are equally astonishing vistas westwards into Lancashire, eastwards to the Derbyshire hills.

STYAL

Cared for by the National Trust, **Styal Country Park** is set in 250 acres of the beautifull wooded valley of the River Bollin and offers many woodland and riverside walks. The Park is open to the public from dawn to dusk throughout the year and is a wonderful place for picnics. Lying within the Park is Quarry Bank Mill, a grand old building erected in 1784 and one of the first generation of cotton mills. It was powered by a huge iron waterwheel fed by the River Bollin. Visitors follow the history of the mill through various galleries and displays within the museum, including weaving and spinning demonstrations, and can experience for themselves, with the help of guides dressed in period costume what life was like for the hundred girls and boys who once lived in the Apprentice House. Also within the park is the delightful factory village of Styal, which was established by the mill's original owner, Samuel Greg, a philanthropist and pioneer of the factory system. He took children from the slums of Manchester to work in his mill, and in return for their labour provided them with food, clothing, housing, education and a place of worship.

WARREN

Just outside the village of Warren is **Gawsworth Hall**, a captivating picture with its dazzling black and white half-timbered walls and lofty three-decker Tudor windows. The Hall was built in 1480 by the Fitton family, one of whose descendants, the celebrated beauty, Mary Fitton is believed to be the Dark Lady of Shakespeare's sonnets. The Bard would no doubt approve of Gawsworth's famous open-air theatre where per-

Gawsworth Hall

formances range from his own plays to Gilbert and Sullivan operas with the Hall serving as a lovely backdrop. Surrounded by a huge park, Gawsworth, to quote its owner Timothy Richards, "is the epitome of a lived-in historic house". Every room that visitors see (which is virtually every room in the house) is in daily use by him and his family. And what wonderful rooms they are. Myriad windows bathe the rooms in light, the low ceilings and modest dimensions radiate calm, and even the richly-carved main staircase is conceived on a human scale. The beautifully sited church, and the lake nearby, add still more to the appeal of this magical place.

WILMSLOW

The oldest building in Wilmslow is **St Bartholomew's Church**, built between 1517 and 1537, and notable for its magnificent ceiling, some striking effigies, and for the fact that Prime Minister-to-be WE Gladstone worshipped here as a boy. A hamlet in medieval times,

164

Wilmslow mushroomed as a mill town in the 18th and 19th centuries, and is now a busy commuter town offering a good choice of inns, hotels and restaurants.

WOODFORD

Just a couple of miles from Woodford is one of the grandest old 'magpie' houses in Cheshire, **Bramall Hall**. This eye-catching, rambling perfection of black and white timbered buildings overlooks some 62 acres of exquisitely-landscaped woods, lakes and formal gardens. The oldest parts of the Hall date from the 14th century: for five of the next six centuries it was owned by the same family, the Davenports. Over the years, the Davenport family continually altered and extended the originally quite modest manor house. But whenever they added a new Banqueting Hall, Withdrawing Room, or even a Chapel, they took pains to ensure that

Bramall Hall

its design harmonised happily with its more ancient neighbours. Along with Little Moreton Hall and Gawsworth Hall, Bramall represents the fullest flowering of a lovely architectural style whose most distinctive examples are all to be found in Cheshire.

The Boars Head | 165

Shrigley Road North,
Higher Poynton,
Cheshire
SK12 1TE
Tel: 01625 876676

Directions:

From Macclesfield
take the A523 north;
turn off on minor
road for Higher
Poynton (just before
Poynton).

This handsome red-
brick public house,
standing alone on a
corner site in the ham-
let of Higher Poynton,
is the first venture into
the licensed trade for
Gordon and Victoria Yoxall, who took over five years ago. The two-storey building dates
back about 120 years and was used as a hostelry for workmen constructing the nearby
railway. Nowadays the clientele comprises regulars from the neighbouring towns and villages, ramblers and motorists enjoying a tour of the attractive countryside south of the
metropolis of Greater Manchester.

Nicely decorated and furnished throughout, the pub benefits not only from the good
atmosphere generated by the congenial hosts but also from the cosy, comfortable surroundings. Gordon is the chef, and dishes from his printed menu and daily specials are available
every lunchtime and evening. Lighter bites include plain or toasted sandwiches, baguettes
with a variety of tasty fillings and an excellent Welsh rarebit served with a crisp green salad.
Main meals comprise pub classics such as a scampi, breaded plaice, prime gammon steaks,
chilli con carne and - swiftly becoming a modern classic! - chicken tikka masala. Larger
parties should book, and children are always welcome.

Visitors can work up an appetite with a pleasant walk along Middlewood Way (the
disused railway track) or beside the Macclesfield Canal. A little further afield are two notable grand houses: the National Trust's Lyme Park at Disley, an Italianate palace with superb
tapestries, Grinling Gibbons wood carvings and an important collection of English clock;
and Adlington Hall, a magnificent house with a stunning Great Hall.

Opening Hours: Lunchtime and evening; all
day Sat, Sun & Bank Holidays in summer.

Food: Bar meals.

Credit Cards: None.

Accommodation: None.

Facilities: Car Park.

Entertainment: None.

Local Places of Interest/Activities:
Macclesfield 6 miles, Lyme Park, Adlington
Hall.

166   The Bull's Head

Mill Lane,
off Town Lane,
Mobberley,
Cheshire
WA16 7HX
Tel: 01565 873134

Directions:

From Knutsford,
B5085 for 2 miles.

Situated off the old main road through the scattered village of Mobberley, **The Bull's Head** started life in the middle of the 18th century as three cottages. Inside, it is splendidly old-world and cosy, and leaseholders Jenny and Ted guarantee a smiling welcome and the best of hospitality.

Looking after the appetites of locals and visitors is the excellent cook Carole, whose menus are available all sessions except Sunday and Monday evenings. Light snacks for quick fillers, but it's best to go for of Carole's hearty main-course specialities, perhaps a curry, a hotpot, braised liver or steak and ale pie. And room should definitely be left for one of her super sweets such as apple and blackberry pie or treacle tart. Children have their own menu, and there's always a choice of hearty Sunday roasts. The 40 seats fill up quickly, so it's best to book, particularly on Friday and Saturday nights. Thirsts are quenched by an excellent selection of ales including four real ales - Tetleys, Boddingtons, Timothy Taylor and a regularly changing guest brew. Lord Ted's Ripping Good Quiz, which is free to enter, starts at 9 o'clock on Thursday, and other diversions include pool, darts, dominoes and an excellent bowling green which costs just £1 per person to hire.

An attraction, hosted at the pub, that should not be missed is the Annual Mobberley Steam Party (held Whitsun Bank Holiday), when steam engine owners bring their machines and their friends to the inn to enjoy a weekend of delights that include live music, pub games and a mini real ale festival.

Opening Hours: All day, every day.

Food: Bar meals (not Sun & Mon eves).

Credit Cards: Diners, Mastercard, Visa.

Accommodation: None.

Facilities: Car Park, games room, bowling green.

Entertainment: Quiz Thursday, annual steam rally. Occasional live music and Morris dancing

Local Places of Interest/Activities: Knutsford 2 miles, Mobberley (church with spectacular woodwork). Hillside Bird Sanctuary across the road.

The Bull's Head 167

Newcastle Road, Smallwood,
Cheshire CW11 2TY
Tel: 01477 500247

Directions:
A534 from Sandbach, right on to A50 at
Arclid Green. Smallwood is situated on the
A50 Newcastle-under-Lyme road.

In its 200-year history this fine building has been a blacksmith's premises and a coaching inn. The interior is immensely appealing, with old black beams, traditional furnishings and Cheshire brick fireplaces.

It has for some years been one of the top eating pubs in the region, with a first-class chef in Ian Evans, who also holds the lease with is wife Sharon. Ian's menu really does provide something for all tastes and appetites, as well as a large specials board which changes daily, featuring local favourites and some more unusual dishes. There's a fine selection of fillings and toppings for the closed and open sandwiches. The main dining room has 70 covers, and in addition there are two lovely light conservatories, one of them looking out over the large award winning beer gardens. Food is served lunchtime and evening Monday to Saturday and from noon to 9 o'clock on Sunday. Booking is recommended for all the weekend sessions.

The choice for ale-quaffers is also impressive, with three real ales and a full range of draught bitters, lagers, stout and cider. To accompany the outstanding food is a wine list chosen for variety and value. This classic English country pub is a popular choice not only as a destination for a drink and a meal but as a venue for wedding parties, family celebrations, business lunches and barbecues.

Opening Hours: Mon-Sat 11.00-15.00, 17.30-23.00; Sun 11.00-22.30

Food: Bar snacks and à la carte.

Credit Cards: Diners, Mastercard, Visa.

Accommodation: None.

Facilities: Function Room, Car Park.

Entertainment: None.

Local Places of Interest/Activities: Sandbach 5 miles, Alsager, Little Moreton Hall (NT).

168   The Buxton Inn

**36 Mottram Old Road,
Gee Cross,
Hyde,
Cheshire
SK4 5NG
Tel: 0161 367 7558**

Directions:

Gee Cross lies
about 1 mile south
of the centre of
Hyde, reached off
the A560 or M67.

Close enough to Manchester to be a convenient base for business trips, but far enough away to enjoy the peace of the countryside, the **Buxton Inn** is the domain of leaseholder Chris Parker. Here since the middle of 2000, he welcomes regulars and newcomers to his atmospheric inn, which was originally called the Buckstone in memory of a favourite hound of a landlord in the 1870s - at that time the inn was the meeting place of the Stalybridge Hunt.

Behind the smart cream-painted exterior the inn has a very inviting feel, with plenty of chairs and banquette seating, local pictures and prints and even a piano in the vault. The inn is a popular place for a snack or a meal, and the across-the-board menu is available lunchtime and evening Monday to Friday and all day Saturday and Sunday. The daily specials are always in demand and could include vegetable and French onion soups, lamb or beef parcels and main dishes such as chicken Dijon or surf 'n' turf. Booking is recommended at the weekend; children are always welcome, and some of the tables are designated non-smoking.

For guests wishing to stay overnight the Buxton Inn offers four letting bedrooms, all upstairs, with showers en suite; available throughout the year, they can be booked on either a Bed & Breakfast or room only basis. Tuesday is quiz nights and there are occasional theme food nights. The inn has good off-road parking, a small patio at the front and, at the back, a beer garden with a children's play area.

Gee Cross is about a mile south of Hyde on the A560. Stockport and Manchester are within easy driving distance, and in the other direction the Peak District National Park beckons.

Opening Hours: All day, every day.

Food: Bar meals and a la carte.

Credit Cards: All the major cards.

Accommodation: 4 en suite rooms.

Facilities: Car Park, beer garden.

Entertainment: Quiz Tuesday.

Local Places of Interest/Activities: Werneth Low Country Park 200 yds, Trans-pennine Trail ¼ mile, Hyde 1 mile, Stockport, Manchester, Peak District National Park.

Internet/Website:
e-mail: buxton@geecross.com

The Church Inn | 169

422 Huddersfield Road,
Millbrook,
Stalybridge,
Cheshire
SK15 3JL
Tel: 0161 338 2813

Directions:

1 mile northeast
of Stalybridge on
a minor road to
the right of the
A635.

There has been an inn on the site since 1740, and the present **Church Inn** was built of local stone in the 1860s. It was taken over in April 2001 by Vicki and Gary Chisnall, both of them very experienced in the licensed and catering trades. They immediately embarked on a programme of improvements that includes top-to-toe redecoration and refurnishing. They also plan to accept credit cards and to introduce live entertainment, quiz nights and themed food nights.

Food is available all day up to 10 o'clock from a menu and specials board that between them offer anything from a sandwich to a steak. Two real ales, Theakstons Mild and a guest, are served at the bar, along with John Smiths Smooth, Boddingtons Creamflow and a range of lagers. Children are welcome at all times. Millbrook is a good base for both business and leisure visitors, with the big cities and the open countryside equally easy to get to. To this end the inn has seven letting bedrooms, all upstairs, with showers en suite. The rooms, available all year round, are let on a Bed & Breakfast basis and the rates (set by room rather than by person) are very reasonable. There's good off-road parking, and the inn can cater for parties and functions - a private room with seats for up to 80 can be hired free of charge.

The recently opened Stalybridge-Huddersfield Canal is set to become a popular local attraction, and it's only a short drive from the Church Inn to the Peak District National Park.

Opening Hours: Lunchtime and evening; all day Saturday and Sunday.

Food: Bar meals.

Credit Cards: Planned.

Accommodation: 7 en suite rooms.

Facilities: Car Park, function room.

Entertainment: None.

Local Places of Interest/Activities:
Stalybridge 1 mile, Stalybridge-Huddersfield Canal, Peak District National Park.

170 The Clarence Hotel

195 Talbot Road,
Newton,
Hyde,
Cheshire
SK14 4HJ
Tel: 01613 682066

Directions:

The hamlet of Newton is located close to Hyde, reached off the A560, M60 or M67.

Situated in the tiny community of Newton, close to Hyde and not far from the motorway network, **The Clarence Hotel** is a neat black and white building dating back to mid-Victorian times. Experienced licensees Carol and Denis Harcourt have held the lease for 10 years, during which time they have really stamped their friendly, outgoing personalities on the place. It's a very comfortable spot, with a traditional look and feel in the bars, allied to the modern diversion of big-screen tvs for sports fans.

Food is served Monday to Friday from 12 to 2, Wednesday to Friday from 5 to 7 and Saturday and Sunday from 1 o'clock to 6. The home-made chilli is one of the most popular dishes on the menu, which is given added choice by the daily specials board. Children are welcome if they are eating, and booking is advisable for larger groups or special occasions. Four real ales are available -Boddingtons, Theakstons, Websters and a weekly changing guest - along with Greenalls Dark Mild, John Smiths Smooth and many more.

The Clarence is a pub with bags of atmosphere, where there always seems to be something going on: pool and darts all through the week, a quiz and a singer on Wednesday and a live performer on Saturday. When the weather is nice, you can enjoy the tranquil beer garden at the rear of the pub. Manchester, Stockport and Glossop are all just a short drive away, but there are also some nearby rural delights, including the Peak District National Park to the southeast, and, a little way north, the narrow finger of land lost to Yorkshire in 1974 that is known as the Panhandle and offers some wonderful Pennine scenery.

Opening Hours: All day, every day.

Food: Bar meals.

Credit Cards: None.

Accommodation: None.

Facilities: Beer Garden

Entertainment: Quiz Wed, live music Wed & Sat

Local Places of Interest/Activities: Manchester, Stockport, Glossop, Peak District National Park.

The Dog Inn 171

Well Bank Lane,
Over Peover,
Nr. Knutsford,
Cheshire
WA16 8UP
Tel: 01625 861421
Fax: 01625 864800

Directions:
Over Peover (pro-
nounced Peever) is 3
miles south of
Knutsford off the A50.
15 minutes from the
M6, J19.

The Dog Inn was originally a row of cottages built almost 200 years ago. In its time the premises of grocers and shoemakers, it became a beer house in 1860, when it was called the New Inn. Later the Gay Dog and finally the Dog Inn, it has established a far-reaching repu-tation for the quality of its food and for the excellent service and value for money provided by the licensees Steve and Rachel Wrigley.

Behind a handsome white-painted frontage adorned with flower boxes and creeper there's a wealth of period character in the cosy, comfortable bars, and seats for over 100, including no-smoking dining areas. An excellent selection of thirst-quenchers includes the products of local brewer Weetwood, Hydes Best Bitter, Moorehouses Black Cat Mild and Addlestones Cloudy Cider. Dishes cooked by Lennie Winstanley, a chef of the old school who combines the best of British produce with classical French technique, are served lunchtime and evening Monday to Saturday and from noon to 8.30 on Sunday. Booking is required for Saturday and for Sunday lunch, and also for the special evenings on the second Friday of the month, when the food and the entertainment are linked to the same country or theme. Thursday and Sunday are quiz nights, and during the happy hours - 5 till 7 Monday to Friday - there are free nibbles at the bar.

With so much to see and do in the vicinity, it's a good idea to have a base, and the Dog Inn offers high-quality overnight accommodation in six en suite bedrooms, four doubles and two twins. Knutsford is very close by, and among other attractions are Jodrell Bank Science Centre, the National Trust's Tatton Park and, in Over Peover itself, Peover Hall with its fine gardens, Georgian stables and private church.

Opening Hours: Lunchtime and evening; all day Sunday.

Food: Bar meals.

Credit Cards: Diners, Mastercard, Visa.

Accommodation: Six en suite rooms.

Facilities: Car Park.

Entertainment: Quiz Thursday and Sunday.

Local Places of Interest/Activities: Peover Hall, Knutsford 3 miles, Tatton Park, Jodrell Bank.

172 The Drum & Monkey

Moss Rose, off Heyes Lane,
Alderley Edge, Cheshire SK9 7LD
Tel: 01625 584747

Fax: 01625 584975

Directions:
To find the pub form the A34 take the first left after the railway bridge as you enter Alderley Edge from the south. Fom the Wilmslow direction follow Heyes Lane and look out for the pub sign on the right.

Previously known as the Moss Rose, this popular pub became the **Drum & Monkey** when the current tenants Simon and Bindu Kalton took over in 1998. Decorated and furnished with taste and style, it's a great place for locals and visitors to socialise over a glass of real ale - the choice is Robinson's Best, Hartleys XB, Hatters Mild or a seasonally changing guest.

They also serve excellent food here with pork pie platters providing tasty quick snacks throughout the day and the rest of the blackboard menu available every session except Sunday and Monday evenings. Simon is the chef, and favourite dishes in his repertoire include fish specials, lamb shanks and steak & kidney pudding. Everything is fresh and appetising, and the pub's popularity means that booking is recommended for Friday and Saturday evenings and Sunday lunch (ask if you want a table in the non-smoking area). Children are welcome until 7.30 in the evening. The food's good, the drink's good, the company's good, and most nights of the week there's even more on offer at the Drum & Monkey: karaoke on Monday, quiz on Tuesday, live entertainment on Wednesday, Irish band every other Thursday, after-dinner entertainment on Saturday. Pool, darts and skittles are among the games played in the bar, and a bowling green is available for patrons' use.

Alderley Edge the village takes its name from Alderley Edge the two-mile escarpment that rises 600 feet above sea level and affords tremendous views over the Cheshire Plain. At nearby Over Alderley, the National Trust's Hare Hill Gardens are well worth a visit.

Opening Hours: All day, every day.

Food: Bar meals (not Sun or Mon eves).

Credit Cards: All the major cards.

Accommodation: None.

Facilities: Car Park, bowling green.

Entertainment: See above.

Local Places of Interest/Activities: Hare Hill Gardens, Wilmslow, Knutsford.

Internet/Website:
e-mail: drumandmonkey@kalton.co.uk

Horseshoe Inn **173**

Fence Lane,
Newbold,
Astbury,
Congleton,
Cheshire
CW12 3NL
Tel: 01260 272205

Directions:

Astbury is on the A34 2 miles southwest of Congleton; Newbold is about a mile from Astbury.

A mile from the village of Astbury and two miles from the National Trust's Mow Cop Castle, the **Horseshoe Inn** is a really delightful place to visit any lunchtime, any evening or all day on Saturday. Set within 11 acres of grounds, it presents an attractive white-painted facade to the world, and beyond the cheerful red door the look is very traditional, with carpeted floors, comfortably upholstered chairs, stools and benches set at neat little tables, and a wealth of horse brasses, old instruments and other ornaments on the walls and on the old black beams.

The Inn dates back to 1774 when licensing records first began and Mervin and Siobhan White have been tenants here since 1995. The greeting is always warm, and all ages are welcome - in the garden is an enclosed area where children can safely romp and climb and explore. Food is served all sessions either in the bars or outside if the weather is fine; the choice is mainly traditional, with gammon steaks and mixed grills among the most popular items, and the printed menu is supplemented by a daily specials board. Prices are very reasonable and portions generous, and to go with the good food is an excellent selection of ales (the pub is CAMRA-listed) including Robinson's Best and the occasional guest ale. A fun quiz starts at 9pm on the last Wednesday of each month. Off-road parking is in the pub's car park across the road.

The town of Congleton is a short drive away, and attractions in the surrounding countryside include the superb parish church of St Mary in Astbury, Little Moreton Hall, perhaps the finest black-and-white moated manor house in the land, and the renowned folly of Mow Cop, a mock ruined castle on a hilltop offering marvellous views.

Opening Hours: Lunchtime and evening, all day Saturday.

Food: Bar meals.

Credit Cards: None.

Accommodation: None.

Facilities: Car Park, beer garden, children's play area.

Entertainment: Quiz last Wednesday each month.

Local Places of Interest/Activities: Congleton 2 miles, Mow Cop 2 miles, Little Moreton Hall, 4 miles

174   The Oakwood

Brook Lane,
Alderley Edge,
Cheshire
SK9 7RU
Tel: 01625 583036
Fax: 01625 583497

Directions:

From Wilmslow, A34
south; just after the
roundabout on
Wilmslow Road turn
right on to Brook
Lane; the Oakwood is
on the left.

A gentleman's residence built in 1887 has been lovingly restored and converted into a fine, substantial public house that's a refreshing landmark in a densely populated area close to Manchester Airport and a few miles south of the city itself. The public rooms are spacious, attractive and very civilised, with notable features including a superb black and amber tiled floor, solid pine tables and chairs, inviting leather sofas, log fires and well-stocked book-shelves.

The proprietor, John Berry, knows precisely what his customers want, and this splendid place has a large and loyal following. Quality is the watchword throughout, with home-cooked food, cask ales including the occasional guest ale and well-chosen wines. The chef at **The Oakwood** mixes skill and inventiveness at a high level, and he seeks out the best and freshest produce from the local markets for a menu that takes its inspiration from all over the world. The Oakwood is open from 11am to 11pm seven days a week; on Thursday night the locals sharpen their brains for the weekly quiz.

Alderley Edge takes its name from the wooded escarpment, almost two miles long, that rises 600 feet above sea level and commands spectacular views over the Cheshire Plain. Other attractions within an easy drive of the hotel include reminders of the area's industrial heritage, notably the National Trust's 15th century Nether Alderley Water Mill, its Victorian machinery restored to full working order, and the Quarry Bank Georgian cotton mill at Styal, near Wilmslow, also in the care of the National Trust and part of the lovely Styal Estate County Park.

Opening Hours: Daily 11am to 11pm.

Food: A la carte menu.

Credit Cards: Amex, Mastercard, Visa.

Accommodation: None.

Facilities: Car Park.

Entertainment: Quiz Thursday.

Local Places of Interest/Activities: Alderley Edge, Nether Alderley 3 miles, Styal 3 miles.

Old Hunters Tavern 175

51-53 Acres Lane,
Stalybridge,
Cheshire
SK15 2JR
Tel: 0161 303 9477

Directions:

A central location in Stalybridge, four miles east of Manchester on the A628.

To the west of Stalybridge lie Ashton-under-Lyne and the great metropolis of Manchester, while to the east, immediately beyond the town boundaries, stretch miles of beautiful open countryside at the southern end of the Pennines, the long-distance Pennine Way footpath, rivers and reservoirs, forests and rugged moorland - ideal for a morning hike to build up a thirst and an appetite before a visit to the **Old Hunters Tavern**.

Occupying a corner site close to the centre of Stalybridge, the fine old redbrick premises, built in 1836 and once a meeting place of the Stalybridge Hunt, have been given a new lease of life by Anne and Derrick Wallwork, tenants since October 2000 and before that managers for two years. Together with son Daniel presiding over the bar and Anne's brother Archie as cook, quizmaster and DJ, they form a particularly friendly, hospitable family team, and in the cosy bar - note the list of innkeepers dating back to 1836 - regulars and visitors can meet and chat over a glass of Robinson's Best or Hatters Mild. At lunchtime Monday to Friday they can accompany their glass of ale with some good heart home cooking; favourites in Archie's repertoire include omelettes, curries and a superior chilli. At the weekend freshly made sandwiches are available at the bar.

Weekly entertainment slots are the quiz on Thursday and DJ-hosted music on Wednesday and Friday; there's a live music evening once a month. Part of the pub has a healthy covering of creeper, and in the spring and summer hanging boxes and window boxes add splashes of colour to the patio. The pub, which has ample off-road parking, is open every lunchtime and evening and all day Friday, Saturday and Sunday. Among the local attractions for visitors is the newly opened Stalybridge-Huddersfield Canal.

Opening Hours: Lunchtime and evening; all day Friday-Sunday.

Food: Bar meals Mon-Fri lunchtime.

Credit Cards: None.

Accommodation: None.

Facilities: Car Park.

Entertainment: Quiz Thursday, DJ Wednesday and Friday.

Local Places of Interest/Activities: Peak District National Park, Ashton-under-Lyne, Manchester.

176 The Poachers Inn

95 Ingersley Road, Bollington,
Cheshire SK10 5RE
Tel: 01625 572086 Fax: 01625 560187

Directions:
From Macclesfield (2 miles) take the A523 north, then the B5091.

Bollington is a delightful little town a short drive north of Macclesfield, and one of the very best reasons for a visit is Helen and Rob Ellwood's **Poachers Inn**. A stone-built country pub dating from about 1800, it occupies a prominent corner site; for all but the last 20 years it was known as the Masonic Arms.

The Ellwoods take great pride in the food on offer here - top-quality dishes served every lunchtime and evening in the bar or in the 25-cover non-smoking Gamekeeper Restaurant. Liver & onions and steak & ale pie are two of the favourite classics, but the menu really does offer something for everyone. Typical choices on an outstandingly imaginative list could include field mushrooms stuffed with a blend of chicken, stilton and garlic set on a leek and garlic sauce; spiced Creole prawns; duck à l'orange; chargrilled fillet of sea bass on a creamy Montbazillac and ginger sauce; Thai-style green chicken curry; and, for vegetarians, spiced vegetable samosas with rice and a chunky sweet and sour fruit sauce. Desserts keep up the good work, and a meal to remember can be accompanied by well-chosen wines or one of the four real ales that are always on tap. Booking is advisable on Friday and Saturday evenings and for the traditional Sunday roast lunch, and is essential for the themed food evenings that take place each month on a Wednesday.

A superb 'hidden' feature of his terrific pub is a rear garden set with parasols and garden furniture. Good off-road parking. Visitors can work up a thirst and an appetite with a walk on the Middlewood Way, a ten-mile traffic-free country trail which uses Bollington's splendid 20-arched viaduct on its way from Macclesfield to Marple.

Opening Hours: Every lunchtime and evening.

Food: Bar and restaurant meals.

Credit Cards: All the major cards.

Accommodation: None.

Facilities: Car Park, beer garden.

Entertainment: None.

Local Places of Interest/Activities: Macclesfield (Silk Museum, Heritage Centre) 2 miles, Peak District National Park.

Internet/Website: www.thepoachersinnbollington.co.uk

Queens Head Hotel 177

*Park Lane,
Congleton,
Cheshire
CW12 3DE
Tel: 01260 272546*

Directions:

On the eastern edge
of Congleton near
the railway station.

The Queens Head Hotel is a smart white-painted licensed premises run with pride by Tony and Anna Gunner, whose first venture it was when they came here as leaseholders four years ago. The public area is smart and comfortable, with an appealingly traditional look, and at the back of the building is by far the largest pub garden in Congleton.

Good food is available throughout the day from the printed menu and specials board, and the liquid refreshment includes no fewer than five real ales. Attached to the main building is a characterful cottage with four letting bedrooms - a single, a twin, a double and a large ground-floor family room - that share two bathrooms. The Queens Head is a great place for traditional pub games, with pool, darts, skittles and shovehapenny all having their keen practitioners, and every month there's live music on a Friday and another session with a local band. On Bank Holidays music is played in the garden.

The pub stands close to the railway station on the A527 towards Biddulph, a ten-minute walk from the town centre and adjacent to the Macclesfield Canal. Moorings can be arranged by the pub, which attracts a regular clientele of boating people. The Macclesfield Canal is one of the highest waterways in England, running for much of its length at more than 500 feet above sea level. Between Macclesfield and Congleton, the Canal, surveyed by Thomas Telford and opened in 1831, descends over 100 feet in a spectacular series of locks at Bosley before crossing the River Dane on Telford's iron viaduct. Just south of Congleton on the Canal are two roving or snake bridges swinging from one bank to the other where the towpath changes sides, allowing horses to cross over without the need to unhitch from their barges.

Opening Hours: All day, every day.

Food: Bar meals.

Credit Cards: None.

Accommodation: 4 rooms in an adjacent cottage.

Facilities: Car Park.

Entertainment: Live music twice monthly.

Local Places of Interest/Activities:
Congleton 1 mile, Little Morton Hall (NT), Biddulph Grange (NT - wonderful gardens) 4 miles.

178   The Rising Sun

*57-59 Stockport
Road East,
Bredbury,
Stockport,
Cheshire
SK6 2AA
Tel: 0161 430 4326*

Directions:

1 mile northeast of
Stockport on the
A560; close to the
M60 (junction 25).

Stockport, Manchester and the Peak District National Park are all within a short drive from the **Rising Sun**, which has been in the same family since 1979. Graham and Linda Booth managed it for 18 months before taking over as tenants in October 2000.

First granted its licence in 1786, it was acquired by the Midland Railway Company in 1873 (it stands next to the railway station) and was later leased to various breweries - the pub's full history is displayed in the bar. The interior is full of period charm, cosy and characterful, with flagstone floors and feature fireplaces and surrounds. Graham is the chef, and his dishes, including daily fish specialities, are available lunchtimes from 12 to 2, till 3 on Sunday, and on Friday evening from 5 till 8; more evening sessions are planned in the future. The Booths also plan to add to the range of real ales on offer. For those who like their spirits, the are special deals in the doubles bar. The regulars play all the usual games in the bar - darts, dominoes, cards - and have to sharpen their wits twice a week, Thursday and Sunday, for the popular quizzes. Twice a month, on a Saturday evening, there's live entertainment. The pub, which is open all day, every day of the week, has a patio garden to the rear and off-road parking next to the railway station.

The proximity of the motorway and other main roads makes the Rising Sun easy to reach from all directions, both from the great metropolis of Manchester and, in the other direction, from the wide open spaces of the Peak District National Park.

Opening Hours: All day, every day.

Food: Bar meals lunchtime and Fri eve.

Credit Cards: Planned.

Accommodation: None.

Facilities: Off-road parking.

Entertainment: Quiz Thursday and Sunday.

Local Places of Interest/Activities: Peak District National Park, Stockport, Manchester.

Robin Hood Inn **179**

*Church Brow,
Rainow,
Macclesfield,
Cheshire
SK10 5XF
Tel: 01625
574060*

Directions:

2 miles north-
east of
Macclesfield on
the B5470 road
towards Whaley
Bridge.

Well known and well liked for its cosy charm and traditional pub food, the **Robin Hood Inn** is situated on the B5470, the road that links Macclesfield with Whaley Bridge and Chapel-en-le-Frith. Teams of horses were stabled here in coaching days, and part of the inn was once a farrier's.

Behind the immaculate white-painted, slate-roofed exterior much of the period appeal remains, with gnarled black beams, open brickwork and stools and chairs set at neat little tables. Steaks are one of the highlights on the menu, which is served lunchtime Monday and Tuesday, lunchtime and evening Wednesday to Saturday and from noon through to 8 o'clock on Sunday. Children are welcome, and food is served throughout the bars - some of the tables are reserved for non-smokers. Three real ales are on tap - Boddingtons, Greenalls and a rotating guest. The Robin Hood Inn is the first venture into the licensed trade for Nick and Sue Rowcliffe, who took over as tenants in the summer of 2000. Sunday night at 9 sees the start of the weekly quiz, and a more specialised quiz, on the theme of music, is held on the last Friday of each month. Pool, darts, a juke box and a fruit machine provide entertainment at any time. The pub's other amenities include terraces front and rear (occasional barbecues), off-road parking and a function room with seats for 80.

The Robin Hood (once called Robin Hood and Little John but Little John had been dropped by 1834!) stands within the Peak District National Park; close to Rainow are the landmarks of Nab Head, which offers magnificent views across east Cheshire, and the round stone tower called White Nancy, affording equally stunning vistas westward into Lancashire and eastward to the Derbyshire hills.

Opening Hours: All day, every day.

Food: Bar meals (not Mon or Tues eves).

Credit Cards: None.

Accommodation: None.

Facilities: Car Park, terraces, function room.

Entertainment: Quiz Sunday.

Local Places of Interest/Activities: Peak District National Park, Macclesfield, Buxton.

Internet/Website:
e-mail: ncr@robin-hood.fslife.co.uk

180
The Royal Oak

134 Longhurst Lane,
Mellor,
Stockport,
Cheshire
SK6 5PJ
Tel: 0161 427 1655

Directions:

Mellor is situated seven miles east of Stockport on a minor road off the A626.

Part of a row cottages built some 300 years ago, the **Royal Oak** became a hostelry about 50 years later. Inside, the old beams, stone floor and real fires paint a splendidly traditional picture, assisted by assorted memorabilia and a show of work by local artists.

Les Smith has been the tenant here for a remarkable 34 years and, ably assisted by Audrey and son Sam, dispenses hospitality and some excellent brews - the real ales are Robinson's Best, Hatters Mild and a regularly changing guest. The pub is open all day, every day in the summer, and Monday to Friday evenings, Saturday and Sunday in the winter. A newly opened major attraction at the Royal Oak is a 40-seat restaurant serving an extensive range of Indian dishes. Extensive is an understatement, as the list runs to some 200 items, and that's not including the sundries - eight breads and eight types of rice. Variations on the lamb, chicken and prawn themes cater for all levels for heat tolerance, from gentle, creamy kormas to fiery vindaloos, and there are even a few dishes for anyone who really insists on an English meal. The restaurant is open from 5 o'clock to 11 Monday to Saturday and from 2 o'clock to 11 on Sunday. A takeaway service is also available.

When the weather is kind the Royal Oak's superb rear garden really comes into its own as a great place for alfresco sipping - a secluded area with tables and chairs set out on a paved area, a lovely lawn and wonderful views. The pub stands less than a mile from the edge of the Peak District National Park.

Opening Hours: Lunchtime and evening; all day in summer; closed Mon-Fri lunchtime in winter.

Food: Indian restaurant.

Credit Cards: None.

Accommodation: None.

Facilities: Beer garden.

Entertainment: Occasional quiz and live entertainment.

Local Places of Interest/Activities: Peak District National Park.

The Stock Dove 181

94 Compstall Road,
Romiley,
Stockport,
Cheshire
SK6 4DE
Tel: 0161 430 2671

Directions:

Romiley lies about 2 miles east of Stockport on the B6106, via A560 or A626/627.

Business partners Mark Vincent and Simon Reeder took over the lease of the **Stock Dove** in June 2000, continuing a tradition of hospitality that goes back to the 18th century. On a prominent corner site in the heart of Romiley, a short drive east of Stockport, the Stock Dove hides a wealth of old-world charm and period detail behind its redbrick frontage: wood is used to great effect in wall panelling, fire surrounds, beams and partitions, and the walls are hung with vintage pictures and prints of local interest.

Food can be enjoyed throughout the pub every weekday lunchtime and every weekday evening except Monday, from noon to 9 o'clock on Saturday and from noon to 7 o'clock on Sunday. The standard printed menu, blackboard specials and the bar snack list provide plenty of choice; it's best to book at the weekend - some areas of the bars are designated no smoking. A well-chosen list of wines accompanies the food. Summer barbecues on the smart patio are always popular occasions, and the Monday quiz draws the crowds all year round. The pub has a good-sized car park.

The pub's name is unique; it commemorates a man called Stock who was an expert at laying bowling greens; his first masterpiece of green-laying was at the back of this pub, which was at the time called The Dove. Stockport, which lies just to the west of Romiley, is well worth exploring, notably for the grand old houses around the market place, the spectacular railway viaduct and the splendid redbrick Church of St George with its sumptuous furnishings and art nouveau details.

Opening Hours: All day, every day.

Food: Bar snacks and meals (not Mon eve).

Credit Cards: All the major cards.

Accommodation: None.

Facilities: Car Park.

Entertainment: Quiz Monday.

Local Places of Interest/Activities:
Stockport 2 miles, Peak District National Park.

182 The Swettenham Arms

**Swettenham, Nr. Congleton,
Cheshire CW12 2LF
Tel: 01477 571284**

Directions:
From Congleton, minor roads off the A53
or A34; about 4 miles.

One of the best-known inns in the whole county, **The Swettenham Arms** has been owned and run by Frances and Jim Cunningham since 1993. It enjoys a tranquil location east of Holmes Chapel, reached on minor roads leading from the A34 and A54. It started life as a nunnery, where relatives would spend the night before burying their loved ones in the churchyard opposite, but for many years it has played a much happier role as one of the top places in the region for a drink and a meal.

The bars are invitingly traditional, with exposed stone walls and ancient blackened timbers. A team of talented chefs seek out the best local produce for the wide-ranging menus that are available lunchtime and evening Monday to Saturday and all day Sunday. The choice is very varied, and smaller portions can be served to children; everything, including the bread, is made on the premises, and the fine food can be accompanied by a glass or two of the excellent real ales, most of which come from small local brewers. It's best to book at all times.

The special theme evenings are always a great success, and on summer Sundays a nostalgic note is struck by the tea dances, when a scrumptious afternoon tea is served in the Lovell Suite to the strains of music from the 20s, 40s and 50s. This suite is also available for private parties.

Sir Bernard Lovell, founder and sometime head of adjacent Jodrell Bank, had a house backing on to the Swettenham Arms and planted many rare specimen trees and shrubs over the years, creating a 35-acre Arboretum that was later acquired by and is now run by the Cheshire Wildlife Trust. The entrance to the Arboretum, a popular year-round attraction, is through he grounds of the inn. Also bordering the inn is a wildflower meadow established two years ago by the Cunninghams.

Opening Hours: Lunchtime and evening; all day summer Sundays.

Food: Bar meals; summer Sunday tea dances.

Credit Cards: All the major cards.

Accommodation: None.

Facilities: Car Park.

Entertainment: None.

Local Places of Interest/Activities: The Jodrell Bank Arboretum and Science Centre, Congleton 4 miles.

Internet/Website: www.cheshireinns.co.uk

Throstles Nest Inn **183**

Buxton Road,
Buglawton,
Congleton,
Cheshire
CW12 2DW
Tel: 01260 272952

Directions:

1 mile east of
Congleton on the
A54 Buxton road.

A short drive east from the centre of Congleton brings motorists to the **Throstles Nest Inn**, which dates from the mid-19th century. Behind the attractive, once-thatched facade, the bar is homely and inviting, a perfect spot for locals and visitors to enjoy a good pint and a lunchtime bite.

The cooking is shared between the tenants Paul and Julie Tyler; Paul was born into the licensed trade and the couple, who arrived here in the autumn of 2000, have given the place a new lease of life. Food is served at lunchtime only, from 11 till 3, and the blackboard choice runs the gamut of bar food from a sandwich to a steak. Children are welcome, and lunch can be taken anywhere in the pub. Two real ales are always available, and there are special offers on beer every Sunday lunchtime.

This is a very sociable sort of place, one of the most popular of local meeting places, and Saturday brings jam sessions or traditional Irish music. Once a month, on a Friday, the karaoke session starts at 7.30. Parking is outside in the street or in the nearby public car park.

In nearby Congleton, once a centre of the textile industry, there's plenty to keep the visitor interested, including the impressive Venetian Gothic-style Town Hall, the Church of St Peter with its splendid Georgian interior, the first silk mill to operate in the town and the curious bridge over the canal that swung to allow horses to change to the opposite towpath without the need to unhitch from their barges. Not far away at Astbury is the National Trust's Little Moreton Hall, one of the most imposing black-and-white half-timbered houses in the country, and known for its role in films such as *Moll Flanders*.

Opening Hours: Open all day every day.

Food: Bar meals lunchtime.

Credit Cards: None.

Accommodation: None.

Entertainment: None.

Local Places of Interest/Activities:
Congleton 1 mile, Astbury (Little Morton Hall) 3 miles.

184   The White Hart

170 Hyde Road,
Woodley,
Stockport,
Cheshire
SK6 1NP
Tel: 0161 406 5921

Directions:
Woodley lies 3 miles
northeast of
Stockport on the
A560.

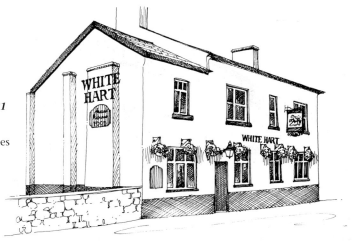

A warm Cheshire welcome is always guaranteed at the **White Hart**, where a local couple, Vincent and Christine Ranson, are the delightful tenants. They came here as managers in the autumn of 2000, bringing with them many years experience in the business.

The pub, which was built in the early 19th century, stands right on the main A560, its smart cream-painted frontage adorned with hanging baskets. Inside, the wood panelling is an eye-catching feature, and above the bar counter is a wooden-framed skylight with stained glass panels. The result is a really attractive, inviting setting for relaxing with a glass of real ale and enjoying a chat with the regulars, who come here from both town and country.

In the bar or in the little non-smoking dining area an across the board menu is available lunchtime and evening Monday to Saturday and from noon to 6 o'clock on Sundays and Bank Holidays. The pub is open throughout the day for drinks, which include Bass real ale, Worthington, Stones and Toby Light keg bitters, Carling and Grolsch, and well-priced spirit doubles.

Woodley is situated on the A560 road that runs from Stockport northeast. Stockport itself, though industrialised, is a place well worth a visit; once famous as a centre of the textile industry and renowned for the production of silk hats, it has many distinguished old buildings, a splendid railway viaduct and the remarkable Church of St George with some fascinating art nouveau features. Closer still is the open countryside and spectacular scenery of the Peak District National Park.

Opening Hours: All day, every day.

Food: Bar meals.

Credit Cards: Diners, Mastercard, Visa.

Accommodation: None.

Facilities: Car Park.

Entertainment: Quiz Thursday.

Local Places of Interest/Activities:
Stockport 3 miles, Peak District National Park.

The Wild Boar
185

Wincle, Macclesfield,
Cheshire SK11 0QL
Tel/Fax: 01260 227219

Directions:
From Macclesfield go south on the A523,
left on to A54. The pub stands about 2
miles along this road.

In a secluded setting by the A54 ten minutes' drive from Macclesfield, the **Wild Boar** is a former coaching inn built about 300 years ago. Diane Trueman, who runs the pub with her son Paul, took over the lease in February 2001, bringing with her 25 years' experience in the licensed trade, gained mostly in the Lake District.

Home cooking is the major attraction at the Wild Boar, with great soups and steak & kidney pie among the most popular items on the menu, which is available every lunchtime and evening. Food is served throughout the pub (the dining room is a no smoking area) and booking is advisable on Friday and Saturday. The place really buzzes on the third Friday of the month, when Irish Folk night with supper thrown in brings in the crowds. The pub is handily placed for access to the towns of Macclesfield, Congleton, Buxton and Leek, and Diane has plans to extend the scope of the Wild Boar by offering overnight accommodation. There will be two upstairs guest rooms, both en suite, decorated and furnished in Victorian style. Lettings will be on a Bed & Breakfast basis, with discounts for extended stays.

The River Dane and the Macclesfield Canal both run nearby, and the area around the pub and the village provides great walks and great scenery in the Peak District National Park. The Wild Boar has a small patio area at the front, a beer garden and ample off-road parking space. The pub is closed on Tuesday in winter.

Opening Hours: Lunchtime and evening; all day Sat, Sun & Bank Holidays. Closed Tuesdays in winter.

Food: Bar meals.

Credit Cards: None.

Accommodation: 2 rooms planned.

Facilities: Car Park, beer garden.

Entertainment: Irish Folk night 3rd Friday of the month.

Local Places of Interest/Activities: Macclesfield 4 miles, Congleton, Buxton, Leek.

186   Ye Olde White Lion

22 High Street,
Congleton,
Cheshire
CW12 1BD
Tel: 01260 272702

Directions:
On the main street
of Congleton.

Amanda Roberts has lived in Congleton for 12 years, and for the past four has been the leaseholder at this historic pub in the centre of a historic town. A tourist attraction in its own right - spot the blue tourist plaque on an outside wall - the pub dates back some 500 years; at one time it was the offices of the solicitors firm of John Bradshaw, who signed the death warrant of King Charles I.

Behind the classic black-and-white frontage the bars are cosy and inviting, with a wealth of horse brasses and other ornaments hanging from the beams and the walls. Amanda does the cooking, producing a good variety of dishes for the printed menu and the daily changing specials board. Food is served Tuesday to Sunday lunchtimes and it's best to book on Friday and Saturday, and also on Sunday, when traditional roasts are among the four main courses on offer. Three or four real ales are always on tap, including Abbot and rotating guest ales, and other brews include Worthington Creamflow and Boddingtons Keg. Happy hour runs from 6 till 8 on Monday and Tuesday. A live band performs every other Sunday evening, and the pub holds occasional quiz nights. At the back is a little gem of a garden; the pub has no parking of its own, but there are public car parks nearby.

Places to see in Congleton, which nestles in the foothills of the Pennines, include the imposing Gothic Town Hall, the first silk mill to work in the town and the Church of St Peter with its handsome Georgian interior.

Opening Hours: All day, every day.

Food: Bar meals Tuesday-Sunday lunches.

Credit Cards: None.

Accommodation: None.

Facilities: None.

Entertainment: Live music every other Sunday.

Local Places of Interest/Activities: Little Morton Hall (NT), Biddulph Grange Gardens (NT) 4 miles.

ALPHABETIC LIST OF INNS

A

The Albion Alehouse	Clayton-le-Moors, nr Accrington, Lancashire	54
The Anchor Inn	Salterforth, nr Barnoldswick, Lancashire	55

B

The Barton Fox	Barton, nr Preston, Lancashire	20
The Basset Hound	Wirral , Cheshire	106
The Beech Tree	Barnton, nr Northwich, Cheshire	138
The Birch and Bottle	Higher Whitley, nr Warrington, Cheshire	139
The Bird in Hand	Guilden Sutton, nr Chester, Cheshire	107
The Black Bull	Caton, nr Lancaster, Lancashire	21
Black Bull Hotel	High Bentham, nr Lancaster, Lancashire	22
Black Bull Inn	Ribchester, Lancashire	23
The Black Swan	Rixton, nr Warrington, Cheshire	140
The Blue Anchor	Bretherton, Lancashire	82
The Blue Anchor Hotel	Bolton-le-Sands, nr Carnforth, Lancashire	24
The Boars Head	Higher Poynton, Cheshire	165
The Boot & Slipper	Wettenhall, Cheshire	141
The Bridge Inn	Lower Tatham, by Lancaster, Lancashire	25
Brook House	Heskin, Lancashire	83
The Bull's Head	Mobberley, Cheshire	166
The Bull's Head	Smallwood, Cheshire	167
The Bulls Head Inn	Clotton, nr Tarporley, Cheshire	108
The Buxton Inn	Gee Cross, nr Hyde, Cheshire	168

C

The Calveley Arms	Handley, nr Tattenhall, Cheshire	109
The Cheshire Cheese	Nantwich, Cheshire	142
The Church Inn	Millbrook, nr Stalybridge, Cheshire	169
The Clarence Hotel	Newton, nr Hyde, Cheshire	170
The Coach & Horses	Bolton by Bowland, nr Clitheroe, Lancashire	26
The Copper Mine	Broxton, Cheshire	110
The Cricketers	Brinscall, nr Chorley, Lancashire	56

D

The Derby Arms	Inskip, nr Preston, Lancashire	27
The Dog Inn	Over Peover, nr Knutsford, Cheshire	171
The Drum & Monkey	Alderley Edge , Cheshire	172

188   *Alphabetic List of Inns*

ALPHABETIC LIST OF INNS

190 ALPHABETIC LIST OF INNS

ACCOMMODATION

ALL DAY OPENING

194   *CHILDRENS FACILITIES*

CREDIT CARDS ACCEPTED

196 CREDIT CARDS ACCEPTED

GARDEN, PATIO OR TERRACE 197

198 | *Garden, Patio or Terrace*

GARDEN, PATIO OR TERRACE | 199

LIVE ENTERTAINMENT

202 RESTAURANT/DINING AREA

RESTAURANT/DINING AREA

INDEX OF PLACES OF INTEREST 205

Hidden Inns Order Form

To order any of our publications just fill in the payment details below and complete the order form *overleaf*. For orders of less than 4 copies please add £1 per book for postage and packing. Orders over 4 copies are P & P free.

Please Complete Either:

I enclose a cheque for £ [   ] made payable to Travel Publishing Ltd

Or:

Card No: [   ]

Expiry Date: [   ]

Signature: [   ]

NAME: [   ]

ADDRESS: [   ]

POSTCODE: [   ]

TEL NO: [   ]

Please either send or telephone your order to:

Travel Publishing Ltd
7a Apollo House
Calleva Park
Aldermaston
Berks, RG7 8TN

Tel : 0118 981 7777
Fax: 0118 982 0077

The Hidden Inns of Lancashire and Cheshire

	PRICE	QUANTITY	VALUE
Hidden Places Regional Titles			
Cambs & Lincolnshire	£7.99	....	....
Chilterns	£8.99	....	....
Cornwall	£8.99	....	....
Derbyshire	£7.99	....	....
Devon	£8.99	....	....
Dorset, Hants & Isle of Wight	£8.99	....	....
East Anglia	£8.99	....	....
Gloucestershire & Wiltshire	£7.99	....	....
Heart of England	£7.99	....	....
Hereford, Worcs & Shropshire	£7.99	....	....
Highlands & Islands	£7.99	....	....
Kent	£8.99	....	....
Lake District & Cumbria	£7.99	....	....
Lancashire & Cheshire	£8.99	....	....
Lincolnshire	£8.99	....	....
Northumberland & Durham	£8.99	....	....
Somerset	£7.99	....	....
Sussex	£7.99	....	....
Thames Valley	£7.99	....	....
Yorkshire	£7.99	....	....
Hidden Places National Titles			
England	£9.99	....	....
Ireland	£9.99	....	....
Scotland	£9.99	....	....
Wales	£11.99	....	....
Hidden Inns Titles			
Central and Southern Scotland	£5.99	....	....
Heart of England	£5.99	....	....
Lancashire and Cheshire	£5.99	....	....
South East England	£5.99	....	....
South of England	£5.99	....	....
Wales	£5.99	....	....
West Country	£5.99	....	....
WelshBorders	£5.99	....	....
Yorkshire	£5.99	....	....
TOTAL			

For orders of less than 4 copies please add £1 per book for
postage & packing. Orders over 4 copies P & P free.

Hidden Inns Reader Reaction

The *Hidden Inns* research team would like to receive reader's comments on any visitor attractions or places reviewed in the book and also recommendations for suitable entries to be included in the next edition. This will help ensure that the *Hidden Inns* series continues to provide its readers with useful information on the more interesting, unusual or unique features of each attraction or place ensuring that their stay in the local area is an enjoyable and stimulating experience.

To provide your comments or recommendations would you please complete the forms below and overleaf as indicated and send to:

The Research Department, Travel Publishing Ltd,

7a Apollo House, Calleva Park, Aldermaston, Reading, RG7 8TN.

Your Name:

Your Address:

Your Telephone Number:

Please tick as appropriate: Comments ☐ Recommendation ☐

Name of *"Hidden Place"*:

Address:

Telephone Number:

Name of Contact:

Hidden Inns Reader Reaction

Comment or Reason for Recommendation:

....

....

....

....

....

....

....

....

....

....